Financial Futures

by
M. Desmond Fitzgerald

Published by Euromoney Publications

Published by
Euromoney Publications Limited,
Nestor House, Playhouse Yard,
London EC4

ISBN 0 903121 43 3

Text set in 10/12 Linotron 202 Bembo, printed and bound
in Great Britain at The Pitman Press, Bath

Contents

		Page
List of exhibits		v
Foreword		vii
Preface		ix
Chapter 1	The development of financial future markets	1
	A. What a financial future is	1
	B. The types of contracts traded	2
	C. Why financial futures contracts have developed	3
	D. The success of the contracts	4
	E. Who uses the financial futures markets	6
	F. More contracts and exchanges expected	8
Chapter 2	The mechanics of financial futures trading	9
	A. The pricing of financial futures contracts	9
	B. Delivery and the clearing house	11
	C. Margins	12
	D. Executing a transaction	15
	E. Types of orders	18
	F. Commissions and transaction costs	23
	G. Price limits	24
	H. The major contracts	25
Chapter 3	Analytical concepts in financial futures	51
	A. Statistical analysis for financial futures	51
	B. Conversion factors and duration for long-term interest rate futures	57
	C. Futures/cash relationships	61
Chapter 4	Hedging with financial futures contracts: the basic principles	67
	A. Elements in making the hedge decision	69
	B. Aggressive hedging strategies	80
	C. The hedge management process	86
Chapter 5	Hedging applications of financial futures	89
	A. Hedging for a commercial bank	89
	B. Hedging by portfolio managers	97
	C. Hedging for a corporation	107
	D. Underwriting applications of financial futures	114
	E. Mortgage hedging with financial futures	115
	F. Conclusions	118
Chapter 6	Trading and speculating in financial futures	119
	A. Open position trading	120
	B. Spread trading	121

		C.	The timing of trading	133
		D.	A strategy of trading	135
		E.	Monitoring and controlling trading performance	135
Chapter 7	Arbitrage with financial futures			137
		A.	Cash and carry arbitrage	139
		B.	Futures and forward-forward arbitrage	146
		C.	Interest and foreign exchange futures combination arbitrage	148
		D.	Short-term and long-term spread arbitrage	149
		E.	Simple inter-market arbitrage	152
		F.	Summing up arbitrage	153
Chapter 8	Investment applications of financial futures			155
		A.	Hedging a yield curve ride	155
		B.	Cash market yields versus futures yields (a strip of futures)	156
		C.	Using the long-term contracts	157
		D.	Complex proxy investments	159
		E.	Conclusions	160
Chapter 9	Accounting and taxation treatment of financial futures★			161
		A.	Accounting issues	161
		B.	Taxation considerations	170
Chapter 10	Regulatory and macro-economic aspects of financial futures			175
Appendix 1	Glossary			182
Appendix 2	Contract specifications			187
Appendix 3	Fundamental and technical analysis of rates			192
Bibliography				195
Index				199
Author's biography				202

★ This chapter was written by Price Waterhouse.

List of exhibits

Exhibit 1.1 Three-month Eurodollar deposit interest rates, 1978–82   3
Exhibit 1.2 $/£ exchange rate, 1974–82   3
Exhibit 1.3 Growth of T-bond futures trading, 1975–82   4
Exhibit 1.4 Growth of T-bill futures trading, 1975–82   4
Exhibit 1.5 IMM foreign exchange futures contract volume, 1972–82   5
Exhibit 1.6 US trading volume for interest rate contracts   5
Exhibit 1.7 LIFFE volume statistics (30 September, 1982 to 31 January, 1983)   6
Exhibit 1.8 Commitments of traders by occupational groups   7

Exhibit 2.1 Example of initial margin calculation   14
Exhibit 2.2 Flow of an order system on a typical exchange   16
Exhibit 2.3 Structure of the clearing process   17
Exhibit 2.4 IMM Treasury bill futures prices   26
Exhibit 2.5 CBT Treasury bond futures prices   33
Exhibit 2.6 Conversion factors for invoicing   34
Exhibit 2.7 Twenty-year interest rate contract—price factors and accrued interest   37
Exhibit 2.8 GNMA equivalent principal balance factors and principal balance
equivalents   40
Exhibit 2.9 GNMA yield equivalents   44
Exhibit 2.10 Correlation matrix in terms of yield   50

Exhibit 3.1 Sterling time deposits and CDs, 1978–81: high correlation   53
Exhibit 3.2 Sterling time deposits and short gilts, 1978–81: fair correlation   53
Exhibit 3.3 Sterling time deposits and stock market yields, 1978–81: low correlation   53
Exhibit 3.4 Scatter diagrams: short-term interest rates   54
Exhibit 3.5 Least squares regression: five-year gilts on sterling time deposits   55
Exhibit 3.6 Typical regression results   55
Exhibit 3.7 Twenty-year interest rate contract—price factors and accrued interest   58
Exhibit 3.8 Conversion factor for invoicing   59
Exhibit 3.9 Cash and futures yield curves   64

Exhibit 4.1a Mismatched book   72
Exhibit 4.1b Matched book   72
Exhibit 4.2 Convergence for sterling deposit contracts   81
Exhibit 4.3 Convergence for US T-bill futures   82
Exhibit 4.4 Cash yield curve versus strip yield curve   83
Exhibit 4.5 Use of orders with a long hedge   84

Exhibit 6.1 Behaviour of straddles through time   125
Exhibit 6.2 Behaviour of T-bill/CD inter-contract spread through time   127
Exhibit 6.3 Behaviour of CD/Eurodollar inter-contract spread through time   127
Exhibit 6.4 Behaviour of T-bond/GNMA inter-contract spread through time   130

Exhibit 7.1   The time/security grid   137
Exhibit 7.2   An example of a closed arbitrage   138
Exhibit 7.3   Cash and carry arbitrage   140
Exhibit 7.4   Forward-forward versus futures arbitrage   147
Exhibit 7.5   T-bond spreads versus short-term rates arbitrage   150

Exhibit A1   Data display—bar chart   193
Exhibit A2   Data display—point and figure (or reversal) chart   193

Foreword

I welcome Dr. Fitzgerald's highly readable book. I am sure it will benefit the professional managers of money that LIFFE has been established to serve.

Financial futures are playing an increasingly important role in the major money markets of the world. They offer businesses a low cost and highly flexible method of controlling the risks to which they are exposed in today's conditions of volatile interest rates and currency values. Yet the manager often lacks the knowledge to use financial futures confidently. Too much that is written on the subject is unclear and over-simplified. The busy manager needs a clear and comprehensive guide and I believe Dr. Fitzgerald's book is just that.

The book explains step by step the ways in which companies, banks and investment institutions can use financial futures to hedge interest rate and currency risks. It illustrates applications for LIFFE's contracts as well as those of other exchanges.

The valuable role played by arbitrageurs and traders in facilitating the execution of hedge transactions is well described. The book offers some sound advice to such participants on how to profit from the market.

Education will play a major part in the continuing development of these new markets. LIFFE in particular has made a substantial investment in developing a comprehensive education programme and I would like to acknowledge the valuable contribution that Dr. Fitzgerald and his colleagues at the City University Business School have made to this undertaking.

March 1983

Michael Jenkins
Chief Executive
LIFFE

Preface

On September 30, 1982, the London International Financial Futures Exchange introduced the world of financial futures trading to Europe. This has lent a new aspect to an industry whose growth has been nothing short of spectacular since the introduction of exchange rate contracts on the Chicago Mercantile Exchange in 1972 and interest rate contracts on the Chicago Board of Trade in 1975. The year 1982 also saw the introduction of stock index futures on several US exchanges, and the approval by the Commodity Futures Trading Commission of a pilot options on futures programme scheduled to begin in 1983. All the signs are that the next five years will see just as much growth in financial futures trading as the last five. As these markets develop, and the scope for hedging interest and exchange rate risk widens, it will be necessary for all bankers, corporate treasurers, portfolio managers and indeed anyone concerned with the management of money to know the features of these markets and how they can be used not just for hedging but for trading, arbitrage and investment strategies as well. This book is designed to provide just that information: from the basic mechanics of futures trading to the sophisticated hedging and trading strategies that are available with financial futures in Chicago, London and elsewhere.

The number of individuals and organizations who helped me in writing this book is legion. I would particularly like to express my appreciation to Roy Batchelor and Gordon Gemmill, my colleagues at City University Business School, and Bernard Reed, Michael Jenkins and others at the London International Financial Futures Exchange. Without the opportunity to get involved in LIFFE's hedging and trading courses, this book would certainly not be as comprehensive as it is—I must thank LIFFE for permission to make use of material prepared for these courses. My thanks are also due to Mark Austen and David Roe of Price Waterhouse for kindly contributing a chapter on tax and accounting aspects of financial futures, to Nancy Rothstein, Bruce Beaumont and Laurie Kroll of the First National Bank of Chicago, and Ian Murray and Kevin McGivern of Hoare Govett Financial Futures. Finally, of course, I must give my sincerest thanks to my indomitable secretary Pat Baker, who has typed excellently a very complex manuscript written in the world's worst handwriting.

M. Desmond Fitzgerald

Chapter 1
The development of financial futures markets

One of the most successful and yet highly controversial innovations in financial markets in recent years has been the introduction of trading in financial futures contracts, i.e. contracts where the underlying asset is not some physical commodity like coffee, cocoa or silver, but fixed interest financial instruments or foreign exchange rates. The first financial futures exchange, the International Monetary Market (IMM), which is a subsidiary of the Chicago Mercantile Exchange, opened in 1972 for the trading of foreign exchange futures. The first traded interest rate future—GNMA collateralized depository receipts (CDR)—began trading on the Chicago Board of Trade (CBT) in 1975. Since then trading in interest rate futures contracts has grown rapidly and continuously, until in value terms it dwarfs many of the cash markets.

This introductory chapter answers basic questions about financial futures and the way in which trading in them has developed in the United States and other centres. This discussion should be seen as a lead-in to the more detailed chapters that follow.

A. What a financial future is

A futures contract is a legally binding contract to take or make delivery of a given quantity and quality of a commodity at an agreed price on a specified date or range of dates in the future.

Thus a typical futures contract might involve an investor agreeing to take delivery of 25 tons of Robusta coffee at a price of £1,500 per ton on 25 April, 1984. The current date is, say, 10 July, 1983. If the futures contract is not cancelled by resale, on 25 April, 1984 the investor, if prices of coffee have not changed, will have to hand over £37,500 cash and take possession of 25 tons of Robusta coffee. Thus, the essence of a futures contract is to fix the price now at which a transaction will take place in the future.

A financial futures contract is simply a binding agreement to buy or sell a financial instrument during a specified month in the future. For example, such a contract might call for delivery of $1 million of US Treasury bills in September 1984 at an invoice price determined by a specific discount yield, say 10.5%.

The markets in which these futures contracts are traded are generally characterized by certain attributes not common to other financial markets.

1. Financial futures contracts are traded by open outcry on a centralized and regulated exchange.
2. Contracts are highly standardized, with trading in specific months for specific quantities of product.
3. Underlying securities are delivered through a clearing system, and the clearing house guarantees the fulfilment of contracts entered into by clearing members.
4. Actual delivery of financial instruments against financial futures contracts tends to be rare.
5. Liquidity must be high for a financial futures contract or the contract tends to 'die'.
6. Trading costs on open outcry markets tend to be very low.

Many of these features are in contrast to the forward markets, particularly the interbank market in forward exchange. The forward market in foreign exchange has no regulatory body or central location. Contracts are written according to individual requirements without any outside guarantee. And, as opposed to futures markets where all prices are publicly disclosed, agreed-upon prices in forward transactions are not publicly disseminated. One final difference is that whereas profits and losses on futures contracts have to be paid daily, a principle known as marking to market (*see* Chapter 2), no payments are made on forward contracts until the contract is finally settled.

B. The types of contracts traded

The first financial futures were foreign currency contracts which began trading on the International Commercial Exchange (ICE) in 1970. These were never actively traded, and the ICE went out of business quickly. Additional foreign currency contracts began trading on the Chicago Mercantile Exchange in 1972 and the New York Mercantile Exchange in 1974. In 1975 the Commodity Futures Trading Commission (CFTC) officially designated nine currencies as contract markets on these exchanges: British pounds, Canadian dollars, Deutschemarks, Dutch guilders, Japanese yen, Mexican pesos, Swiss francs, French francs and Italian lira.

Interest rate contracts were first designated by the CFTC in 1975. Both GNMA CDR contracts on the Chicago Board of Trade and T-bill contracts on the Chicago Mercantile Exchange were approved in 1975. In 1977 the CBT Treasury bond contract and 90-day commercial paper contracts were approved. In 1978 four more contracts were approved: a one-year T-bill contract (CME), a 30-day commercial paper contract (CBT), and two more GNMA contracts (Amex Commodities Exchange, CBT). In 1979, a further six contracts were approved: a long-term bond contract (ACE), a GNMA contract (COMEX), two additional 90-day T-bill contracts (ACE, COMEX) and two Treasury note contracts (CBT, CME). In 1980, the CFTC designated three more contracts: a 20-year bond contract (New York Futures Exchange), a 90-day bill contract (NYFE), and a two-year Treasury note contract (COMEX). In August 1980 trading ceased on the Amex Commodities Exchange.

Among other designations in the period 1981–82 were: domestic certificates of deposit (CBT, CME, NYFE), Eurodollar deposits (CBT, NYFE, CME), one-year T-bills (COMEX), long-term Treasury notes (CBT), stock index futures (CME, NYFE, CBT, Kansas City Board of Trade) and several others.

However, very few of these designated contracts have proved successful in terms of trading volume; in fact, a majority of the contracts mentioned above are virtually moribund. Below is a list of those financial futures contracts which are actively traded at the present time.

United States
US Treasury bond (Chicago Board of Trade)
GNMA (Chicago Board of Trade)
$6\frac{1}{2}$–10 year Treasury note (Chicago Board of Trade)
90-day Treasury bill (IMM)
Domestic certificate of deposit (IMM)
Eurodollar time deposit (IMM)
Foreign exchange contracts (IMM): sterling, Canadian dollar, Deutschemark, yen, Swiss franc.
Stock index futures (IOM, New York Futures Exchange, Kansas City Board of Trade)

United Kingdom
London International Financial Futures Exchange (LIFFE)
Sterling three-month time deposit
Eurodollar three-month time deposit
20-year gilt-edged stock
Foreign exchange contracts ($): sterling, yen, Deutschemark, Swiss franc.

Canada
Canadian T-bill (Winnipeg, Toronto, Montreal)
20-year, 9% Canadian government bond (Toronto, Montreal)
5-year government bond (Toronto)

Australia
  Foreign exchange contract: Australian $/US$ (Sydney)
  Banker's acceptances (Sydney)

The range of contracts traded is wide, and can be expected to grow further over the next few years.

C. Why financial futures contracts have developed

Futures contracts fulfil two primary purposes. First, they allow investors to hedge the risk of adverse price movements in the cash market. Secondly, they allow speculators to back their forecasts with a high degree of leverage. The more volatile the underlying asset prices, the more hedging demand will develop. In response to this increased risk, financial futures markets have developed which allow holders of cash positions to hedge their interest rate, exchange rate and stock market risk, and traders to speculate in a very volatile commodity. Exhibits 1.1 and 1.2 show how volatile UK and US interest rates and exchange rates have become over the last few years. The growth of financial futures trading has been a natural response to this sort of volatility.

Exhibit 1.1: Three-month Eurodollar deposit interest rates, 1978–82

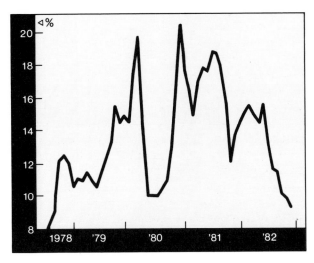

Exhibit 1.2: $/£ Exchange rate, 1974–82

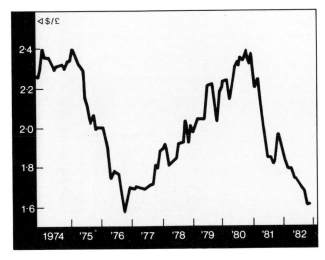

D. The success of the contracts

Volume growth in foreign exchange and interest rate contracts on the Chicago markets has been spectacular over the past five years. By 1980, annual trading volume in all types of financial futures amounted to nearly 17 million contracts, representing some 18% of all futures trading in the United States. Further advances in trading volume were recorded in 1981 and 1982, with the volume of trading in the most popular contracts comfortably exceeding total trades in the underlying cash markets. Exhibits 1.3–1.5 show the explosive growth of futures trading in Chicago. Exhibit 1.6 gives volume figures for the most popular interest rate contracts for 1980, 1981 and 1982.

Exhibit 1.3: Growth of T-bond futures trading, 1975–82

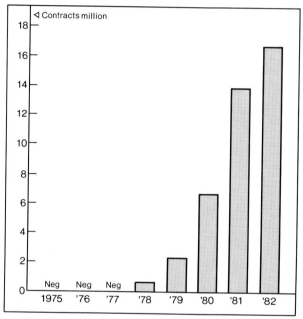

Neg—negligible
Source: Chicago Board of Trade

Exhibit 1.4: Growth of T-bill futures trading, 1975–82

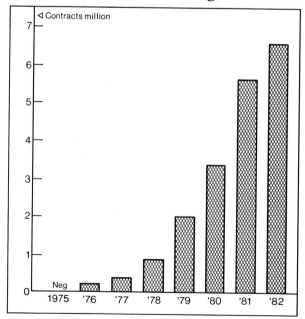

Source: International Monetary Market

4

Exhibit 1.5: IMM foreign exchange futures contract volume, 1972–82

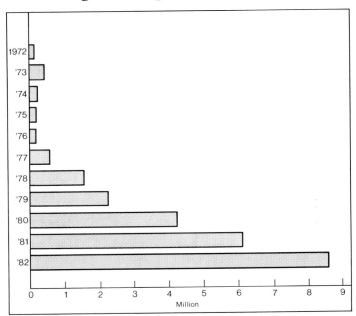

Source: International Monetary Market

Exhibit 1.6: US trading volume for interest rate contracts

	1980	1981	1982
GNMA (CDR): Chicago Board of Trade ($100,000)	2,325,892	2,292,882	2,055,648
Treasury bonds: Chicago Board of Trade ($100,000)	6,489,555	13,907,988	16,739,695
Treasury bills (90-day): IMM ($1,000,000)	3,338,773	5,631,290	6,598,848
Domestic certificates of deposit: IMM ($1,000,000)	—	423,718	1,556,327
Foreign exchange contracts: IMM (various)	4,211,641	6,121,938	8,690,285

What is notable about these statistics, however, is how concentrated the volume has been in a very few interest rate contracts, and how difficult it has proved for markets outside Chicago to develop sufficient liquidity for a viable market. Already the American Stock Exchange financial futures operation has been absorbed into COMEX. Similarly, the much publicized New York Futures Exchange (NYFE), which opened in August 1980, failed to establish any significant volume of trading in any contract, until the opening of trading in stock index futures in 1982.

The interest rate contracts which appear capable of developing liquidity to rival the big three in interest rate futures in the United States are the domestic CD contract on the IMM, which was trading around 4,000 contracts a day in mid 1983 with open interest over 20,000, and the new Treasury note contract on the Chicago Board of Trade, which was trading between 3,000 and 5,000 contracts per day in mid 1983 with open interest of over 10,000. The development of this latter contract is being watched particularly keenly by futures market professionals, since if it succeeds it will be the first medium–term interest rate contract to establish itself. Its relative success tends to confirm the split between the Chicago Board of Trade as the specialist exchange in discount priced interest rate contracts and the IMM as the specialist exchange in index priced interest rate contracts.

The most recent success story of futures trading for the US exchanges, however, has been the commencement of trading stock market index contracts. The most successful has been the Standard and Poor's 500 index futures on the Chicago Mercantile Index and Options Market, which in mid 1983 was trading well over 40,000 contracts per day, but both the New York Futures Exchange and the Kansas City Board of Trade have been trading good volume at around 15–20,000 and 3,000 contracts per day respectively. Stock index futures trading seems destined to continue to show rapid expansion over the next couple of years.

Another important event for world financial futures trading in 1982 was the long-awaited opening of the London International Financial Futures Exchange on 30 September. London commenced trading with three interest rate contracts and four foreign exchange rate contracts. Although the volume of trading has not been high by Chicago standards in the initial months, all the interest rate contracts have traded in large enough volume for traders to buy and sell contracts reasonably easily, and by mid 1983 the exchange looked fairly well established. Exhibit 1.7 shows some volume statistics for LIFFE contracts since its inception.

Exhibit 1.7: LIFFE volume statistics (30 September, 1982 to 31 January, 1983)

		30/9/82–31/3/83	1/4/83–30/9/83	30/9/82–30/9/83
Gilt contract	Cumulative total	113,235	255,190	368,425
	Daily average	1,132	2,025	1,645
Eurodollar deposit	Cumulative total	205,442	229,081	434,523
contract	Daily average	1,644	1,847	1,731
Sterling deposit	Cumulative total	112,916	85,922	198,838
contract	Daily average	1,129	693	880
FX contracts	Cumulative total	104,687	105,432	210,119
	Daily average	844	851	847

Source: LIFFE

In terms of seat purchases, LIFFE can already be deemed a success, with virtually all the major City of London financial institutions purchasing seats on the exchange.

With the volume of trading in financial futures seemingly expanding without limit, and with the apparent success of several new contracts, and the opening of the London market to complement Chicago, all the signs are that financial futures trading will enjoy as much success in the future as in the past.

E. Who uses the financial futures markets

There are broadly two types of users of financial futures: hedgers and traders. Traders are generally referred to as speculators in the United States.

Hedging is aimed at reducing the risk of adverse interest rate or exchange rate movements by taking a position in the futures market that is opposite to existing or anticipated positions in the cash market. This makes use of the idea that financial futures prices move inversely with interest rates. Hence, if an investor is worried that his investments will lose value if interest rates rise and he does not want to sell them, he could sell financial futures and make an offsetting profit when the futures prices fall as interest rates rise. Some of the types of hedger who might use these markets are:

1. Retailers: To protect interest rates on an anticipated seasonal cash surplus.
2. Corporations: To protect the interest rate on a forecast temporary cash surplus; and to lock in the borrowing rate on a planned issue of commercial paper.
3. Pension funds: To protect the yield on a planned investment in gilts or Treasury bonds; and to insulate an equity portfolio against an overall decline in the market.
4. Exporters: To protect the exchange rate on payments for expected shipments.
5. Investment banks: To sell a large amount of short-term assets which the cash market seems unlikely to absorb fully at current prices.
6. Property companies: Planning a convertible loan stock issue but fearing interest rates will rise before it is completed.
7. Mortgage bankers: To protect a GNMA pool against adverse movements in mortgage rates before origination is complete.

This list is not exhaustive, but it does provide a flavour of the widely differing types of institutions who may find the futures market useful for hedging interest rate, exchange rate or stock market risk.

In contrast to hedging, trading in the financial futures market is aimed at taking positions in the markets to benefit from absolute or relative changes in interest rates or exchange rates. Conventionally financial futures trading is divided into three types.

1. Arbitrage: Taking advantage of temporary mispricing of cash instruments and futures contracts to earn almost riskless profits.
2. Spreading: Taking a view on the evolution of the price difference between different futures prices.
3. Position trading: Betting on absolute interest or exchange rate movements by buying and selling futures contracts.

Both hedgers and traders are necessary to the efficient operation of the financial futures market. Traders provide liquidity to the market, allowing hedgers to buy or sell in volume without difficulty.

In practice the use of these markets will vary greatly between potential participants. According to a recent study by the Commodity Futures Trading Commission, the dominant commercial users of interest-rate futures markets are government securities dealers who use the markets for both speculative and hedging purposes. The dominant commercial users of foreign currency futures appear to be foreign exchange dealers, primarily commercial banks, who use the markets for the purpose of profiting from differences in exchange rates between the forward and futures markets, as well as for hedging purposes. Hedging use of interest rate contracts amounts, according to the CFTC, to between 15–35% of open interest at any one time, and around 10–20% of foreign currency contracts. Exhibit 1.8 shows the usage of the financial futures markets for the most popular contracts on 30 March, 1979, the date surveyed in the CFTC study. There is little evidence to suggest a similar survey now would produce very different results.

Exhibit 1.8: Commitments of traders by occupational groups

Occupations	CBT Treasury bond			CBT GNMA–CDR			IMM T-bill		
	Number of traders	Positions long	short	Number of traders	Positions long	short	Number of traders	Positions long	short
Commercial traders									
Commercial banks	14	1,365	1,578	13	565	745	24	796	2,366
Securities dealers non-FCM*	20	4,327	4,522	16	2,592	2,223	18	3,145	4,180
Securities dealers FCM*	12	4,395	3,209	11	1,128	2,596	11	1,175	2,692
Savings and loans	2	788	0	33	3,696	1,304	6	201	70
Mortgage bankers	9	352	308	35	1,169	1,774	4	962	987
Pension funds/insurance	2	100	5	4	100	30	4	140	15
Other financial	28	1,264	1,251	29	1,462	1,338	58	5,981	3,975
Real estate interests	8	359	401	8	289	285	12	454	474
Non-financial commercial	13	365	217	12	277	225	37	1,221	1,151
Sub-total	108	13,295	11,491	161	11,278	10,520	174	174	15,910
Non-commercial traders	129	11,573	14,276	138	22,108	20,118	132	7,407	9,462
Commodity pools and funds	53	9,431	9,536	75	8,580	13,614	98	5,404	5,877
Individual traders	298	10,874	9,962	459	16,882	16,108	774	16,468	14,704
Sub-total	480	31,878	33,774	672	47,570	49,840	1,004	29,279	30,043
Total	588	45,173	45,265	833	58,848	60,360	1,178	43,354	45,953

* FCM—Futures commission merchants
Source: CFTC market survey

The relatively small usage made of financial futures markets by commercial users is evident:

	T-bond	GNMA	T-bill	All contracts
			(%)	
Commercial	27.4	18.3	33.6	25.6
Futures industry	28.6	35.4	18.9	28.4
Commodity pools and funds	21.0	18.6	12.6	17.5
Individuals	23.0	27.7	34.9	28.5

These percentage figures show that trading in financial futures is dominated by individual traders, commodity funds and the futures industry. Although it is likely that commercial usage of the market has been growing more recently, there is clearly considerable potential for increasing the hedging use of financial futures dramatically.

F. More contracts and exchanges expected

Although the history of financial futures trading is littered with contracts and exchanges that did not quite make it, it appears that the number and type of contracts and exchanges is expanding. New contract activity in financial futures seems likely to concentrate largely in the stock index futures contracts. The Chicago Board of Trade plans to introduce stock index futures based on various industry indices. Along similar lines the Chicago Mercantile Exchange has proposed six further stock index futures to the CFTC. Three of these are based on Standard and Poor's indices—financials, transport and utilities—and three others will be based on indices produced by the exchange—high technology, consumer staples and energy. The New York Futures Exchange also has plans before the CFTC for additional stock index contracts based on sub-indices for particular industries, while COMEX plans to introduce a stock index future.

In the United States, apart from one or two interest rate contracts, such as Eurodollar deposits and two-year Treasury notes on the CBT, the main activity, in addition to stock index futures, will be the development of the extensive options on futures programme authorized by the CFTC. Although option strategies are outside the scope of this book, it is clear that this will be a field of rapid growth over the next few years.

New developments outside the United States will primarily involve several new exchanges opening, and some interesting new contracts being introduced on existing exchanges. After much delay the all-computerized financial futures exchange INTEX, based in Bermuda, is scheduled to open in 1983. The initial intention is to trade in gold futures and long-term US T-bond futures. Subsequent contracts are also scheduled to include such exotica as a world freight index future, which would be a general freight index based on several leading commodities, a representative number of trade routes and vessel sizes, and dry bulk cargo only, plus perhaps a Eurobond index future.

In addition to INTEX, a working party in Hong Kong has been reviewing the possible establishment of a local financial futures market. Whether plans for such an exchange go ahead will probably largely depend upon the success of LIFFE in developing trading volume.

Toronto is introducing a fascinating new stock index future which actually calls for physical delivery of a portfolio consisting of 100 share units of several leading Canadian stocks. This concept of a physical delivery stock market index future is unique. The Australian financial futures market in Sydney has introduced a stock market index future, while LIFFE is rumoured to be looking at various possibilities for new contracts including a Eurobond index future.

The message seems to be that there is no letting up in the proliferation of new types of financial futures and new financial futures exchanges. Nonetheless, all the new contracts and exchanges outside Chicago still have to prove themselves. There is as yet no concrete evidence that financial futures trading outside the Chicago Board of Trade and the Chicago Mercantile Exchange can develop sufficient liquidity to be useful to commercial hedgers. Thus the next two to three years should prove to be the most interesting to the professional futures markets' observer since interest rate futures began to trade. The rest of this book hopes to provide the basis for such an observer to analyse the success of these new markets, as well as to provide would-be hedgers and traders with the information needed to use existing markets.

Chapter 2

The mechanics of financial futures trading

This chapter is concerned with the basic elements of trading financial futures: first, the general principles involved; then, an examination of the most heavily traded individual contracts on the US and UK markets. A full list of currently traded contracts is given in Appendix 2.

A. The pricing of financial futures contracts

It is important for an investor to know how the pricing of financial futures contracts is carried out, because futures pricing systems sometimes differ considerably from those used in the cash market. This section looks at three basic types of financial futures traded: short-term interest rate contracts, long-term interest rate contracts, and foreign exchange rate contracts.

Short-term interest rates

The short-term interest rate contracts such as the Treasury bill contract on the IMM, the sterling deposit contract on LIFFE, and the Eurodollar contracts on the IMM and LIFFE, are all priced on an index basis, i.e. the price of a futures contract written on a short-term instrument is always given as (100 − implied interest rate). This method of pricing preserves the normal inverse relationship between prices and interest rates. The higher the implied interest rate, the lower is the futures price.

For instance, a March sterling time deposit rate can be locked in at 13.5% by purchasing a March sterling time deposit future at a price of 86.5 (100 − 13.5). If the price moves to 86.25, the implied time deposit interest rate has risen to 13.75 (100 − 86.25).

Virtually all the exchanges define the minimum price movement, called a tick, of such contracts as one basis point, or one hundredth of 1%. To facilitate efficient trading, the exchanges also ensure that each tick has the same money value, calculated as the tick size times the face value of the contract, which is generally $1,000,000 for dollar interest rate futures and £250,000 for sterling deposit futures.

Three-month Eurodollar interest rate

Tick size = 0.01% of interest for 3 months
Value of tick = $25 (0.0001 × 3/12 × $1,000,000)

Three-month sterling interest rate

Tick size = 0.01% of interest for 3 months
Value of tick = £6.25 (0.0001 × 3/12 × £250,000)

Example 1

A trader buys 10 three-month Eurodollar contracts at a price of 84.15. Ten days later the position is closed at a price of 84.05.

Profit or loss: 10 contracts × 10 ticks loss, (i.e. 84.05 − 84.15) × $25 per tick
Total loss = $2,500

Example 2

A trader sells five three-month sterling interest rate futures at a price of 86.27. Ten days later the position is closed at a price of 86.00.

Profit or loss: 5 contracts × 27 ticks gain (i.e. 86.27 − 86.00) × £6.25 per tick
Total gain = £843.75

Long-term interest rates

By contrast, futures contracts written on longer-term financial instruments such as the CBT Treasury bond contract, the CBT GNMA contract and the 20-year gilt contract on LIFFE are priced on the same discount basis as in the cash market. In each case, what is priced is an instrument with a standard coupon yield and a standard maturity. For instance, the gilt contract on LIFFE is priced as a percentage of face value, on the assumption of a standard 12% coupon yield and a 20-year maturity. Suppose the observed price of the LIFFE December 1983 gilt future was 99–16 on 15 November, 1983. This tells the trader that the market is willing to pay £99 16/32nds for £100 nominal of a 12% 20-year gilt. Longer-term instruments such as the gilt futures contract are priced in 32nds. In a similar manner the CBT Treasury bond contract is based on a standardized 8% 20-year Treasury bond, while the GNMA contract is based upon an 8% coupon with a 30-year maturity prepaid in 12 years.

The minimum price movement, or tick size, for these contracts is specified as 1/32nd per 100 units nominal. Once again the value of the tick is found by multiplying the tick size by the face value of the futures contract.

20-year gilt contract (LIFFE)

Tick size = 1/32 of 1%
Value of tick = £15.625 (1/32 × 0.01 × £50,000)

20-year Treasury bond contract (CBT)

Tick size = 1/32 of 1%
Value of tick = $31.25 (1/32 × 0.01 × $100,000)

Example

A trader buys five gilt contracts on LIFFE at a price of 97-28. A month later the position is closed at a price of 98-06.

Profit or loss: 5 contracts × 10 ticks gain (i.e. 98-06 minus 97-28) × £15.625 per tick
Total gain = £781.25

Foreign exchange contracts

Foreign exchange contracts, both on the IMM and LIFFE, are simply priced in terms of the underlying exchange rate. The trader observes the September 1983 dollar/sterling future quoted one day at 1.7000, and perhaps the next day at 1.7150. The pricing system is therefore exactly parallel to the ordinary foreign exchange forward market, save that foreign exchange futures price all currencies in terms of the number of dollars per unit of foreign currency. However, because of the very different values of different currencies in terms of dollars, tick sizes differ between the different contracts. The tick value is the same for all contracts except for Canadian dollars and Mexican pesos on the IMM, and sterling on LIFFE.

Sterling-dollar contracts

Tick size = 0.05 cents per £1/IMM: 0.01 cents per £1/LIFFE
Value of tick = $12.50 (0.0005 × £25,000)/IMM: $2.50 (0.0001 × £25,000)/LIFFE
Face value of contract = £25,000

Deutschmark-dollar contracts

Tick size = 0.01 cents per DM 1
Value of tick = $12.50 (0.0001 × DM 125,000)
Face value of contract = DM 125,000

Mexican peso-dollar

Tick size = 0.01 per Pesos 10
Value of tick = $10 (0.0001 × 1/10 × Pesos 1,000,000)
Face value of contract = Pesos 1,000,000

Example

A trader buys two sterling-dollar exchange rate contracts on the IMM at a price of $1.70. Eight days later the position is closed at a price of $1.75.

Profit or loss: 2 contracts × 100 ticks gain (i.e. $1.7500 − $1.7000/0.0005 per tick) × $12.50 per tick
Total profit = $2,500

In all cases, the profit or loss on a financial futures market transaction is determined by multiplying the number of contracts by the number of ticks the price has changed by the tick value. The standard size of the tick values makes it very easy for hedgers and traders to calculate the cash change in a futures position implied by a given change in the interest or foreign exchange rate.

B. Delivery and the clearing house

Although very few financial futures contracts, with the possible exception of the Treasury bill contract on the IMM, actually go to delivery, the delivery process is important in determining the relationship between cash and futures prices. For instance, there are many financial futures contracts which allow a wide variety of financial instruments to be delivered against a futures contract. Some financial instruments will be cheaper to acquire for the purpose of making delivery than others. Logically, the holder of a short futures position will deliver the instrument which costs him the least to acquire. Thus the market price of the futures contract will tend to trade off the price of what is called the cheapest deliverable instrument.

Were it not for the physical fact of possible delivery, no mechanism would exist for ensuring that cash and futures prices converge within the delivery month. During the delivery month—that month designated by the relevant exchange as the month within which physical delivery will take place—cash and futures prices will be approximately the same, or significant arbitrage profits will be possible. All exchanges determine a given sequence of calendar months as delivery months—the most common is a quarterly cycle of March, June, September and December, although different contracts on different exchanges may operate different cycles. The period or actual day within the delivery month on which delivery takes place, and the question whether the delivery process is to be initiated by the short or the long, also varies between different exchanges and contracts.

For most contracts, with the exception of cash settlement contracts, delivery in the futures market is the settlement of a contractual obligation. In general the exchange in question will specify a predetermined and fixed sequence of events, and each step in the process must be completed by a specific deadline. In virtually all cases, the process calls for notification by the long or short of intention to take or make delivery (which one depending on the rules of the individual contract) to the clearing house. This is followed by the matching by the clearing house of the long and short, and a notification to the other chosen party to expect to make or take delivery by a particular time. The delivery process is then completed by the short presenting either to the clearing house or directly to the long a suitable eligible financial instrument, and receiving payment for that instrument at an appropriate invoice price. The eligibility of particular financial instruments for delivery is determined in accordance with the rules of the exchange. For details of precise delivery methods on particular financial futures contracts, *see* the discussion of the more widely traded contracts later in this chapter.

Intention to make and take delivery on a financial futures contract is done through the clearing house. The role of the clearing house is crucial in the organization of a financial futures market where trading is by open outcry, and where there is no opportunity on the floor of checking the creditworthiness of individuals or firms with which contracts are made. The role of the clearing house can best be seen by quoting from the LIFFE discussion document on financial futures, September 1980.

> "A clearing house performs the following crucial functions on an exchange.
> (a) It carries out the function of matching and processing all trades. It registers and confirms all trades transacted on the market each day, thus providing an up-to-date record, both centrally and for each clearing member, of the current agreed position.
> (b) The clearing house becomes a party to every trade transacted by the principle of substitution: thus every trade is effectively done with and guaranteed by the clearing house. This virtually eliminates all credit risk and the necessity to assess the worth or integrity of the other party to a trade. (Note: as the clearing house is party to all transactions, it is always totally matched and fully margined with no position of its own). This procedure also enables any transaction or position to be reversed without any reference to the party with whom the original deal was done."

It is this process of substitution that enables the open outcry financial futures market to operate. In addition to matching and guaranteeing financial futures trades, the clearing house is also responsible for operating the system of daily evaluation and settlement of profits and losses on outstanding futures contracts. This margin and marking to market system is explained in detail in the next section.

The clearing house also plays a crucial role in the delivery system. At delivery an outstanding long position has to be matched with a short position for the exchange of deliverable instrument for cash to take place. Once notification of intention to deliver has been made by a clearing member to the clearing house, it is the role of the clearing house to match the long and the short according to specified rules.

The clearing house organization structure differs from one exchange to another. The tendency in the United States has been for the clearing house to be owned by the clearing members of the exchange concerned. For example, the Chicago Board of Trade Clearing Corporation is composed of 140 individuals and firms that are also members of the Chicago Board of Trade. Similarly the clearing house of the IMM is a subsidiary operation of the Chicago Mercantile Exchange. LIFFE, by contrast, has chosen to clear through the International Commodities Clearing House, which is a wholly-owned subsidiary of the UK clearing banks, and is thus completely financially independent of the London International Financial Futures Exchange.

The rule on all exchanges is that only clearing members will be able to clear trades at the clearing house, and that all other members will have to clear through a clearing member. The clearing house guarantee applies only to the clearing member who is a party to a futures transaction. Clearing members have to display a particular net worth requirement and fulfil any other exchange conditions. (See *Executing a transaction* on p. 15 for more details of this system.)

Whatever the particular clearing system adopted, they have all worked well in the past to protect futures market customers. Since the foundation of the Clearing Corporation of the CBT and the Clearing House on the IMM, there has never been an incidence of a financial loss due to default on a futures contract.

C. Margins

The high leverage available with financial futures has been mentioned. For example, an initial margin of only $2,000 is required to set up a long position of $1,000,000 (one contract) in Eurodollar time deposit futures. If Eurodollar interest rates fell by half a percentage point (or 50 basis points), the price of the futures contract would rise by the same amount. The buyer's futures position would be showing a profit of $1,250 (50 ticks × $25). On the other hand, if rates had risen rather than fallen 50 basis points, the buyer would have suffered a loss of $1,250. To cover that, it would be necessary for the buyer to deposit a further sum of $1,250 to his futures account to bring it back to a positive balance of $2,000. Futures profits and losses are calculated at the end of each business day and the resultant payments necessary to maintain the initial margin are called variation margin.

Example

Purchase of one three-month sterling deposit contract, with a face value of £250,000.

	Margin (£)	
	Initial	**Variation**
At time of initial transaction		
Buyer	£500	—
Seller	£500	—
If market value declines by £1,250		
Buyer	£500	£1,250 debit
Seller	£500	£1,250 credit

Initial margin levels

Three-month sterling time deposit (LIFFE):	0.2% of the nominal amount of the contract or £500 per £250,000 nominal.
Eurodollar deposit rate (IMM, LIFFE)★:	0.2% of the nominal amount of the contract or $2,000 per $1,000,000 nominal.
90-day Treasury bill (IMM):	0.2% of the nominal account of the contract or $2,000 per $1,000,000 nominal.
Gilt future (LIFFE):	3% of face value of contract or £1,500 per £50,000 nominal.

These margins can be changed and should be checked. Any dealer in financial futures must know exactly how much cash will be needed to set up the desired futures position, and work out the interest cost of financing this cash in relation to potential gains. The US exchanges often charge different margins for speculative positions and *bona fide* hedge positions.

The US exchanges also use a concept of maintenance margin, which is the minimum balance required in a futures account for a single open position, which is slightly less than the original initial margin. A classic example is the 90-day Eurodollar time deposit contract on the IMM, where the initial margin is $2,000 and the maintenance margin is $1,500. A series of Eurodollar futures prices illustrates how this works.

	Price	**Margin account**	**Debit or credit**	**Variation margin call**
Day 1	85.00	$2,000	—	—
Day 2	84.88	$1,700	− $300	—
Day 3	84.68	$1,200	− $500	$800
Day 4	84.68	$2,000	—	—
Day 5	84.78	$2,250	+ $250	− $250

On day 1, a futures position was set up for an initial margin payment of $2,000. On day 2, the price fell from 85 to 84.88, resulting in a loss of $300. The margin account was reduced to $1,700, but because this is still above the maintenance margin of $1,500, no margin call occurred. However, on day 3 the price of the future fell further and the money in the margin account fell to $1,200. Since this is below the maintenance margin level, a margin call of $800 was issued to bring the value of the margin account up to the initial level of $2,000. Finally, on day 5 the account showed a level of $2,250, entitling the holder of the financial future to withdraw $250 from the account. Exchanges such as LIFFE, which insist on margin accounts being kept up to the full initial margin on a daily basis, are simply keeping initial and maintenance margins at the same level.

In addition, even lower margins are required for what are termed straddle positions. A straddle position is defined as a simultaneous long and short position in different months of a single futures contract. Thus a typical straddle might be long 1 September three-month Eurodollar time deposit contract and short 1 December three-month Eurodollar contract. The initial margin on each pair of contracts is often substantially less than half the initial margin on

---

★ Since this book went to press, the LIFFE Eurodollar initial margin has changed to 0.1% on $1,000.

an outright position in a single contract. For instance, the spread margin of a IMM T-bill straddle has been only $400 initial and $200 maintenance, compared with $2,000 and $1,500 respectively for an outright T-bill position.

On LIFFE all straddle margins are 50% of the initial margin on a single futures contract. The reason for the low level of straddle margins is that the difference in price between the delivery months of a single contract is often less volatile than the absolute price of either month.

Finally, on the US markets initial, maintenance and spread margins in the delivery months for certain contracts may be substantially different from non-delivery months. Given the complexity of margin requirements and the frequency of changes in required margins, any trader should contact his broker to find the current state of initial margins before the commencement of trading.

The margins discussed so far are simply minimum levels determined by the exchange. Initial margins may be raised if interest and exchange rates appear to have become unduly volatile, or if the exchange believes undue speculative activity is taking place and over-large speculative positions are being built up. The basic reason for the size of margin payments is to protect the clearing system against default; initial margins are generally supposed to be at least the normal daily trading range of a financial futures contract.

While individual traders will be interested in the level of margin payments on financial futures trading, margin management can be of crucial importance to clearing members of the exchange. This is because the clearing house will often net off a clearing member's positions before determining margin requirements. Exhibit 2.1 gives a typical example for a clearing member trading in the Eurodollar contract and the gilt contract on LIFFE.

Exhibit 2.1: Example of initial margin calculation

	Three-month Eurodollar				20-year gilt			
	Open contracts		Uncovered		Open contracts		Uncovered	
	Bought	Sold	Bought	Sold	Bought	Sold	Bought	Sold
Spot month	20	10	10		20	50		30
Back months								
1	2	20		18	10	2	8	
2	10		10		15	40		25
3	20	4	16			2		2
4	5		5		22	10	12	
		Total	31	18		Total	20	27

Initial margin required

Spot month	10 × $1,000 = $10,000	30 × £1,500 = £45,000
Back months		
straddle	18 × $500 = $9,000	20 × £750 = £15,000
non-straddle	13 × $1,000 = $13,000	7 × £1,500 = £10,500
	$32,000	£70,500
Total due	£70,500	
	$32,000	

Although 91 Eurodollar contracts and 171 gilt contracts are outstanding, both long and short, total margin payments are only $32,000 and £70,500 compared with the $91,000 appropriate for 91 Eurodollar contracts and £256,500 associated with 171 gilt contracts. This is because not only are long and short positions in the same delivery months netted off, but long and short positions matched among different delivery months are counted as straddles and hence attract smaller margins. The clearing member, on the other hand, will be entitled to demand full margins from both the short and long positions bought and sold through him by non-clearing members and outsiders. In other words, this netting off process may well provide the clearing member with substantial uncommitted funds available for investment. The management of margin accounts can thus provide both clearing members, and non-clearing members dealing for non-members, with substantial extra profits.

What constitutes an adequate deposit against margin requirements varies substantially between different financial futures exchanges. Most of the US exchanges allow initial margin payments to be put in the form of acceptable interest bearing securities such as Treasury bills; in other words, the trader does not lose interest income on his initial margin payments. However, additional or variation margin payments must generally be made in cash, and interest will not be paid to the holder of the contract. A surplus on the margin account can be withdrawn or reinvested to earn additional returns.

In the UK the situation on initial margin is similar. While initial margin payments may be made in cash and earn interest, margin payments made in non-cash deposits will bear substantial penalties, although bank guarantees can be used as margin in certain circumstances. Once again the trader in financial futures needs to be aware of the individual requirements of different exchanges for margining financial futures positions.

The level of variation margin calls is determined by what is called the settlement price of the financial futures contract, which is the daily price the clearing house uses to clear all trades. The settlement price is determined by reference to the high and low prices at which transactions take place during a period at the end of a trading session officially designated by the exchange as the close. The trader should also be aware that he must meet adverse variation margin calls immediately. If a customer fails to come up with variation margin within an appropriate time frame, a position can be closed out and any loss sustained deducted from the balance in the margin account. Any further shortfall would also have to be met by the customer.

Exchange rules on initial and variation margin payments apply only between clearing members of the exchange and the clearing house or system. Margin relationships, amounts and payments between non-clearing members and a clearing member are technically negotiable, as are arrangements between non-members and members of the exchange.

Frequently a broker will insist on higher initial margin payments or deposits than are determined by the exchange and the clearing system. However exchange rules generally insist that such margins may not be less than the clearing member pays to the clearing system. Both the buyer and seller of a futures contract need to maintain a minimum balance of the initial margin in their futures account as long as the position remains open.

D. Executing a transaction

Once a potential participant in financial futures trading is fully familiar with the principles of pricing of interest rate and foreign exchange rate contracts and the exchange requirements of initial, maintenance and variation margins, he will be ready to place an order. This section considers the basic steps involved in the purchase of a single futures contract.

The first step in trading financial futures for a non-member of the exchange is to open a futures trading account with a member firm. The choice of a broker is an important decision for the individual customer, yet it is difficult to provide hard and fast rules for choosing through whom to deal. It will partly depend on the nature of the individual customers—some brokers will only be prepared to handle institutional business. Additionally, brokers may demand widely different margins and deposits from different types of customers. Some brokers will provide a full research service but may charge high commissions; others may do nothing but execute customers' orders without trying to advise on customers' strategies.

The important thing is to find a broker whose methods of operation are consistent with a customer's requirements. This will also partially depend upon the rates of commission and margin requirements the broker is willing to grant to the customer, since on all major exchanges these are subject to individual negotiation.

The first step for a customer is to place an order with a registered representative of a member firm. Such an order will specify whether it is to buy or sell contracts, which contracts and how many. It may also contain restrictions on the price at which the order is to be transacted, and how long an order is to remain open. The member will check that the order is consistent with any restrictions or limits on the customer's account, and possibly whether the customer's deposit is sufficient to cover the order. The order will be confirmed to the customer orally, and subsequently in writing, normally time-stamped. Orders may also be originated within a member firm, and the same checking procedure will be followed.

As soon as the order is originated, it is immediately transmitted to the member's booth on the floor of the exchange, where details will be written on a standard order slip, which is immediately time-stamped. The order slip will contain a clear instruction as to the type of order, the price or price range within which it may be executed, and if appropriate a customer account number. One or two copies of the order slip will be kept at the booth, while the other will be sent through a "runner" to a member of the trading staff or a pit broker for execution.

Once the order has been executed, the broker in the pit will complete the details of the execution on the order slip and sent it back to the booth. When it is confirmed that the order has been executed in line with the customer's instructions, an official exchange clearing slip will be prepared giving full details of the transaction and identifying codes of the counterparty to the transaction. Both the buyer and seller of a financial futures contract will be responsible for preparing an official exchange clearing slip for the transaction which will be presented to the exchange, or directly to the clearing house, for matching.

Coincident with the preparation of the official exchange clearing slip, the staff on the floor will confirm execution of the order and the terms of execution to the member's office, which will in turn confirm to the customer details of the transaction carried out on his behalf. Secondly, a written record of the transaction will be remitted to the member's office to enable reconciliation with the clearing system and as an entry into the firm's customer accounting system. Exhibit 2.2 shows the flow of this order system on a typical exchange.

Exhibit 2.2: Flow of an order system on a typical exchange

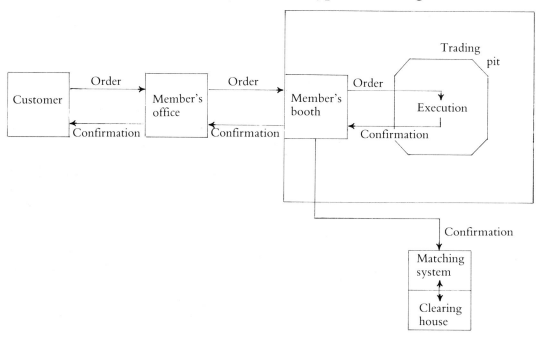

The process of matching the official clearing slips or trade confirmation cards varies between different exchanges. The London International Financial Futures Exchange carries out the process of matching orders itself continuously throughout the day, and itself transmits matched pairs of orders to the clearing house. The exchange staff are responsible for identifying any invalid clearing slips, or slips for which an exact match cannot be found, in order to correct any mismatches as quickly as possible. The aim is to ensure that all transactions are matched and entered into the clearing system on the same day.

In most US exchanges, the process of matching and transaction verification is carried out by the clearing house itself rather than the exchange; however, the process of matching orders is identical in both systems.

Once verified transactions are entered into the clearing system, the members of the exchange cease to deal with each other but deal only with the clearing house: the clearing house interposes itself as the second party to any futures contract position. Exhibit 2.3 gives the basic structure of the clearing process.

Exhibit 2.3: Structure of the clearing process

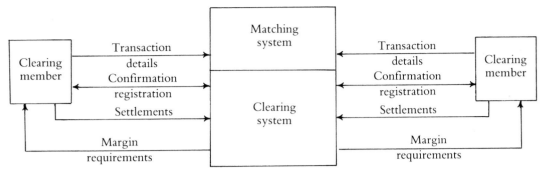

Soon after the end of a trading day, the clearing house provides each clearing member with full details of all trades registered that day in the name of the clearing member or those non-clearing members who clear through him. Following confirmation by the clearing member of these registered transactions, plus receipt of the required margins on the transactions, the clearing house guarantee of performance of these future contracts comes into force. Once this happens, the carrying out of contract obligations of a clearing member is guaranteed by the clearing house, regardless of any failure on the part of the original parties to the transactions to fulfil their obligations.

The clearing house is able to provide this guarantee to clearing members because of four major elements, two of which arise out of the margin system for financial futures we have discussed earlier. The system of initial margins from both buyer and seller of contracts, and the system of daily marking to market, serves to minimize the net exposure of the clearing house in the event of a default by a clearing member.

Any loss that cannot be met out of margin deposits will be met out of the capital resources of the clearing house, and subsequently from the resources of its shareholders and clearing members. Given the large capital requirements a clearing member of any futures exchange has to display, the financial resources backing the clearing house guarantee are generally very large and more than adequate.

Exchange members who do not choose to be clearing members must have their trades cleared by another member who is a clearing member. So, whenever a non-clearing member carries out and registers a transaction on the trading floor, the transaction will be included in a clearing member's account for the purpose of registration by the clearing house as if the non-clearing member were simply another customer of the clearing member. However, the clearing house guarantee of contract fulfilment only applies to the clearing member. Hence a customer dealing through a non-clearing member of the exchange will need to assure himself of the creditworthiness of the member.

In addition to providing guarantees, the clearing house of a financial futures exchange carries out three further functions. First, it determines the margin requirements, both initial and variation, that clearing members are required to deposit with the clearing house. The method an individual clearing house uses to determine the amount of required margin varies. The ICCH for LIFFE clearing members will allow major offsets of contracts, including the spot months, in determining margins. Some US exchange clearing houses, on the other hand, require margins on a gross basis from clearing members, i.e. 10 long and 10 short in the same delivery month requires 20 initial margins. Each clearing house will provide full details of its margin offsets on request.

Clearing members pass on margin requirements to non-clearing members who clear through them, and to direct customers. All exchanges have a rule that the margin requirements from clearing members to non-clearing members and customers must be no less, although they can be more, than those imposed on the clearing member by the clearing house.

The clearing house also controls the closing out of contracts by settlement. This works by pairing long and short positions for the same delivery month. A member who is long five sterling March deposit contracts on LIFFE can sell five March contracts and request settlement. The clearing house matches the opposing futures positions and cancels the original obligation, releasing any margin monies held with respect to the original long position. The vast proportion of outstanding financial futures contracts are liquidated or cancelled by settlement.

Finally the clearing house is also responsible for organizing and carrying out the delivery process for financial futures (see *The major contracts* on p. 25).

The steps involved in purchasing a single financial futures contract are:

1. Order given to member. Order confirmed to customer by member.
2. Order transmitted to exchange. Time-stamped order executed if possible in pit.
3. Official clearing slip prepared. Execution and terms confirmed to member's office. Execution confirmed to customer.
4. Clearing slips matched by exchange or clearing house. Transaction registered to clearing member.
5. Clearing member confirms transaction to clearing house. Clearing house guarantee is triggered.
6. Clearing member deposits required initial margin with clearing house. Clearing member requires margin from non-clearing member or customer.
7. Non-clearing member deposits initial margin with clearing member. Non-clearing member requires margin from customer.
8. Customer deposits initial margin with member.

Steps 6, 7, 8 of this structure will be repeated daily with respect to variation margin.

E. Types of orders

The order slip specifies the price range and time within which the transaction must be carried out. Various types of order have developed in trading financial futures, and the most important of these are described in this section.

The major elements in any order are: buy or sell, the exchange, the underlying asset, the number of contracts, the delivery month, the price, and the duration. The most common type of order is the *market* order. This is simply an order to buy or sell a financial futures contract at the best available price in the market.

Example of typical market order to buy

Exchange	Buy/Sell	Quantity	Type	Price	Order type	Duration
LIFFE	Buy	5	June sterling time deposit	Market		

The floor broker receives an order to buy five sterling time deposit contracts at market. These are currently trading at bid 89.65 and ask 89.70. He might try to get a lower price than 89.70: if he cannot, he will buy the five contracts at 89.70 if possible. However, he might be able to buy only two contracts at 89.70 and the other three at 89.72. A market order to sell would follow exactly the same pattern. Once a transaction is agreed, each floor or pit broker will record on a trading card or order slip the name and number of the other broker, the contract, the delivery month, the contract and the price.

Sometimes, however, a customer may wish to buy or sell only at a specified price, and in this case he would use what is called a *limit order*. Such an order tells the broker to buy or sell only at a particular price or one even more favourable to the customer. Thus a *limit order to buy* will be placed below the current market price, with the transaction to take place at or below the limit. A *limit order to sell* would be placed above the current market price, with the transaction to take place at or above the limit.

Example of typical limit order to sell

Exchange	Buy/Sell	Quantity	Type	Price	Order type	Duration
CBT	Sell	2	June T-bond	89 14/32	Limit	

The floor broker is instructed to sell June T-bond futures at or above 89 14/32nds. The current price is 88 20/32nds. The broker does nothing. However, if the price rises to 89 14/32nds, he will sell two T-bond contracts. If no duration is specified, as in this example, the order is automatically presumed to be what is called a *day* order. In a day order, if the price limit is not reached within one trading session (day), and therefore the order cannot be executed, it is automatically cancelled.

The success of limit orders depends to a considerable extent on the skill of the floor broker. The fact that a price at or above a sell limit is observed does not necessarily mean that the broker will have got in at that price.

An alternative type of order that combines some of the characteristics of the market order and the limit order is the *market if touched* (MIT). This type of order does not necessarily need to be carried out at the price limit. It is an order that turns into a market order once there is one trade in the market at the price limit.

Example of a typical MIT order

Exchange	Buy/Sell	Quantity	Type	Price	Order type	Duration
IMM	Buy	3	March 90-day T-bill	90.00	MIT	

The market is trading at 91.00 and the customer has a short position in three March T-bill contracts. He places an MIT order to buy at 90.00. The broker observes prices dropping and a transaction is carried out at 90.00. He immediately enters the market to get the best possible price for his customer. However 90.00 turns out to be the low for the day, and he buys the three contracts at a price of 90.05. Unlike a limit to buy order, the MIT order can be fulfilled at a price above that stated in the order.

A similar type of order to the MIT order is the *stop* order. An MIT order to buy is triggered if the price reaches or goes above the stated price. Similarly a stop order to sell is triggered if the price reaches, or goes below, the stated price. When the price is reached, like the MIT order, the stop order turns into a market order.

Example of a stop order to sell

Exchange	Buy/Sell	Quantity	Type	Price	Order type	Duration
LIFFE	Sell	2	March Eurodollar time deposit	89.50	Stop	GTC

A customer has a long position in two March Eurodollar futures, and wishes to cut his losses if the market moves against him. Thus he enters a *stop sell* order for two contracts at 89.50: the current price is 90.00. At first, the broker does nothing. Later in the day the market trades at 89.50; the broker enters the market and sells two contracts at 89.49. The duration of this stop order is GTC or *good till cancelled*. This type of order is not cancelled at the end of a trading day, but remains with the floor broker as an active order until cancelled by the customer himself.

Stop orders can also be entered as limit orders. There are two basic types: *stop-limit* and *stop and limit*. In both cases a stop order becomes a limit order rather than a market order when the stated price is reached. The difference is that in the stop–limit order the stop price and the limit price are different, while in the stop and limit order the stop price and the limit price are identical.

Example of a stop-limit order

Exchange	Buy/Sell	Quantity	Type	Price	Order type	Duration
LIFFE	Buy	2	March Eurodollar time deposit	89.50	Stop limit 89.70	GTC

Consider a customer who is short two Eurodollar contracts when the price is 88.80. On receiving the order the broker does nothing. As soon as a price of 89.50 is observed in the market, the order is converted into a limit order to buy at 89.70, i.e. the broker will now attempt to purchase the two contracts at a price at or below 89.70. If he cannot fill the order until the price exceeds 89.70, he does not attempt to fill the order again until the price falls back into the 89.50–89.70 range. This is known as a good till cancelled (GTC) order.

Example of a stop and limit order

Exchange	Buy/Sell	Quantity	Type	Price	Order type	Duration
IMM	Sell	2	March 90-day T-bill	90.00	Stop and limit	Month

Consider a customer who is long two March T-bill contracts at 90.50. He is worried about prices falling sharply and decides to limit his losses by putting in a stop and limit order at 90.00. As soon as a trade or bid is heard in the market at 90.00, the limit order is triggered and the broker will attempt to sell the two contracts at or higher than the limit price. This is a *month* order: it will remain open until the last trading day of the month, when it will be automatically cancelled.

It can be seen how combinations of these orders can be used to protect both sides of a financial futures trader's position. Consider a customer who purchases five IMM March T-bill contracts at a price of 90.00. He wants to protect himself against possible losses but also to take profits if the T-bill price goes to a certain level. Consider the following combination of orders:

Example of a combination of orders

Exchange	Buy/sell	Quantity	Type	Price	Order type	Duration
IMM	Sell	5	March 90-day T-bill	92.00	MIT	GTC
IMM	Sell	5	March 90-day T-bill	89.00	Stop	GTC

The customer has placed an MIT order to sell at 92.00 and a stop order to sell at 89.00. If the market trades up to 92.00, the MIT order will trigger and the broker will liquidate the contracts at the best price available. If the market trades down to 89.00, the stop will trigger and the broker will also liquidate the contracts at the best possible price. Although the investor is not certain of getting exactly the stated prices, he will in all likelihood have circumscribed his potential losses or taken significant profits. The use of stop orders to limit financial futures risk is absolutely necessary if the customer cannot maintain very close contact with the market.

There are also other specified duration orders. The most notorious of these is the *fill-or-kill* or FOK order. Sometimes this is known as an *immediate-or-cancel* or *quick* order. This is a specific order with a determined price which can be offered or bid on the floor only three times; if it is not executed, it is immediately cancelled. If part of the order can be executed, that is done and the rest cancelled.

Example of FOK order

Exchange	Buy/Sell	Quantity	Type	Price	Order type	Duration
LIFFE	Buy	2	March sterling time deposit	91.00	Limit	FOK

The customer institutes a FOK limit order, i.e. he orders the broker to buy two contracts at a price of 91.00 or lower on a fill-or-kill basis. The broker succeeds in buying only one contract at that price, and cancels the other half of the order. He immediately reports the transaction to the customer together with the latest price.

Other time specific orders are *at the opening* or *at the close* orders. These are orders that must be executed during the official opening or closing periods of the financial futures market in question. If they are market orders, the execution price must fall within the range of prices within those official periods. If limit or stop orders, and the broker is unable to execute the order within the closing or opening period, the order is once again automatically cancelled.

Examples of at the opening and at the close orders

Exchange	Buy/Sell	Quantity	Type	Price	Order type	Duration
CBT	Buy	5	March T-bond	Market		Opening only
CBT	Sell	5	March T-bond	89 16/32	Limit	At the close

Sometimes a trader may use a combination of such orders; for example, he might want to put in a limit to buy order for the trading day, which would turn into a market at the close order if not fulfilled.

Example of combined time specific orders

Exchange	Buy/Sell	Quantity	Type	Price	Order type	Duration
CBT	Buy	5	March T-bond	89 16/32	Limit or Market on the close	

The order is to buy five T-bond contracts at a limit price of 89 16/32nds; however, if the broker cannot fulfil the limit he is instructed to fill the order at the close at the best available price. If the price remains at 90 1/32nd all day, the broker must fill the order at that price during the close.

In addition to the orders already described, which are characterized by specified prices or duration or both, there are also more complex orders which are *contingent* on other orders being fulfilled. The most common of these orders is the *scale* order, where the broker is instructed to buy or sell further contracts on a price scale related to the price at which the first transaction is executed.

Example of scale order

Exchange	Buy/Sell	Quantity	Type	Price	Order type	Duration
IMM	Buy	2	March T-bill and 2 each 10 pts lower: total 8	Market		GTC
IMM	Buy	2	March T-bill and 2 each 10 pts lower: total 8	90.00	Limit	GTC

The first order calls for the broker to buy two March T-bills at market. If he gets a price of 89.90, immediately three separate limit orders to buy are set up for two contracts each: the first at 89.80, the second at 89.70 and the final third at 89.60. The second order gives the broker a limit order to buy two contracts at 90.00. If he achieves a price of 89.98, a further three limit orders to buy are set up for two contracts each: this time the first will be at 89.88, the second at 89.78 and the third at 89.68.

Another type of contingent order is the *alternative* order. This involves two separate orders, but linked in the sense that if one order is triggered, the other is automatically cancelled. Its main role is when a customer wishes to put a stop-loss and profit-taking order on simultaneously. In a previous example, a holder of a long position in T-bills bought at 90.00 decided to simultaneously put an MIT sell order at 92.00 and a stop-sell order at 89.00. If the customer's position was closed out by taking profits at 92.00, he would not necessarily want to open a new short position if the price fell to 89.00.

Example of an alternative order

Exchange	Buy/Sell	Quantity	Type	Price	Order type	Duration
CBT	Buy	3	March T-bond	88.00	Limit or Stop 88 6/32 OCO	GTC

Suppose the current market price is 88 3/32nds: the customer wants to take advantage of a drop in the market price to buy, so he puts in a limit order to buy at 88-00. On the other hand he does not want to miss out on a sudden upward trend, so he also puts in a stop-buy at 88 6/32nds. However, if the market does advance and the broker purchases three T-bond contracts at 88 6/32nds, the order to buy at 88-00 is immediately cancelled (OCO stands for *one cancels other*).

The types of contingent orders discussed so far are relatively easy for any competent floor broker to execute. Other types of contingent orders, where the execution of one order actually depends on the execution of another, are much more difficult to handle, and some contingent orders are not acceptable on certain exchanges. Any customer wishing to use such orders will need to check which types of orders are allowed on which exchanges. In general a broker will not accept responsibility for simultaneous or exact execution.

There are two types of such orders: first, those involving the simultaneous purchase and sale of two contracts, basically spread or straddle orders, and second the orders that require the execution of one order before another.

Some examples of orders instituting and cancelling spreads and straddles are shown below. (*See* Chapter 6 for a more detailed discussion of spreads.)

Example of a straddle order

Exchange	Buy/Sell	Quantity	Type	Price	Order type	Duration
LIFFE	Buy	2	March sterling time deposit			GTC
LIFFE	Sell	2	June sterling time deposit	June 50 pts under or less		GTC

This is a simple order calling for the simultaneous (or as near simultaneous as the broker can manage) purchase of two March contracts and sale of two June contracts when the difference between the March and June contract price is 50 basis points or less. (The difference is March price minus June price.) This spread could be unwound with an order in the following form:

Example of a straddle unwinding order

Exchange	Buy/Sell	Quantity	Type	Price	Order type	Duration
LIFFE	Buy	2	June sterling time deposit	June 100 pts under or more		GTC
LIFFE	Sell	2	March sterling time deposit			GTC

The instruction to the broker is to unwind the straddle if the difference between the March and June contracts widens to 100 basis points or more. In some markets, there are spread brokers who will quote an actual spread and themselves take on the risk of putting the two sides of the transactions on simultaneously. If the spread brokers do not exist, then although a broker will do his best to buy and sell the contracts to achieve the required spread, the customer has no guarantee that he will be able to. Spread orders could also involve the simultaneous purchase and sale of different futures contracts on the same exchange, or identical or different futures contracts on two different exchanges. The order structure would, however, be identical.

A *switch* order is used to move an existing position in one month into a similar position in a different month. It differs from a spread or straddle in that the customer already has a futures position and wishes to swap it for another one.

Example of a switch order

Exchange	Buy/Sell	Quantity	Type	Price	Order type	Duration
IMM	Switch buy	5	June T-bill			GTC
IMM	Sell	5	March T-bill	June 10 basis points under or less		

The customer is long five March T-bills. He instructs the broker to switch him into June T-bills as soon as the difference between March and June futures price is 10 basis points or less.

Finally, there are contracts involving the purchase or sale of a futures contract and the simultaneous setting-up of a limit order to liquidate the position.

Example of a contingent order

Exchange	Buy/Sell	Quantity	Type	Price	Order type	Duration
LIFFE	Buy	5	March gilt when done	89 16/32	Limit	GTC
LIFFE	Sell	5	March gilt	91 2/32	Limit	GTC

The customer has ordered the broker to buy five March gilt contracts at a price of 89 16/32nds or lower. If, and only if, the first limit order is carried out, then a second limit order to sell at or above a price of 91 2/32nds is triggered.

This section has described the most common types of orders. Individual brokerage firms may not be willing to accept all these orders, or may offer other orders to customers as an extra service. Not all such orders are acceptable on all exchanges. However, any competent trader in financial futures must be aware of different types of orders if he wishes to manage his position in an optimal manner.

F. Commissions and transaction costs

One of the most important elements in financial futures trading for non-members is the question of commissions and transactions costs. There are no fixed commissions on any major futures exchange trading financial futures. Thus the precise level of commissions is entirely subject to discussion between individual clients and the broker or member. However, it is likely that higher rates of commission will apply for non-members trading with a member of the exchange, than will apply between members.

Nonetheless there are some elements relating to commissions on financial futures. First, a commission will generally be quoted for a round-turn, i.e. commissions are paid only after both a buying and selling transaction are completed. For instance, supposing an investor sells a T-bill future in anticipation of a decline in price: one commission will be paid either when the T-bill contract is repurchased or when delivery is made. The level of commission is also generally not influenced by the price of the underlying contract. Finally, reduced commissions will generally be charged for day trades, when a position is opened and closed out on the same day, and for spread and straddle trades.

As far as a non-member transaction is concerned, the level of commission negotiated with a broker or member, plus the level of required margin deposits, are the only relevant items. For the members of the exchange, certain direct fees have to be taken into account and fitted into the cost structure of trading. Each contract cleared through the clearing house will require the payment of a clearing fee. In addition, on LIFFE where the clearing house and the exchange are separate, the exchange also levies a fee on individual transactions. Finally, it is likely that clearing members will levy a charge per transaction on non-clearing members clearing through them. Although such fees are small—for example, the current LIFFE fees are a 28–30p per transaction clearing fee and a 10p per transaction LIFFE levy—they can make a significant difference to scalping operations.

Any investor considering dealing in financial futures must be careful to work a precise and detailed schedule of commissions with his broker or member before commencing trading.

G. Price limits

Virtually all futures contracts traded on an organized exchange are subject to daily price limits, i.e. restrictions on the amount the price of the commodity can rise or fall during the course of a trading day relative to the settlement price on the previous day. Transactions can take place only within the prescribed range, which is determined by the authorities of the exchange concerned and promulgated through its set of rules and regulations. Such limits will vary from one exchange to another and from one financial future to another. Thus, on the IMM, the daily price limit on the 90-day Treasury bill contract is equal to 60 basis points above or below the previous day's settlement price, while the Eurodollar time deposit contract price limit is 100 basis points above or below the settlement price.

Example

IMM Eurodollar time deposit contract

10 May	Settlement price = 88.67
11 May	Maximum price for a transaction 89.67
	Minimum price for a transaction 87.67

On virtually all US exchanges when the daily price limit is reached in either direction, trading ceases for that trading day. The aim of price limits is to ensure an orderly market and limit undue speculation. In particular, it forces traders to take time to evaluate the impact of a particular piece of information on the price, rather than introduce an immediate full assessment into the price. It also has the effect of evening out large random fluctuations in prices. For instance, suppose the following set of prices for IMM Eurodollar time deposit futures would have occurred in the absence of price limits.

Example A

	10 May	11 May	12 May	13 May	14 May
June Eurodollar future	88.67	85.50	86.00	87.00	87.20

Now suppose we impose a price limit of 100 basis points and examine the sequence of settlement prices.

Example B

	10 May	11 May	12 May	13 May	14 May
Settlement price	88.67	87.67	86.67	87.00	87.20
Price range permitted		87.67	86.67	85.67	86.20
		89.67	88.67	87.67	88.20

The pattern of prices has been smoothed out, and the sudden drop down to 85.50, which was reversed over the next couple of days, has been to a large extent eliminated. This is one of the prime aims of price limits as used in the United States—to try and remove the impact of sudden, large fluctuations in future prices.

Occasionally, however, the price limits may serve to interfere with a prolonged fundamental upturn or downturn in the market. In such a case, the simple continuation of the standard limits day after day could lead to no trading on the exchange for several days. When no trading takes place, it is impossible for investors to close out their positions either to take profits or cut losses. To handle this problem, most exchanges have a system of expanded daily limits when prices are moving particularly strongly over a period in a particular direction.

For instance, if we take the domestic CD contract on the IMM, the standard daily trading limit is 80 basis points up or down. However, the exchange rules state that whenever any contract month closes at the normal daily limit in the same direction on two consecutive days, an expanded daily limit schedule goes into effect. On the third day, the daily limit is 150% of the normal limit, and on the fourth day and thereafter 200% of the normal limit for as long as any contract remains limit-up or limit-down. As soon as all contracts close at prices within the expanded limits on a given day, the normal daily limit is reinstated on the following day. This can be illustrated with an example. Suppose, in the absence of limit trading, the following set of prices for domestic CD futures would be observed.

Example

	10 May	11 May	12 May	13 May	14 May	17 May	18 May
June CD future	88.67	86.67	84.67	83.67	83.50	83.40	83.42

Now let us look at the daily price limits and their impact on the settlement price.

	10 May	11 May	12 May	13 May	14 May	17 May	18 May
Settlement price	88.67	87.87	87.07	85.87[a]	84.27[b]	83.40[c]	83.42
Price range		87.87	87.07	85.87	84.27	82.67	82.60
		89.47	88.67	88.27	87.47	85.87	84.20

[a]On the third day, 13 May, after two days of consecutive limit-down prices, the daily price limit is raised to 120 basis points giving a range of 240 basis points (85.87–88.27).
[b]On the fourth day, 14 May, after another limit-down price, the daily price limit is raised to 160 basis points giving a range of 320 basis points (84.27–87.47).
[c]On the fifth day, 15 May, the final price closes within the prescribed daily range of 320 points (82.67–85.87).

The normal price limit of 80 basis points and daily range of 160 points is reinstated on 18 May.

This system can lead to substantial differences between settlement prices and fundamental equilibrium prices for significant periods, when there is a fundamental shift in a particular direction in the futures price. In the example above, the settlement price was not equal to the underlying price until 17 May; for the whole period 11 May–14 May, there would have been no trading in this contract. The daily settlement price is the determinant of the daily variation margin payments. Many US exchanges, however, also specify that there will be no price limits in operation within the spot or delivery month.

The LIFFE system interferes much less with the movement of futures prices in response to new information. The effect of limits is merely a brief pause, to allow positions to be assessed. In contrast to the US system of limits, there is little or no interference with the ability of investors to liquidate outstanding futures positions. It seems likely that a prolonged period of limit-up or limit-down prices in, say, the Eurodollar time deposit contract in Chicago would lead to many investors offsetting their positions, which cannot be closed in the normal way on the IMM, on the London exchange.

Anyone trading financial futures should, however, be aware of the existence of these price limit systems, and hence the possibility that they will not be able to close out positions to take profits or cut losses at will. Precise details of normal and expanded price limits for individual contracts are available from the individual exchanges.

H. The major contracts

1. Treasury bill futures contracts (IMM)

The IMM US Treasury bill contract, written on 90-day Treasury bills, has by far the biggest trading volume of any short-term interest rate contract. The IMM T-bill contract is traded on a December, March, June, September two-year cycle.

Pricing
In keeping with the general principles of pricing of short-term interest rate contracts, the Treasury bill futures contract is priced on an index basis:

$$\text{Treasury bill futures price} = 100 - \text{discount yield}$$

Thus a futures price of 87.50 is equivalent to an annual discount yield on a 90-day Treasury bill of 12.50%. The index price for the Treasury bill future determines the profits and losses to an open futures position.

The tick value for a Treasury bill contract is calculated in the usual manner for a tick size of 0.01% or one basis point:

$$\text{Tick value} = \frac{\text{T-bill face value} \times \text{Tick size} \times \text{Days to maturity}}{360}$$

$$\text{Tick value} = \frac{\$1,000,000 \times 0.0001 \times 90}{360} = \$25$$

Example

A trader buys two March T-bill contracts on the IMM at 88.50 and sells them 10 days later at 88.72.

$$\text{Gain on each contract} = 22 \text{ ticks } (88.72 - 88.50)$$
$$\text{Profit} = 2 \text{ contracts} \times 22 \text{ ticks} \times \$25 \text{ tick value}$$
$$= \$1,100$$

Exhibit 2.4 gives a typical set of data for IMM Treasury bill contracts for 10 March, 1982, and illustrates most of the important points concerning these contracts. Consider first the March 1982 contracts: an opening price of 87.85, a high for the day of 87.92, and a low of 87.68. The settlement price is 87.75, i.e. the price at which the IMM Clearing House clears all the trades. The settlement price is based upon the closing range of trading on 10 March, 1982. The price change on the day is (18) basis points, i.e. the 10 March settlement price of 87.75 is 18 basis points lower than the previous day's settlement price of 87.93. The opening price of the March contract is already 8 basis points lower than the settlement price of the previous day.

Exhibit 2.4: IMM Treasury bill futures prices

Wednesday, 10 March, 1982
Open interest reflects previous trading day Treasury bills (IMM)—$1 million; pts of 100%

	Open	High	Low	Settle	Change	Discount Settle	Discount Change	Open Interest
March 82	87.85	87.92	87.68	87.75	−.18	12.25	+.18	6,149
June	87.70	87.80	87.55	87.69	−.14	12.31	+.14	21,054
Sept.	87.50	87.55	87.36	87.43	−.14	12.57	+.14	6,277
Dec.	87.27	87.35	87.19	87.25	−.11	12.75	+.11	2,940
March 83	87.20	87.27	87.15	87.20	−.07	12.80	+.07	1,784
June	87.24	87.27	87.16	87.20	−.05	12.80	+.05	973
Sept.	87.21	87.25	87.18	87.23	−.07	12.77	+.07	138
Dec.	87.26	87.27	87.25	87.27	−.08	12.73	+.08	33

Est. vol. 32,215; vol. Mon. 30,794; open interest 39,348; +989

Source: International Monetary Market

The settlement price change determines all variation margin payments to the Clearing House: a trader holding a long position in one March contract would have his margin account debited $450 on the evening of 10 March (18 ticks × $25 tick value). On the other hand, a trader with a short position in one December 1982 T-bill would have his account credited with $275 (11 ticks × $25 tick value).

The volume and open interest figures for this series of contracts are also interesting. The daily trading volume is vastly in excess of the daily change in open interest. A considerable amount of contracts traded during a day are closed out before the close of trading (*see* Chapter 6 for scalping and trading activities that give rise to this level of volume).

The pattern of open interest in individual contract months also displays a conventional pattern. Open interest is invariably high in the nearby months and decreases quite rapidly through the deferred months. The March 1982 open interest is low and decreasing because we are already within the delivery month, and most financial futures contracts are closed out before delivery.

All US 90-day T-bill futures contracts have as delivery day the third business day following the Federal T-bill auction of the third week of the delivery month. This pattern of open interest, which will be found duplicated in other futures contracts, has important implications for hedging strategies.[1]

All financial futures exchanges operate a system of price limits. While price limits may be varied by the exchanges under certain circumstances, the price limit for US T-bill contracts is normally 60 basis points up or down. In other words, the maximum possible daily range of prices is 120 basis points. So, if a March T-bill closes at 89.00, the next day the price can move to a maximum of 89.60 or a minimum of 88.40 before trading is brought to a halt. Similarly, although exchanges do vary margins from time to time in line with market conditions, the usual initial margin on T-bill contracts in recent months has been 0.20% of contract face value or $2,000. Firms may well require substantially higher initial margins than this exchange minimum.

Delivery

Although the pricing of T-bill contracts is identical with other short-term financial instruments, the fact that Treasury bills are discount rather than coupon instruments makes a big difference to the delivery process. The US 90-day Treasury bill futures contract calls for the delivery of a 90-day Treasury bill, or at the option of the short position holder, a 91-day or 92-day Treasury bill. The delivery is carried out through the book entry system operated by the Federal Reserve. Under this system, banks who are members of the Federal Reserve system hold their Treasury securities in accounts at the Federal Reserve. Thus transactions between banks can be carried out simply by debiting and crediting these accounts.

When a customer decides to take delivery of Treasury bills on his futures contract, he will instruct his bank accordingly. When the bank is informed by wire that their account has been credited with the appropriate bills, they will credit the customer accordingly and debit his account for payments. The T-bills themselves will never leave the Federal Reserve.

The process of delivery for T-bills on the IMM is:

1. On the last trading day, which is two business days after the Federal T-bills auction in the third week of the delivery month, the short will notify the clearing house of *intent to deliver*. This will specify a Chicago or New York bank registered with the IMM and a member of the Federal Reserve System, and the name of the account from which the delivery will take place.
2. On the last trading day, the long will give to the clearing house a *delivery commitment*, including bank and account details to which the delivery will be made.
3. The short gives *orders to expect* to his bank informing them of the impending delivery, and instructing them to be prepared to wire T-bills and accept payment from the long's bank as identified by the clearing house via wire.
4. The clearing house will instruct the bank of the short as to which bank the T-bills should be wired.
5. The clearing house will instruct the bank of the long as to which bank the Federal Funds payment should be wired.
6. The clearing house converts the official settlement price on the exchange to a discount yield to be used in pricing the T-bills.
7. The clearing house contacts the bank of the short to determine the face value and maturity of the bills to be delivered. It combines this information with the discount yield to determine the invoice price.

---

[1] This will change in June 1983: "the first delivery day shall be the first day of the spot month on which a 13-week Treasury bill is issued, and a one-year Treasury bill has 13 weeks remaining to maturity."

8. The clearing house instructs the bank of the long as to the exact amount of funds to be wired to the bank of the short.
9. By 11:00am (Chicago time) on the day of delivery, the short's bank transfers the T-bills by wire to the long's bank.
10. By 11:00am (Chicago time) on the day of delivery, the long's bank transfers by wire the invoice amount to the short's bank.
11. The delivery process is then complete.

The final question is: how does the clearing house calculate the invoice price on a single contract, face value $1,000,000, of T-bills? The settlement price gives an equivalent annual discount yield. The invoice price is found in the following way:

$$\text{Invoice price} = \$1,000,000 - \frac{\$1,000,000 \times \text{Days to maturity} \times \text{T-bill discount yield}}{360}$$

Consider two cases: first where a 92-day bill is delivered when the discount yield is 12%; second, where a 90-day bill is delivered with a discount yield of 10%. The two invoice prices will be:

$$\text{First price} = \$1,000,000 - \frac{\$1,000,000 \times 92 \times 0.12}{360}$$

$$= \$969,333.33$$

$$\text{Second price} = \$1,000,000 - \frac{\$1,000,000 \times 90 \times 0.10}{360}$$

$$= \$975,000$$

The annual discount yield is not the actual yield an investor will earn over the life of the Treasury bill. This will be given by the effective or bond equivalent yield. This is calculated as follows:

$$\text{Effective T-bill yield} = \frac{\text{T-bill par value} - \text{Invoice price}}{\text{Invoice price}} \times \frac{365}{\text{Days to maturity}}$$

In the case of these two deliveries, the effective yield to the bill on the long taking delivery would be:

$$1. \quad \text{Yield} = \frac{\$1,000,000 - \$969,333.33}{\$969,333.33} \times \frac{365}{92}$$

$$= 0.1255 \text{ or } 12.55\%$$

$$2. \quad \text{Yield} = \frac{\$1,000,000 - \$975,000}{\$975,000} \times \frac{365}{90}$$

$$= 0.1040 \text{ or } 10.40\%$$

Thus, when buying a T-bill contract, an individual will have to put up at least an exchange minimum initial margin of $2,000, and will own an instrument that will go up and down in value by $25 for every basis point change in price or equivalent discount yield. If the investor decides eventually to take delivery, he receives in exchange for the appropriate invoice price a US Treasury bill of face value $1,000,000 maturing between 90 and 92 days after the delivery date.

The IMM also trades, although with little liquidity, one-year Treasury bills in denominations of $250,000. All the essential principles of trading and pricing described above for the 90-day T-bill contract apply also to these bills.

2. Eurodollar time deposits (IMM, LIFFE)

The three-month Eurodollar time deposit contracts traded on the IMM and LIFFE are essentially similar with only a few minor differences. Both are based upon a $1,000,000 face value Eurodollar time deposit, with pricing based upon the familiar index system already described. Both exchanges trade Eurodollar futures on the March, June, September and December cycle with minimum price fluctuations of 0.01% or 1 basis point. In normal circumstances, the initial margin on the Eurodollar contract on each exchange is 0.2% of face value or $2,000.★ Normal daily price limits are 100 basis points above or below the previous close in London and in Chicago. Both margin levels and price limits can be changed by the exchanges in the light of prevailing trading conditions.

Delivery

The Eurodollar contract, then, looks like a conventional short-term interest rate future traded on both exchanges. However, there are major differences in delivery procedures between the two exchanges. Whereas the London International Financial Futures Exchange contract calls for physical delivery, although with a cash settlement option at the behest of the long, the IMM contract is strictly cash settlement.

a. IMM delivery system

Any Eurodollar futures contracts still open at the termination of trading in that contract, which will occur on the second London business day before the third Wednesday of the delivery month, will be settled by cash settlement. The cash settlement will occur in conjunction with a final settlement price for the last day of trading determined by the clearing house. The clearing house determines the London interbank offered rate (Libor) for three-month Eurodollar time deposits both at the termination of trading in a contract, and at a randomly selected time within the last 90 minutes of trading. The final settlement price will be 100 minus the arithmetic mean, rounded to the nearest basis point, of the Libor at the two times.

According to the rules of the IMM, the clearing house will obtain Libor by selecting a random 12 reference banks from a list of not less than 20 participating banks which are major banks in the Eurodollar market. Each reference bank will quote to the clearing house the rate at which three-month Eurodollar time deposit funds are offered by the market to prime banks. After confirmation of these rates by telex, they may be used to determine the final settlement price. After the two highest and two lowest quotes are eliminated, the arithmetic mean of the remaining eight quotes is regarded as the appropriate Libor rate at that time. Final settlement of open positions is then made by the usual variation margin system based on a settlement price equal to the final settlement price.

The delivery or final settlement system works exactly like the normal marking to market system, save that the final settlement price is determined not by the futures market, but a representative sample of Eurodollar rates in the cash market. The system can be explained easily by considering a trader who purchases one IMM Eurodollar contract two days prior to the final day of trading.

Day 1 Trader purchases at the close one March Eurodollar contract at 89.25.
Initial margin = $2,000
Settlement price = 89.25

Day 2 Settlement price = 89.15
Trader's margin account is debited $250 (10 ticks loss × $25 tick value)
Margin account = $1,750
No variation margin calls because maintenance margin is only $1,500.

Day 3 (Last day of trading)
1. Clearing house at a randomly chosen time of 2:36pm London time checks Libor rate with representative banks. Mean rate = 11.50%

★ In May 1983, LIFFE adjusted initial margin to 0.1% or $1,000.

2. At 3:30pm London time trading in March Eurodollar futures ceases. Clearing house again checks Libor rate with representative banks. Mean rate = 11.46%.
3. Clearing house determines final settlement price as

$$100 - 11.48\% \left(\frac{11.50 + 11.46}{2} \right) = 88.52$$

4. Trader's margin account is debited $1,575, i.e. (63) ticks (88.52 − 89.15) × $25 tick value.
5. Residual value of margin account, equal to $175, is returned to trader and position is closed.

Thus the Chicago delivery system via cash settlement is extremely simple and easy to operate, and is merely an extension of the normal mark to market system, with the final settlement price being determined by the cash market rather than the futures market.

b. LIFFE delivery system

The delivery system for Eurodollar time deposit contracts on LIFFE, on the other hand, does give the possibility for physical delivery. It is up to the holder of the long position to decide whether he decides to take cash settlement or physical delivery. Although there is no official reason why the option of physical delivery has been retained, it seems probable that it is because the UK gaming laws, which make gambling debts non-recoverable in law, could apply to purely cash settlement contracts. Thus, though in practice only one or two LIFFE Eurodollar contracts outstanding at the close of trading are settled by cash settlement, a full physical delivery system does exist on LIFFE.

There are two major reasons why the cash settlement option is likely to be favoured. First, the exchange specifies a large number of Eurodollar prime banks whose Eurodollar time deposits are regarded by the exchange as being of deliverable quality. It is inevitable that from time to time individual banks will be perceived by the market as having different degrees of creditworthiness. Since the invoice price will depend upon the actual yield on the time deposit delivered, time deposits delivered will be those of banks perceived by the market as less creditworthy than the average. This is because such banks need to pay slightly more than average to attract funds, and any extra accrues to the benefit of the seller whose contractual commitment is only to arrange a deposit facility at the average rate. Such time deposits are also ones which the long least wishes to take delivery of: hence the cash settlement option will appear more attractive.

The second reason why physical delivery is liable to be restricted is that the long taking delivery does not know into which bank his money will be placed. This can cause problems on credit limits. Each major financial institution, especially banks, will have credit limits for institutions with whom money is deposited.

Consider a Eurodollar bank with a credit limit to another bank of, say, $500 million, and a net deposit position with that bank of $490 million. The first bank holds 20 Eurodollar contracts and decides to take physical delivery. Suppose what is delivered is 20 time deposits at the second bank: the first bank's deposit position with the second bank is raised to $510 million—$10 million above its credit limit. Again the danger of this will tend to make the cash settlement option the most attractive.

The process of arriving at the final LIFFE settlement price is almost the same as for the IMM. The last trading day for Eurodollar contracts on LIFFE is the second business day, common both to New York and London, immediately preceding the settlement or delivery day of the delivery month, and trading ceases at 12:00pm London time on that day. The settlement or delivery day is normally the second Wednesday of the delivery month, save when that is not a business day in London and New York, when it is the next business day common to both centres. The final settlement price is determined from a sample of 16 Libor quotes obtained during the closing one and a half hours of dealing on the last trading day, subtracting 0.25% and deducting the resultant rate from 100.

1. **One day before the last trading day**

   Each clearing member will inform the clearing house of the maximum number of contracts on which delivery will be required.

2. **Last trading day**

   The long will inform the clearing house of the number of contracts on which cash settlement option is being exercised.

   The long will give the clearing house a delivery commitment indicating the number of contracts to be settled by physical delivery, plus an irrevocable payment order issued by an approved bank confirming an amount equal to the value of the outstanding contracts will be paid on settlement day to the account of the clearing house at a bank designated by them in New York.

3. **Last trading day**

   The clearing house will inform the short how many actual time deposits need to be delivered against outstanding contracts, and how many will be settled in cash.

   The short will inform the clearing house as to where required time deposit facilities have been established together with their yield and maturity.

   The clearing house will confirm time deposit details with the short's bank and request details as to where payment is to be affected.

4. **Last trading day**

   The clearing house will announce the final settlement price.

5. **Settlement or delivery day**

   Final variation margins payments based on the final settlement price will be made by the long and the short.

   The clearing house will advise the long, where relevant, of the details of any time deposit allocated to him; time deposits will be allocated to shorts *pro rata* to their gross open positions.

6. **Day after delivery day**

   The clearing house will receive confirmation that the time deposit was made.

All variation margins and initial margins will be paid to long and short, plus or minus any adjustment on differences between the interest rate on the time deposit delivered and the settlement price. Two cases illustrate this where the trader is long one March Eurodollar contract: the first where the long opts for cash settlement; the second where he requires physical delivery. In both cases the closing price on the day before the last trading day is 90.20.

Case 1

1. By the opening of the last trading day, the long has met variation margins on his open position and his margin account stands at $1,000.
2. The final settlement price is announced as 90.40, i.e. a yield of 9.60% per annum.
3. The long's margin account is credited with positive variation margin of $500 (20 ticks × $25 tick value).
4. The total margin account of $1,500 is released to the long and the position is closed.

Case 2

1. The long's margin account is credited with positive variation margin of $500, taking the account to $1,500.
2. The long is informed he has been allocated at AB Bank a 91-day Eurodollar time deposit with a yield of 9.70%.
3. The long transfers $1,000,000 to AB Bank.
4. Finally the long receives his $1,500 margin less an amount to compensate for the difference between the settlement yield and the actual yield on the time deposit.

$$\text{Settlement amount payable by buyer} = \left[\frac{M \times (D - S) \times C}{36,000}\right] \bigg/ \left[1 + \frac{(S \times M)}{36,000}\right]$$

where M = days to maturity of time deposit
D = annual percentage yield on time deposit
S = annual percentage settlement yield
C = value of contract = $1,000,000

In our case this would be

$$\text{Settlement amount} = \left[\frac{91 \times (9.70 - 9.60) \times \$1,000,000}{36,000}\right]\bigg/\left[1 + \frac{(9.60 \times 91)}{36,000}\right]$$

$$= \$246.79$$

Hence the long would receive a final payment of $1,253.21 ($1,500 − $246.79).

Given the extra complexities and lack of clear advantage of physical delivery, most longs will continue to choose to take the cash settlement option. Legal reasons appear to be the main reason for not having a purely cash settlement system on LIFFE, as is the case on the IMM.

3. The sterling time deposit (LIFFE)

The sterling time deposit futures contract traded on LIFFE is similar at present in structure to the Eurodollar contract. In particular, the delivery system with optional cash settlement at the option of the long is exactly the same. The only real difference is that the formula for determining the payment from buyer to seller arising from a difference between the actual yield on the time deposit and the settlement yield is altered because sterling time deposits are traded on a 365-day basis. The revised settlement formula is:

$$\text{Settlement amount} = \left[\frac{M \times (D - S) \times C}{36,500}\right]\bigg/\left[1 + \frac{(S \times M)}{36,500}\right]$$

All the terms are defined as for the Eurodollar contract, save that the face value of the sterling time deposit contract is £250,000. Although the tick size is still one basis point, the value of the tick will be £6.25 because of the different face value of the contract.

Apart from this, the delivery months and delivery day are identical with the LIFFE Eurodollar contract, and the normal exchange minimum initial margin is 0.2% of contract face value, or £500. The price limits are also identical at 100 basis points above or below the previous day's close. The delivery cycle is the same as for the Eurodollar contract, but takes one day rather than two, with trading continuing until 11:00am on the day before delivery.

4. US Treasury bond futures (CBT)

The CBT US Treasury bond futures contract is the single most heavily traded financial futures contract. It is traded on a March, June, September, December, three-year cycle. The face value of the contract is $100,000 and the minimum price movement, or tick, is 1/32nd of 1%. This gives a tick value of $31.25.

$$\text{Tick value} = \text{Face value of contract} \times 1/32 \text{ of } 1\%$$
$$= \$100,000 \times 0.0003125 = \$31.25$$

Pricing

The price of the Treasury bond contract, like all long-term interest rate futures, is quoted as a percentage of par. The maximum daily price limit is 64/32nds above or below the previous close. Exhibit 2.5 gives a typical set of trading information for T-bonds on the CBT.

Consider the nearby March contract. The opening price is 85-00, i.e. the futures market is willing to pay $85 per $100 nominal of the Treasury bond. The settlement price has risen to 85-19, which is a rise of 19/32nds or 19 ticks. Hence a trader with a single long position in June T-bond futures would be showing a profit on the day of $593.75 (19 ticks × $31.25 tick value). In contrast to the short-term financial instruments, the change in yield is not equal to the change in the settlement price. The question, then, is what is the T-bond contract pricing?

Exhibit 2.5: CBT Treasury bond futures prices

Wednesday 4 March

Treasury bonds (CBT)—$100,000; pts 32nds of 100%

	Open	High	Low	Settle	Change	Yield Settle	Yield Change	Open interest
March	85-00	85-21	85-00	85-19	+19	9.638	−0.076	37,026
June	85-12	85-31	85-12	85-30	+20	9.594	−0.080	56,542
September	85-22	86-10	85-22	86-08	+22	9.554	−0.088	23,311
December	85-31	86-20	85-31	85-17	+18	9.518	−0.072	19,654
March	86-08	86-26	86-08	86-24	+16	9.491	−0.063	15,272
June	86-16	87-03	86-16	87-00	+15	9.460	−0.058	13,540
September	86-24	87-12	86-24	87-10	+16	9.421	−0.062	16,871
December	86-31	87-21	86-31	87-17	+16	9.393	−0.063	13,260
March	87-05	87-24	87-05	87-22	+15	9.374	−0.058	11,102
June	87-11	87-29	87-11	87-27	+14	9.355	−0.054	7,860
September	87-17	87-31	87-17	87-31	+12	9.339	−0.047	4,200
December	87-23	88-06	87-23	88-05	+10	9.316	−0.039	1,320

Est. vol. 93,891; vol Tues 94,620; open interest 219,958 + 1,325

Source: Chicago Board of Trade

The T-bond futures price is the price the market is willing to pay for a Treasury bond of 20-year maturity and a standard 8% yield for delivery on the appropriate date. Such an instrument with this particular maturity and yield may not actually trade in the cash market, but that is irrelevant for the futures market. The futures market is simply showing what it would be willing to pay for such a standard instrument if it did exist.

The settlement yield shown in the exhibit is thus just the effective yield to maturity on a standard 20-year 8% T-bond with a price equal to the settlement price. Looking at the June contract again: the yield to maturity on a 20-year 8% bond priced at 85-19 is 9.638%, which is 0.076% lower than the yield to maturity on the bond based on the previous day's settlement price.[2]

The exhibit also illustrates that the long maturity of the instruments naturally results in substantial price changes in the financial futures contracts for very small changes in the yield to maturity. Hence initial and maintenance margin requirements on these contracts are much higher than on the short-term interest rate contracts. The initial margin on the CBT contract is $3,000, equivalent to 3% of the face value of the contract. However, exchange minimum margins are subject to change, and margins required by member firms may exceed CBT minimum contract margins.

Delivery

Because the T-bond futures contract is based upon a standard 20-year 8% T-bond, which may not actually be trading in the cash market, the delivery process is defined in terms of actually traded T-bonds, with the invoice amount being determined relative to the settlement price of the standard bond.

The Board of Trade contract calls for delivery of either non-callable Treasury bonds with a minimum maturity of 15 years, or callable bonds with at least 15 years to the first call date. If a particular bond is callable, the Treasury can redeem it before it reaches maturity any time after the call date. For example, the 11¾% 2005-10 Treasury bond matures on 15 February, 2010, but is callable after 15 February, 2005. All the bonds delivered against a single futures contract must be of the same issue.

The next step is to translate the final settlement price on the T-bond futures contract into an equivalent price for the T-bond actually being delivered. This is done by using a conversion

---

[2] Yield books giving all combinations of price and yields to maturity for 20-year 8% T-bonds are readily available.

factor, which is obtained by determining the price at which the particular bond being delivered will display a yield to maturity of 8%.

1. We know that at a price of 100, the standard 20-year 8% bond will have a yield to maturity of 8%.
2. We wish to find the conversion value for a 7⅝% bond with maturity of 21 years and six months. The price at which such a bond has an 8% yield to maturity is 96.18.
3. Therefore the conversion factor for use in invoicing is 0.9618.

This conversion factor will be used in determining the invoice price for a T-bond delivery. (Chapter 3 contains more details on conversion factors and how they are derived.) An example of a table of conversion factors is shown in Exhibit 2.6.

Exhibit 2.6: Conversion factors for invoicing

PRICES TO YIELD 8.000%

TERM	7%	7⅛%	7¼%	7⅜%	7½%	7⅝%	7¾%	7⅞%
			COUPON RATES					
15	.9135	.9243	.9352	.9460	.9568	.9676	.9784	.9892
15-3	.9126	.9235	.9344	.9453	.9562	.9671	.9780	.9889
15-6	.9121	.9231	.9340	.9450	.9560	.9670	.9780	.9890
15-9	.9112	.9222	.9333	.9444	.9555	.9666	.9776	.9887
16	.9106	.9218	.9330	.9441	.9553	.9665	.9777	.9888
16-3	.9098	.9210	.9323	.9435	.9548	.9660	.9773	.9885
16-6	.9093	.9206	.9319	.9433	.9546	.9660	.9773	.9887
16-9	.9084	.9198	.9313	.9427	.9541	.9655	.9770	.9884
17	.9079	.9195	.9310	.9425	.9540	.9655	.9770	.9885
17-3	.9071	.9187	.9303	.9419	.9535	.9651	.9766	.9882
17-6	.9067	.9183	.9300	.9417	.9533	.9650	.9767	.9883
17-9	.9059	.9176	.9294	.9411	.9528	.9646	.9763	.9881
18	.9055	.9173	.9291	.9409	.9527	.9645	.9764	.9882
18-3	.9047	.9166	.9285	.9404	.9522	.9641	.9760	.9879
18-6	.9043	.9163	.9282	.9402	.9521	.9641	.9761	.9880
18-9	.9035	.9156	.9276	.9396	.9517	.9637	.9757	.9878
19	.9032	.9153	.9274	.9395	.9516	.9637	.9758	.9879
19-3	.9024	.9146	.9268	.9390	.9511	.9633	.9755	.9876
19-6	.9021	.9143	.9266	.9388	.9510	.9633	.9755	.9878
19-9	.9014	.9137	.9260	.9383	.9506	.9629	.9752	.9875
20	.9010	.9134	.9258	.9381	.9505	.9629	.9753	.9876
20-3	.9004	.9128	.9252	.9377	.9501	.9625	.9749	.9874
20-6	.9000	.9125	.9250	.9375	.9500	.9625	.9750	.9875
20-9	.8994	.9119	.9245	.9370	.9496	.9621	.9747	.9873
21	.8991	.9117	.9243	.9369	.9495	.9622	.9748	.9874
21-3	.8984	.9111	.9238	.9364	.9491	.9618	.9745	.9871
21-6	.8981	.9109	.9236	.9363	.9491	.9618 ⟨	.9745	.9873
21-9	.8975	.9103	.9231	.9359	.9487	.9614	.9742	.9870
22	.8973	.9101	.9229	.9358	.9486	.9615	.9743	.9872
22-3	.8967	.9095	.9224	.9353	.9482	.9611	.9740	.9869
22-6	.8964	.9093	.9223	.9352	.9482	.9611	.9741	.9870
22-9	.8958	.9088	.9218	.9348	.9478	.9608	.9738	.9868
23	.8956	.9086	.9217	.9347	.9478	.9608	.9739	.9869
23-3	.8950	.9081	.9212	.9343	.9474	.9605	.9736	.9867
23-6	.8948	.9079	.9211	.9342	.9474	.9605	.9737	.9868
23-9	.8942	.9074	.9206	.9338	.9470	.9602	.9734	.9866
24	.8940	.9073	.9205	.9338	.9470	.9603	.9735	.9868
24-3	.8935	.9068	.9201	.9334	.9466	.9599	.9732	.9865
24-6	.8933	.9066	.9200	.9333	.9466	.9600	.9733	.9867
24-9	.8928	.9061	.9195	.9329	.9463	.9597	.9730	.9864
25	.8926	.9060	.9194	.9329	.9463	.9597	.9731	.9866
25-3	.8921	.9055	.9190	.9325	.9459	.9594	.9729	.9863
25-6	.8919	.9054	.9189	.9324	.9460	.9595	.9730	.9865
25-9	.8914	.9050	.9185	.9321	.9456	.9592	.9727	.9863
26	.8913	.9049	.9184	.9320	.9456	.9592	.9728	.9864
26-3	.8908	.9044	.9180	.9317	.9453	.9589	.9725	.9862
26-6	.8906	.9043	.9180	.9316	.9453	.9590	.9727	.9863
26-9	.8902	.9039	.9176	.9313	.9450	.9587	.9724	.9861
27	.8900	.9038	.9175	.9313	.9450	.9588	.9725	.9863
27-3	.8896	.9034	.9171	.9309	.9447	.9585	.9722	.9860
27-6	.8895	.9033	.9171	.9309	.9447	.9585	.9724	.9862
27-9	.8890	.9029	.9167	.9306	.9444	.9583	.9721	.9860

How is the invoice price at delivery worked out in a specific case.[3] Suppose the short chooses to deliver against a futures contract on 11 June, 1980, the $7\frac{5}{8}$% T-bond with maturity 15 February, 2002–07. The settlement price is 83-16.

1. Determination of maturity
The bond is callable on 15 February, 2002. This is 21 years, 8 months and 14 days from 11 June, 1980. Since the clearing house rounds down to the nearest quarter, this becomes 21 years and 6 months.

2. Choice of conversion factor
Looking at the table, the conversion factor for a 21 year 6 month $7\frac{5}{8}$% T-bond is 0.9618.

3. Calculation of accrued interest in bond
The short also invoices the long for any accrued interest contained in the bond. The bond issue in question pays interest on 15 February and 15 August. Hence the bond contains 117 days of accrued interest: the period between 15 February–11 June.

$$\text{Daily accrued interest} = \frac{\$3,812.50 \begin{pmatrix} \text{semi-annual coupon} \\ \text{payment on } \$50,000 \end{pmatrix}}{182 \quad \text{(days in half-year)}}$$

$$= \$20.9478022$$

$$\text{Bond accrued interest} = 117 \text{ days} \times \$20.9478022$$
$$= \$2,450.89$$

4. Calculation of invoice for principal

$$\text{Principal} = \text{Settlement price} \times \text{Face value} \times \text{Conversion factor}$$
$$= 0.835 \ (83\text{-}16) \times \$100,000 \times 0.9618$$
$$= \$80,310.30$$

5. Determination of total invoice amount

$$\text{Invoice amount} = \text{Principal} + \text{Accrued interest}$$
$$= \$80,310.30 + \$2,450.89$$
$$= \$82,761.19$$

These tables of conversion factors, plus knowledge of the maturity, yield and interest payment schedule of the delivered bond, enable an exact invoice amount to be calculated at delivery. However, the trader holding a long position through to delivery will not necessarily know until delivery the exact amount of cash he will have to transfer and the T-bonds he will actually receive. This is because the choice of which bond to actually deliver is at the option of the holder of the short position. This uncertainty will tend to limit the number of T-bond contracts actually going to delivery.

As with the Treasury bill contract on the IMM, the delivery process on the CBT T-bond contract is carried out through the Federal Reserve book entry system. T-bonds for delivery can either be purchased by the short through a Federal Reserve member bank, or the short could convert actual bonds into book entry bonds by depositing them with such a bank. The delivery process takes three days and can be initiated by the short during a period which begins two days prior to the first business day of the month. The period ends one day before the last business day of the month. The procedure is similar to that on the IMM and is itemized below.

Day 1 Position day
The short informs his clearing member he intends to make delivery. The clearing member files an intent to deliver notice with the clearing house.

Day 2 Notice of intention day
1. The short invoices the long based on the position day settlement price.
2. The clearing house matches the oldest long to the short and notifies both clearing members.
3. The long provides the short with his bank name and location.

---

[3] The numbers in this example are drawn from the Chicago Board of Trade publication *Understanding the Delivery Process in Financial Futures.*

Day 3 Delivery day

1. The short deposits the bonds to be delivered and instructs his bank to wire them to the long's account.
2. The long's bank accepts the bonds and pays the invoice amount by wire to the short's account.

The delivery process is then complete, except for the release of any margin monies by the clearing house to the long and the short. One important feature of this delivery process is that it can be started on any day of the delivery month, or two days before it. Thus any person holding a long position in T-bonds is in danger of being called to take delivery, unless he cancels his position three business days before the delivery month. All traders should bear this fact in mind.

Finally there is the question of which bond will be delivered. Because the conversion factor method equalizes the yield to maturity, it is probable that differential yields in the cash market will make some bonds cheaper to deliver than others.

5. The long-term gilt contract (LIFFE)

The long-term gilt contract traded on LIFFE is very similar to the T-bond contract traded on the Chicago Board of Trade. However, the contract traded is based on a standard 20-year 12% gilt-edged stock. The face value of the contract is £50,000 and the minimum price movement, or tick size, is again 1/32nd of 1%. However, because of the different face value of the contract, the tick value is £15.625.

$$\text{Tick value} = \text{Face value} \times \text{Tick size}$$
$$= £50,000 \times 0.0003125 \ (1/32 \text{ of } 1\%)$$
$$= £15.625$$

Thus if a trader purchases a LIFFE gilt contract at 92-15 and closes out his position at 93-02, that represents a rise of 19 ticks or 19/32nds. The trader would have a profit of £296.88 (19 ticks × £15.625 tick value).

As on the CBT, the price limit is two points or 64/32nds above or below the previous day's closing price. No price limit applies to trading in the period four weeks prior to the first delivery day. The standard exchange minimum initial margin is 3% of the face value of the contract or £1,500. The delivery months are March, June, September and December, and delivery may take place at the discretion of the seller on any business day in the delivery month.

Delivery

The delivery process calls for the delivery of £50,000 nominal value of a gilt-edged stock with maturity not less than 15 years and not more than 25 years on the first day of the delivery month. Where the stock has an optional redemption date, the relevant maturity date is the earliest possible redemption date. No variable rate or index-linked or convertible stocks may be delivered. No partly paid stocks may be delivered, and a stock is not deliverable if the delivery date falls within three weeks and one day prior to the ex-dividend date. Finally interest on the delivered stock must be payable half-yearly.

Given that the futures market is pricing a standard 20-year 12% instrument, then once again a conversion factor will be necessary to translate the settlement price on the futures market into an invoice for the actual gilt to be delivered. As with the CBT T-bond contract, the LIFFE conversion factors are based upon determining the price at which the deliverable gilt will have a 12% yield to maturity. Once a conversion factor has been chosen for a particular gilt, then the invoice amount is worked out using the following formula:

$$\text{Invoice amount} = \left[\text{Settlement price} \times \text{Conversion factor} \times \text{Nominal value}\right] + \text{Accrued interest}$$

Unlike the CBT, LIFFE issues at regular intervals tables of conversion factors and accrued interest for all gilts deliverable on the gilt contract. A typical example of these tables is given in Exhibit 2.7.

Exhibit 2.7: Twenty-year interest rate contract—price factors and accrued interest

Contract month: March 83

Stock				Price factor	Daily accrued	Initial accrued
Treasury	15½%	30 Sept.	1998	1.2446110	21.2329	−636.99
Exchequer	12%	20 Nov.	1998	1.0000623	16.4384	1,643.84
Treasury	9½%	15 Jan.	1999	0.8245612	13.0137	572.60
Exchequer	12¼%	26 March	1999	1.0179052	16.7808	−436.30
Treasury	10½%	19 May	1999	0.8939428	14.3836	1,452.74
Treasury	13%	14 July	2000	1.0724969	17.8082	801.37
Treasury	14%	22 May	98-2001	1.1384685	19.1781	1,879.45
Exchequer	12%	22 Jan.	99-2002	1.0001983	16.4384	608.22
Treasury	13¾%	25 July	2000-03	1.1268837	18.8356	640.41
Treasury	11½%	19 March	2001-04	0.9620974	15.7534	−299.32
Funding	3½%	14 July	99-2004	0.3504174	4.7945	215.75
Treasury	12½%	21 Nov.	2003-05	1.0380064	17.1233	1,695.21
Treasury	8%	5 Oct.	2002-06	0.6882427	10.9589	−394.52
Treasury	11¾%	22 Jan.	2003-07	0.9806478	16.0959	595.55
Treasury	13½%	26 March	2004-08	1.1145726	18.4932	−480.82

Daily accrued: accrued interest per day on $50,000 face value
Price factor: price factor expressed as a fraction of par
Initial accrued: accrued interest on £50,000 face value as of the last day of the month prior to the delivery month
Invoicing formula: invoicing amount = [(settlement price) × (price factor) × 500] + initial accrued + [(daily accrued) × (delivery month)]

Source: LIFFE/Investor Intelligence Systems

This table provides conversion factors, the amount of accrued interest contained in £50,000 nominal of the given stock on the last day of month prior to the delivery month, plus the extra accrued interest per day.

Example

Suppose the Treasury 13%, 14 July, 2000, is to be delivered against a March 1983 gilt futures contract on the 15 March, 1983. The settlement price is that on the second business day before delivery, in this case 97-08.
From the table, the conversion factor for the stock is 1.0724969. The accrued interest up to 28 February is £801.37, and the daily interest accrued is £17.8082.
Hence the invoice amount contains three elements.

$$\text{Principal} = 0.9725 \ (97\text{-}08) \times 1.0724969 \times £50,000$$

$$= £52,150.16$$

$$\text{Accrued interest up to end February} = £801.37$$

$$\text{Extra 15 days accrued interest to 15 March} = £267.12 \ (15 \times £17.8082)$$

$$\text{Total invoice amount} = £53,218.65$$

The delivery cycle is similar to that on the T-bond contract and also occupies three business days. There are some minor differences. First, rather than the longs for delivery being allocated on an oldest position first basis, the clearing house will allocate longs *pro rata* to the gross open positions and then, if there is more than one type of stock delivered, on a random basis to the individual contracts. Second, because of the lack of a book entry system in the UK, the seller may deliver to the clearing house either a stock transfer form certified by the Bank of England, or actual certificates of title. Otherwise the delivery procedure follows the standard pattern.

The GNMA contract (CBT)

The fourth most popular financial futures contract in the United States is the GNMA contract traded on the Chicago Board of Trade. The delivery system for this contract is rather complex owing to the nature of the underlying instrument.

Pricing

The GNMA futures contract on all exchanges is priced on the basis of a standard 8% GNMA certificate of 30-years' maturity with expected prepayment in 12 years. The futures price is given on the same basis as the T-bond contracts, i.e. an observed price of 90-08 indicates the market is willing to pay $90.25 per $100 face value of 8% GNMA certificates with a 30-year life and an expected prepayment in 12 years. The face value of the contract is $100,000 and the minimum price movement is 1/32nd of 1% on the CBT. Thus the respective tick value is $31.25 determined in the usual way.

$$\text{Tick value} = \text{Face value} \times \text{Tick size}$$
$$= \$100,000 \times 0.0003125 \ (1/32 \text{ of } 1\%)$$
$$= \$31.25$$

The standard daily price limit is 64/32nds above or below the previous close. This may vary according to market conditions.

Thus, just like the T-bond, an investor who buys a single GNMA contract on the CBT at 90-08 and closes out his position at 90-16 will realize a profit of $250.00 (8 ticks × $31.25 tick value).

The GNMA market

The Government National Mortgage Association (GNMA) takes pools of mortgages and issues certificates that guarantee that the principal and interest from the mortgage pool will be paid to the certificate holder. If payments of principal and interest are not received from the mortgages in the pool, the GNMA will make payments promptly to the holders of the certificate. The originator of a pool of mortgages may either issue directly mortgages to home buyers, builders or developers, or may purchase mortgages produced by other financial institutions. Payments of principal and interest to the certificate holder are paid monthly, with the first payment due 45 days after the issue date. Any prepayments by mortgages in the pool, or prepayments associated with defaults and the invoking of the guarantee, are distributed *pro rata* to the holders of the certificate.

Calculating the effective yield on such a security is complex. First, the regular payments involve both principal and interest payments. Second, major prepayments of mortgages in certain pools can occur. Falling interest rates can substantially affect the usual pattern of prepayment on a mortgage pool, as can changing patterns of home ownership and other institutional factors. Although 12.5 years is generally taken to represent the average life of a 30-year mortgage, many mortgage pools may have average lives substantially different to the figure.

The two most common ways to measure the rate of return on a GNMA certificate are the pass-through or GNMA yield, and the bond equivalent yield. The pass-through yield is derived on the basis of three assumptions. First, that during the first 12 years of life of the certificate, all interest and principal payments are received on the appropriate day. Second, that the investor re-invests all payments at the same coupon yield as the original GNMA certificate. Third, that the entire set of mortgages in the pool is prepaid at the end of 12 years. Under these circumstances, the pass-through yield is:

$$\text{Percentage annual yield} = \frac{\text{Net annual interest}}{\text{Invested principal}}$$

Example

1. An 8% GNMA under the above assumption is purchased at 98-06

$$\text{Pass-through yield} = \frac{\$8,000}{\$100,000 \times 0.981875 \ (98\text{-}06)}$$
$$= 8.15\%$$

2. A 10.5% GNMA purchased at 106-16.

$$\text{Pass-through yield} = \frac{\$10,500}{\$100,000 \times 1.0650 \ (106\text{-}16)}$$
$$= 9.86\%$$

Converting simple pass-through yields to bond-equivalent yields necessitates taking into account two factors. First, that GNMA interest payments are not made until the 15th of the month. Second, that interest and principal payments are received monthly rather than on a six-month basis. Tables of bond equivalent yields for given pass-through yields are readily available. The table below gives a few examples of the differences between the two types of yield.

GNMA pass-through yield (%)	Bond equivalent yield
7.75	7.88
8.75	8.91
9.75	9.95
10.75	10.99
11.75	12.04
12.75	13.09
13.75	14.15
14.75	15.21
15.75	16.28

GNMA certificates are offered to the investor either directly by the pool originator or by dealers. The cash GNMA market is essentially a dealer market. There are also *standby* and *forward* markets for GNMA certificates.

The standby market essentially involves commitments by one party to standby to purchase a GNMA from the other party at a specific price on a specific date. The seller will generally pay a cash commitment fee to the buyer. Normally the commitments will also contain a yield maintenance clause allowing the seller to deliver any particular GNMA but only at the yield specified in the original commitment. Additionally there is frequently a *par cap* provision within these commitments meaning that the buyer will not have to pay more than par for any coupon GNMA unless specifically negotiated at the time of the commitment.

Example

A trader commits himself to receive a 10% GNMA at a price of 98-16, with a par cap provision, i.e. the buyer will not pay more than 100-00 regardless of what coupon GNMA is delivered.

$$\text{Pass-through yield} = \frac{\$10,000}{\$98,500} = 10.15\%$$

Therefore the maximum coupon GNMA certificate that can be delivered without loss to seller is 10.15%.

A forward market in GNMA certificates also exists between dealers, with no payment of commitment fees in this case, but with no right on the part of the buyer or the seller to cancel the transaction. The difference between the two markets is essentially the difference between an option market and a forward market.

GNMA collateralized depository receipt

The most liquid contract is the GNMA collateralized depository receipt (CDR) contract traded on the CBT, which was the first interest rate futures contract ever traded. In this contract, when delivery takes place, the long receives not actual GNMA certificates, but a collateralized depository receipt. This CDR is a document prepared, signed and dated by the depository—an authorized bank—to verify that the originator has placed in safekeeping $100,000 principal balance of GNMA 8% or the equivalent on the indicated date. This equivalent balance for non-8% GNMAs is the dollar amount of a particular GNMA of $100,000 face value required to give the same yield as GNMA 8% when priced at par, under the usual assumptions of a 30-year life certificate prepaid in the 12th year. Tables for determining these equivalent balances have been prepared by the Chicago Board of Trade (see Exhibit 2.8).

Exhibit 2.8: GNMA equivalent principal balance factors and principal balance equivalents

GNMA Interest Rate	Factor *	Amount Equivalent to $100,000 Principal Balance of GNMA 8s
9½	.900322	$90,032.20
9¾	.885609	$88,560.90
10	.871460 ❲	$87,146.00 ❲
10¼	.857143	$85,714.30
10½	.843289	$84,328.90
10¾	.830450	$83,045.00
11	.817439 ❲	$81,743.90
11¼	.804829	$80,482.90
11½	.793021	$79,302.10
11¾	.781250	$78,125.00
12	.769724	$76,972.40
12¼	.758534	$75,853.40
12½	.747664	$74,766.40
12¾	.736920	$73,692.00
13	.726744	$72,674.40
13¼	.716846	$71,684.60
13½	.707214	$70,721.40
13¾	.697350	$69,735.00
14	.688231	$68,823.10
14¼	.679117	$67,911.70
14½	.670578	$67,057.80
14¾	.661888	$66,188.80
15	.653595	$65,359.50

* Multiply the factor by $100,000 to obtain the equivalent principal balance to $100,000 of GNMA 8s for the corresponding coupon.

Source: Chicago Board of Trade Rules and Regulations

The short can obtain a CDR for delivery from an originator or originate a CDR himself. However, anyone choosing to originate a CDR must meet CBT requirements and obtain exchange approval. A deliverable CDR needs to be properly registered with the CBT and endorsed by the originator, the depository, and the clearing member making delivery.

The invoice amount for a CDR on delivery of a GNMA futures contract is found in the following way:

$$\text{Invoice amount} = (\text{Settlement price} \times \$100,000) + \text{Accrued interest}$$

Example

On position day 25 September, a short decides to make delivery of one GNMA CDR futures contract; the settlement price on position day is 88-06.

$$\text{Principal invoice amount} = 0.881875 \ (88\text{-}06) \times \$100,000$$
$$= \$88,187.50$$

All CDRs accrue interest at the rate of $635 per month. Hence to find interest accrued, divide $635 by 30 (number of days in September) and multiply by number of days between first day of delivery month and the 25th.

$$\text{Accrued interest} = \frac{\$635}{30} \times 25$$
$$= \$529.17$$
$$\text{Total invoice amount} = \$88,187.50 + \$529.17$$
$$= \$88,716.67$$

The delivery procedure for a GNMA CDR futures contract can be itemized in the usual way.

Day 1 Position day
> Short notifies clearing member of intention to deliver. Clearing member gives notice of delivery to clearing house.

Day 2 Notice of intention day
> 1. Clearing house matches short to oldest long and informs both clearing members.
> 2. Long clearing member provides short with necessary delivery information.
> 3. Short invoices long using system described above.

Day 3 Delivery day
> Short delivers CDR to long clearing member. Long makes payment via Federal Funds for invoiced amount.

The delivery process is then complete.

With GNMA transactions the story does not end there. The long now holds a CDR upon which he will receive $635 per month in interest. He will not receive any principal payment until the CDR is surrendered. The CDR may be surrendered for actual GNMA certificates at the office of the originator's depository or a correspondent. After surrender, the originator must provide the required GNMA certificates within 15 days. The originator must provide either between $97,500 and $102,500 principal balance of GNMA 8%, or the equivalent principal balance of another coupon GNMA for each CDR. Discrepancies within the tolerance limit are settled in cash.

This requirement means that the originator of the CDR must maintain the dollar value of the GNMA certificates deposited at $100,000 or equivalent, even though the mortgages may be paid down in the interim.

In these two examples of surrender, a holder of a single CDR surrenders it.

Example 1

The originator exchanges $78,500 of $11\frac{3}{4}$% GNMA certificates for the CDR.
From the table of equivalent balances given above, $100,000 of GNMA 8% certificates is equivalent to $78,125 of $11\frac{3}{4}$% certificates.
To find the equivalent principal balance of GNMA 8% certificates:

$$\text{Equivalent principal balance of GNMA 8\%} = \frac{\text{Principal balance of GNMA } 11\frac{3}{4}\%}{\text{Factor for GNMA } 11\frac{3}{4}\%}$$
$$= \frac{\$78,500}{0.78125}$$
$$= \$100,480$$

Hence end result is for a holder of a CDR to make a cash payment of $480 ($100,480 − $100,000) to the originator and receive $78,500 of GNMA $11\frac{3}{4}$% certificates.

Example 2

The originator exchanges $71,000 of 13¾% GNMA certificates for a CDR.
From the table of equivalent balances, $100,000 of GNMA 8% certificates is equivalent to $71,684.60 of 13¼% certificates.

$$\text{Equivalent principal balance of GNMA 8\%} = \frac{\$71,000}{0.716846}$$

$$= \$99,045$$

Hence end result is for a holder of a CDR to receive $71,000 of GNMA 13¼% certificates plus a cash payment of $955 ($100,000 − $99,045) from the originator.

The decision to surrender a CDR for GNMA certificates is entirely up to the holder of the CDR. As far as the originator is concerned, this is a perpetual obligation to maintain the deposit account up to $100,000 principal or equivalent and pay the holder of the CDR $635 per month interest. However, each year the CDR must be renewed. On the final interest date before the one year anniversary of the CDR's creation, it must be presented to the originator for renewal. At that time, the originator if he so wishes may replace it with a new CDR originated by himself or another originator.

Movements in market mortgage rates will have a major influence upon decisions to surrender CDRs. The CDR holder receives a fixed rate of interest regardless of the actual rate of interest on the mortgage pools backing the GNMA certificates with the depository. If mortgage rates are high, it will be worthwhile for the CDR holder to surrender his CDRs and receive the benefits of higher interest rates and possibly faster prepayments of principal. Similarly, on removal, it will be worthwhile for the originator to replace an old CDR with a new CDR as mortgage rates decline.

All the other GNMA interest rate contracts call for physical delivery of GNMA certificates.

GNMA certificate delivery contracts

The delivery process for GNMA certificate delivery contracts on the Chicago Board of Trade is similar to those traded on other US exchanges. With these contracts, the delivery day is either the 16th of the delivery month or the business day immediately preceding that day. Delivery can be made with any GNMA certificate with a coupon at or below the current GNMA production rate.

If the current production rate is lower than the previous production rate, the previous production rate is also deliverable in the next three months following the month in which the production rate was lowered.

If the production rate increases, GNMA certificates created after the effective rate change are immediately deliverable. However, certificates bearing the new rate, but dated and issued before the rate change, are not deliverable until 45 days after the rate change.

How is the invoice value of the deliverable certificate determined?[4] A short decides to make delivery on 16 June, 1980 using an 8% coupon GNMA certificate with an original principal balance of $110,000 and a pool payment factor of 0.9181812. This pool factor indicates the proportion of the certificate balance still outstanding.

$$\text{Remaining principal balance} = \text{Face value} \times \text{Pool payment factor}$$

$$= \$110,000 \times 0.9181812$$

$$= \$101,000$$

The $101,000 principal balance falls within the tolerance limits for delivery of $100,000 ± $2,500.

The invoice principal amount is now calculated on the basis that the yield on the deliverable certificate will be the same as the yield on the standard 8% coupon GNMA implied by the

---

[4] The examples described here are taken from the Chicago Board of Trade publication, *Understand the Delivery Process in Financial Futures*.

settlement price. So, if the GNMA CD contract settlement price implies a yield of 11%, then a 10% coupon GNMA certificate delivered will be priced to yield 11%. In the first example, this adjustment is not made because an 8% coupon GNMA certificate is being delivered.

The relevant settlement price is 80-00. Hence the principal invoice price is calculated as:

$$\text{Principal invoice price} = \text{Remaining principal balance} \times \text{Settlement price}$$
$$= \$101,000 \times 0.8000 \ (80\text{-}00)$$
$$= \$80,800.00$$

Next, the interest amount is calculated. This is simply the daily interest in dollars on the certificate times the numbers of days between the beginning of the month and the delivery day (excluding the delivery day itself).

For the 8% certificate with principal balance of $101,000:

$$\text{Daily interest} = \frac{0.08 \times \$101,000}{360}$$
$$= \$22.444$$
$$\text{Total interest} = 15 \times \$22.444 \text{ per day}$$
$$= \$336.66$$

Hence the total amount invoiced for this particular 8% coupon GNMA certificate would be:

$$\text{Invoice amount} = \$80,800.00 + \$336.66$$
$$= \$81,136.66$$

Now suppose the short chooses to deliver a GNMA certificate with a coupon of 9% and an unpaid principal balance of $100,000 with the same settlement price. Using the yield tables (*see* Exhibit 2.9), the yield on a GNMA 8% coupon certificate at a settlement price of 80-00 is 11.115%. The price of a 9% coupon certificate to give the same yield is 86.175.

$$\text{Principal amount} = \$100,000 \times 0.86175 \text{ (Equivalent settlement price for 9\% GNMAs)}$$
$$= \$86,175$$
$$\text{Interest amount} = \$25 \left(\frac{0.09 \times \$100,000}{360}\right) \times 15 \text{ days}$$
$$= \$375.00$$
$$\text{Total invoice amount} = \$86,175 + \$375$$
$$= \$86,550.00$$

Apart from this difference in invoicing, the delivery mechanism is standard save for the fact that it takes five days rather than three, and that the clearing house employs an agent bank to match long and short positions, and handle the transfer of payments and GNMA certificates.

What is apparent from actual trading experience in these contracts is that the CD contracts display very low liquidity relative to the CDR contracts, and secondly that the incidence of actual delivery on the CDR contracts is almost non-existent. This may not be too surprising, given the complexities of the delivery process. There are also additional financing costs in making delivery of GNMA certificates through the futures market rather than selling them directly into the cash market. Restrictions on the number of pools that can make up a GNMA certificate in the cash market, as compared with the CBT contract, may also cause problems for the long taking delivery of a GNMA futures contract; for all these reasons, it is likely that these markets will rarely be physical delivery markets.

Exhibit 2.9: GNMA yield equivalents

8.00% 30 year Security based upon a 8.50% Mortgage .50% Service
Prepaid in 12 years

PRICE 32nds	YIELD	PRICE 32nds	YIELD	PRICE 32nds	YIELD	PRICE 32nds	YIELD
78.00	11.491	80.00	11.115	82.00	10.752	84.00	10.401
1	11.485	1	11.109	1	10.746	1	10.396
2	11.479	2	11.104	2	10.741	2	10.390
3	11.473	3	11.098	3	10.735	3	10.385
4	11.467	4	11.092	4	10.730	4	10.379
5	11.461	5	11.086	5	10.724	5	10.374
6	11.455	6	11.081	6	10.719	6	10.369
7	11.449	7	11.075	7	10.713	7	10.363
78.25	11.444	80.25	11.069	82.25	10.707	84.25	10.358
9	11.438	9	11.063	9	10.702	9	10.353
10	11.432	10	11.058	10	10.696	10	10.347
11	11.426	11	11.052	11	10.691	11	10.342
12	11.420	12	11.046	12	10.685	12	10.337
13	11.414	13	11.040	13	10.680	13	10.331
14	11.408	14	11.035	14	10.674	14	10.326
15	11.402	15	11.029	15	10.669	15	10.320
78.50	11.396	80.50	11.023	82.50	10.663	84.50	10.315
17	11.390	17	11.017	17	10.658	17	10.310
18	11.384	18	11.012	18	10.652	18	10.304
19	11.378	19	11.006	19	10.647	19	10.299
20	11.372	20	11.000	20	10.641	20	10.294
21	11.366	21	10.995	21	10.636	21	10.288
22	11.360	22	10.989	22	10.630	22	10.283
23	11.355	23	10.983	23	10.624	23	10.278
78.75	11.349	80.75	10.977	82.75	10.619	84.75	10.272
25	11.343	25	10.972	25	10.613	25	10.267
26	11.337	26	10.966	26	10.608	26	10.262
27	11.331	27	10.960	27	10.602	27	10.256
28	11.325	28	10.955	28	10.597	28	10.251
29	11.319	29	10.949	29	10.591	29	10.246
30	11.313	30	10.943	30	10.586	30	10.241
31	11.307	31	10.938	31	10.581	31	10.235

9.00% 30 year Security based upon a 9.50% Mortgage .50% Service
Prepaid in 12 years

PRICE 32nds	YIELD	PRICE 32nds	YIELD	PRICE 32nds	YIELD	PRICE 32nds	YIELD
80.00	12.249	82.00	11.868	84.00	11.501	86.00	11.145
1	12.243	1	11.862	1	11.495	1	11.140
2	12.236	2	11.856	2	11.489	2	11.134
3	12.230	3	11.851	3	11.484	3	11.129
4	12.224	4	11.845	4	11.478	4	11.124
5	12.218	5	11.839	5	11.472	5	11.118
6	12.212	6	11.833	6	11.467	6	11.113
7	12.206	7	11.827	7	11.461	7	11.107
80.25	12.200	82.25	11.821	84.25	11.456	86.25	11.102
9	12.194	9	11.816	9	11.450	9	11.096
10	12.188	10	11.810	10	11.444	10	11.091
11	12.182	11	11.804	11	11.439	11	11.086
12	12.176	12	11.798	12	11.433	12	11.080
13	12.170	13	11.792	13	11.427	13	11.075
14	12.164	14	11.787	14	11.422	14	11.069
15	12.158	15	11.781	15	11.416	15	11.064
80.50	12.152	82.50	11.775	84.50	11.411	86.50	11.058
17	12.146	17	11.769	17	11.405	17	11.053
18	12.140	18	11.763	18	11.399	18	11.048
19	12.134	19	11.758	19	11.394	19	11.042
20	12.128	20	11.752	20	11.388	20	11.037
21	12.122	21	11.746	21	11.383	21	11.031
22	12.116	22	11.740	22	11.377	22	11.026
23	12.110	23	11.735	23	11.372	23	11.021
80.75	12.104	82.75	11.729	84.75	11.366	86.75	11.015
25	12.098	25	11.723	25	11.360	25	11.010
26	12.092	26	11.717	26	11.355	26	11.004
27	12.086	27	11.711	27	11.349	27	10.999
28	12.080	28	11.706	28	11.344	28	10.994
29	12.074	29	11.700	29	11.338	29	10.988
30	12.069	30	11.694	30	11.333	30	10.983
31	12.063	31	11.688	31	11.327	31	10.978

Reproduced from *Net Yield Table for GNMA Mortgage Backed Securities*, Pub. No. 746 and Pub. No. 746 revised © 1979, Financial Publishing Co., Boston MA.

7. The foreign currency contracts (IMM, LIFFE)

The foreign currency futures contracts traded both on the International Monetary Market and the London International Financial Futures Exchange provide a degree of competition for the widely used forward market in foreign exchange. The contracts traded on both the IMM and LIFFE are essentially similar, albeit with a few differences.

Pricing

All currency futures contracts traded on either exchange have prices quoted on the basis of the US system of quotation, i.e. prices are quoted in dollar units per one foreign currency unit. Thus the price of a sterling/dollar contract on LIFFE might be quoted as $1.6200, while a French franc contract on the IMM might be quoted as $0.1358. In keeping with this system of quotation, the contract size or face value is standardized according to foreign currency amount. The contract sizes currently traded are listed below.

Currency	IMM	LIFFE
Sterling	£25,000	£25,000
Deutschemark	DM125,000	DM125,000
Yen	Y12,500,000	Y12,500,000
Swiss franc	Swfr125,000	SF125,000
French franc	Ffr250,000	—
Dutch guilder	Dfl125,000	—
Canadian dollar	C$100,000	—
Mexican peso	MP1,000,000	—

Because of the very different face values of the currency contracts, it is not possible to keep to the same minimum price movement or tick size for all contracts. Instead, the exchanges generally attempt to preserve the same dollar value for ticks on all contracts: the only exceptions are the Canadian dollar and Mexican peso on the IMM, and sterling on LIFFE. The table below gives the tick sizes, tick values and normal daily price limits for the currency contracts

Currency	IMM			LIFFE		
	Tick size	Tick value	Price limit	Tick size	Tick value	Price limit
Sterling	0.0005¢	$12.50	0.05($1,250)	0.0001¢	$2.50	0.05($1,250)
Deutschemark	0.0001¢	$12.50	0.01($1,250)	0.0001¢	$12.50	0.01($1,250)
Yen	0.000001¢	$12.50	0.001($1,250)	0.000001¢	$12.50	0.0001($1,250)
Swiss franc	0.0001¢	$12.50	0.015($1,875)	0.0001¢	$12.50	0.01($1,250)
French franc	0.00005¢	$12.50	0.005($1,250)			
Dutch guilder	0.0001¢	$12.50	0.01($1,250)			
Canadian dollar	0.0001¢	$10.00	0.0075($750)			
Mexican peso	0.00001¢	$10.00	0.0015($1,500)			

As usual, there is no price limit in the spot month.

It may be useful to give a couple of examples of how profits and losses will be determined for these foreign currency contracts.

Example 1

A trader purchases one sterling/dollar contract on LIFFE at a price of $1.6200. He closes out his position at a price of $1.6315.

$$\text{Exchange rate change} = \$0.0115 \ (\$1.6315 - \$1.6200)$$

$$\text{Number of ticks} = \frac{\$0.0115}{\$0.0001} = 115$$

$$\text{Profit} = 115 \text{ ticks} \times \$2.50 \text{ tick value}$$
$$= \$287.50$$

45

Example 2

A trader sells one Canadian dollar contract on the IMM at a price of $0.9230. He closes out his position at a price of $0.9203.

$$\text{Exchange rate change} = -\$0.0027$$

$$\text{Number of ticks} = \frac{-\$0.0027}{\$0.0001}$$
$$= 27$$

$$\text{Profit} = 27 \text{ ticks} \times \$10.00 \text{ tick value}$$
$$= \$270.00$$

Delivery

The delivery cycle of the currency contracts varies somewhat between the exchanges. LIFFE follows a conventional cycle of delivery months of March, June, September and December. The IMM trades delivery months of January, March, April, June, July, September, October and December.

There are no basic differences between the two exchanges on the delivery system. However, there is a one-week difference between delivery days. The delivery day on the IMM is the third Wednesday of the delivery month, or if this is not a business day, then the next business day common to Chicago and major financial centres. The delivery day on LIFFE is the second Wednesday of the delivery month. The delivery system is itemized below; this is common to both exchanges.

Day 1 Last day of trading
1. Clearing house announces settlement price for the foreign exchange contract. The short gives notice of delivery to the clearing house. The long gives notice of taking delivery to the clearing house.
2. The long instructs bank to deposit sufficient dollar funds with the clearing house.
3. The short arranges for currency to be delivered to the clearing house.

Day 2 Clearing house is informed of receipt of US dollars from long bank by its bank.

Day 3 Delivery day
1. Clearing house pays to the long currency to provide cleared funds that day in the relevant delivery centre.
2. Clearing house pays US dollars to the seller to provide cleared funds that day.
3. Margin accounts are receipted to long and short.

The delivery process is then complete.

Hence, the foreign exchange futures market is essentially similar to the forward market for foreign currency with the exception of the standard daily marking to market. The invoice amount for a currency delivery is:

$$\text{Invoice amount} = \text{Face value of contract} \times \text{Settlement price} \times \text{Number of contracts}$$

Example

The holder of a single long position in sterling/dollar on LIFFE decides to take delivery. The settlement price is 1.6312.

$$\text{Invoice amount} = £25,000 \times \$1.6312$$
$$= \$40,780.00$$

8. Domestic certificate of deposit futures (IMM)

The domestic certificate of deposit futures contracts traded on the IMM are based on a $1 million face value certificate of deposit issued by an eligible bank. As usual with short-term interest rate contracts, the pricing is based on the index system. CD futures are traded on the March, June, September and December quarterly cycle. The minimum price fluctuation is 0.01,

46

or one basis point, and the tick value is $25 based on the usual calculation for a notional three-month instrument:

$$\text{Tick value} = \$1,000,000 \times 0.0001 \times 3/12 = \$25$$

The CD futures contracts resembles the Eurodollar time deposits futures and Treasury bill futures. The essential differences arise out of the definition of certificates of deposit available for delivery and the invoicing procedure at delivery.

Delivery

The specifications of delivery quality certificates of deposits on the IMM are very precise:

1. Deliverable banks are announced two business days before the 15th day of the delivery month. Deliverable CDs are determined by polling of dealers in the cash market.
2. CDs delivered must mature between the 16th and last day of the month three months after the delivery month.
3. Deliverable maturity range is approximately two and a half to three and a half months.
4. CDs may only be delivered with no more than 185 days of accrued interest.
5. Variable rate and discount CDs are deliverable if and when yields are equivalent to the "no name" run.

Physical delivery may be made at the behest of the short from the 15th through the last day of the delivery month. In addition to the above conditions, the deliverable CD must have a fixed maturity value not less than $1,000,000 and not greater than $1,200,000, and should have not interest payments between the delivery date and the maturity date.

Most domestic certificates of deposits are add-on in the sense that they pay principal plus interest at maturity. Thus, a six-month $1,000,000 CD with an add-on yield of 10% would have a maturity value of:

$$\text{Maturity value} = \$1,000,000 \left\{ 1 + (0.10)\ \frac{(180)}{360} \right\}$$

$$= \$1,050,000$$

Suppose this particular CD were delivered with 90 days remaining to maturity at a futures settlement price of 87.50 equivalent to an add-on yield of 12.50%. The IMM would determine the invoice price to the long in the following way:

$$\text{Invoice price} = \frac{\$1,050,000}{\left[1 + (0.125)\ \frac{90}{360} \right]} = \$1,018,181.80$$

Below is a typical delivery procedure for an open CD contract on the IMM:

1. The short's clearing member will present to the clearing house one business day before the delivery day by 2:00pm a seller's delivery commitment.
2. Upon receipt of the seller's delivery commitment, the clearing house will match it to the oldest long position and inform the long accordingly.
3. Upon receipt of this notification from the clearing house, the long's clearing member will deliver to the clearing house by 5:00pm one business day before the delivery day a buyer's delivery commitment that includes the buyer's name and account number, and the New York bank to which the delivery unit is to be transferred.
4. By 12:00 noon on the delivery day, the short's clearing member delivers an appropriately eligible CD to the bank notified by the buyer.
5. By 12:45pm on the delivery day, the long's clearing member will present to the short's clearing member's designated bank a wire transfer of Federal funds for the net invoicing price.

The delivery process is then complete. At the beginning of 1983 the margins for a $1,000,000 CD contract on the IMM were $2,500 initial and $2,000 maintenance, with a daily price limit of 80 basis points.

9. Stock market index futures (IOM, NYFE, Kansas City BOT)

The stock market index futures traded on the Index and Options Market (IOM) of the CME, NYFE and the Kansas City Board of Trade amongst others, are the only financial futures contracts written on instruments that have no physical existence. Hence there is no element of physical delivery with these contracts: all contracts left outstanding in the delivery month will be closed out by cash settlement along similar lines to the IMM Eurodollar time deposit contract. All the stock index futures contracts are similar in construction, except that contracts on different exchanges tend to be based on different underlying stock market indices.

The stock index future traded on NYFE is based on the New York Stock Exchange Composite index, while the IOM contract is based on the Standard and Poor's 500 index. Calculations by the IOM estimate a 0.989 correlation coefficient between movements in the two indices in the period 1971–82, which suggests that future prices on the two exchanges will tend to move closely in parallel.

The Kansas City Board of Trade futures contract is based upon the Value Line index, which differs somewhat from the other indices in being an unweighted geometric average covering a much larger number of stocks.

Since their inception on the Kansas City Board of Trade in February 1982, stock index futures have shown the most rapid growth of any newly introduced contract; in January 1983, the IOM contract traded over 20,000 contracts per day, the NYFE contract around 10,000 and the Kansas City Board of Trade contract was trading around 3,000 per day.

Both the IOM and NYFE plan to introduce various new index futures in 1983, while the Chicago Board of Trade also hopes to introduce stock index futures (following delays caused by legal problems). This section will describe the IOM stock index future, which is the most widely traded; differences with the other major contracts will be mentioned where relevant.

The Standard and Poor's 500 index is a market-value weighted geometric index of 500 firms (generally the largest firms) quoted on the New York Stock Exchange. The index is calculated using the base years 1941–43 = 10. The S + P 500 index has recently been trading at over 140.0. The IOM stock index future is valued at $500 times the futures contract price.

Example

20 May   The S + P 500 index close = 144.26

June index futures price = 145.10

Sept. index futures price = 145.62

Value of June future = $72,550 ($500 × 145.10)

Value of September future = $72,810 ($500 × 145.62)

The NYFE index future is also based on a value of $500 times the futures contract price. But because the level of the NYSE composite index is substantially lower than that of the S + P 500 index, the value of a futures contract traded on NYFE is significantly less in dollar terms. For instance on 10 December, 1982 the closing level of the NYSE composite was 80.49 and that of the S + P 500, 139.57. Thus the dollar value of two futures contracts, assuming the contract price was equal to the actual spot level of the underlying indices, would have been $40,245 and $69,785 respectively. The relative sizes of the index futures contracts will influence the relative demand for these contracts from institutional investors and retail participants.

In keeping with the valuation system described above, stock index futures prices are quoted in terms of the underlying stock index. For both the IOM and NYFE contracts, the tick size is 0.05 points per contract, which is equivalent to $25 per tick.

Example

1. On 14 May, September S + P 500 index futures are traded at 147.25. An investor buys 10 contracts.
2. On 20 May, September S + P 500 index futures are priced at 149.10. The investor closes his position by selling 10 contracts.

Change in price = 37 ticks (1.85/0.05)

Profit = 37 ticks × $25 per tick × 10 contracts

= $9,250

All the exchanges trade their stock index futures contracts on the March, June, September, December quarterly cycle. The last day of trading on the IOM contract is the third Thursday of the contract month, which is also the settlement day. On NYFE the last trading day is the day prior to the last business day of the delivery month, which is also the settlement day.

There is no physical delivery. All contracts outstanding at the close of trading on the last day of trading will be closed by cash settlement based on the settlement price, which in both the IOM and NYFE contracts is simply $500 times the equity index underlying the contract at the close of trading of the New York Stock Exchange for NYFE, and at 3:00pm central time for the IOM.

Thus the cash settlement system is exactly like the standard variation margin system, save that the settlement margin is determined by the difference between the delivery month futures settlement price on the day before the last day of trading and the actual closing level of the underlying index on the last day of trading. Although on the IOM contract the tick size of the contract is 0.05 points, the settlement will be carried out at the precise level of the index at 3:00pm central time.

Example

Wednesday 19 June	S + P 500 close = 139.24
	June S + P index future = 139.30
Thursday 20 June	S + P 500 (3:00pm central time) = 138.93
	June S + P index future close = 138.95

Final settlement payment to short from long = $185 (0.37 × $500)

There are currently no limits on daily stock index futures price changes.

10. Other financial futures contracts

One feature of the financial futures contracts already described, which includes all those with major trading volume, is that they are either very short-term or long-term interest rate contracts. It has proved difficult to develop good liquidity in medium-term contracts, say between two and 10 years. The failure of the four- to six-year Treasury note contract on the Chicago Board of Trade is a typical example of this.

Nevertheless, some new contracts have developed sufficient trading volume to provide evidence that this gap in the market may soon be filled. The $6\frac{1}{2}$–10 year Treasury note contract, introduced in the Chicago Board of Trade on 3 May, 1982, traded 881,235 contracts in 1982. On an equivalent annual volume basis this is approximately at a volume level of 1.5 million contracts per annum. This is not far short of the 2.06 million GNMA CDR contracts traded on the CBT in 1982, and represents a substantial start for a newly introduced contract.

The CBT $6\frac{1}{2}$–10 year Treasury note contract is designed along similar lines to the CBT Treasury bond contracts. The contract is based on a standardized 10-year 9% Treasury note of $100,000 face value and priced on a discount basis. Treasury rates of maturity between six and a half and 10 years can be delivered, and the settlement amount is determined by price factors in the same manner as the Treasury bond contract. The tick size of 1/32nd of a point, or $31.25 per contract, and the price limit of 64/32nds, are also identical to the Treasury bond contract. But the current initial margin of $1,500 is $500 less than the T-bond margin, reflecting the generally lower volatility of T-note prices to interest changes. Delivery is made through the Federal Reserve book entry wire transfer system. Given its early success, this contract looks like showing strong growth over the next few years.

Another new contract introduced on the Chicago Board of Trade, which also holds considerable potential, is the two-year Treasury note contract. This contract is rather different to the T-bond and 10-year T-note contracts. It is traded in face values of $400,000, with the price quoted as a percentage of par for a standardized two-year 8% instrument. However, the price basis is 1/128th of a point rather than 1/32nd; this preserves for the $400,000 face value a standard tick value of $31.25.

$$\text{Tick value} = \$400,000 \times 0.0000781 \ (1/128 \text{ of } 1\%)$$

$$= \$31.25$$

US Treasury notes and non-callable US Treasury bonds with an actual maturity of not less than one year, nine months and not more than two years can be delivered. As usual, delivery is through the Federal Reserve book entry transfer system, with the invoice amount adjusted for coupon rates and maturity dates, and accrued interest pro rated. Again, a standard conversion factor system is used, which is the price at which a note with the same coupon and maturity as the standard issue would yield 8%. Initial margin is currently $3,000 and maintenance margin $2,000. The daily price limits are 96/128ths of a point.

One of the reasons this contract is expected to be successful is the substantial increase in the use of T-notes for federal funding in recent years. As of December 1982, the Board of Trade estimated the total deliverable supply of two-year notes as $57,900 million. Moreover, recent correlation studies by the Board of Trade (see Exhibit 2.10) suggest that the contract will provide valuable hedge opportunities. Although cash two-year T-notes correlated well with other two-year instruments, there is also a high correlation with two-year T-bills and four-year T-notes.

Exhibit 2.10: Correlation matrix in terms of yield

	(0)	(1)	(2)	(3)	(4)	(5)	(6)	(7)	(8)	(9)	(10)
2-year Treasury note	1.000										
4-year Treasury note	0.976	1.000									
20-year Treasury bond	0.905	0.968	1.000								
8% GNMA	0.902	0.960	0.986	1.000							
3-month T-bill	0.859	0.758	0.621	0.624	1.000						
6-month T-bill	0.926	0.840	0.713	0.714	0.984	1.000					
12-month T-bill	0.973	0.910	0.803	0.802	0.943	0.984	1.000				
2-year Fed. Agency	0.990	0.965	0.890	0.888	0.843	0.914	0.964	1.000			
1-year secondary CD	0.965	0.905	0.794	0.793	0.930	0.974	0.989	0.963	1.000		
2-year secondary CD	0.990	0.983	0.930	0.925	0.927	0.965	0.984	0.981	0.986	1.000	
10-year Treasury note	0.935	0.985	0.992	0.972	0.668	0.758	0.842	0.922	0.836	0.963	1.000

Daily time series

Source: Chicago Board of Trade

Financial futures trading outside the United States and the UK has been relatively slow to take off. However, the volume of trading on the Toronto Exchange developed fairly rapidly in 1982 in both the long Canadian bond contract and the Canadian Treasury bill contract. The mid-term bond contract has not been able to develop any significant liquidity. The long-term bond contract, which is based on a standardized 9% 18-year bond with a $100,000 face value, is the most widely traded, and was averaging over 4,000 contracts per month in the second half of 1982. Treasury bill contracts, based on a conventional 91-day T-bill in $1 million units, have been averaging 30-40 contracts per day, though figures in excess of 200 contracts have been traded on some days.

The only other significant futures market for financial instruments is in Sydney, Australia, where there is modest trading in futures based on bankers' acceptances and the US dollar/ Australian dollar exchange rate. All these contract specifications are shown in detail in Appendix 2.

Chapter 3
Analytical concepts in financial futures

A. Statistical analysis for financial futures

There are two primary uses for statistical analysis in financial futures trading. First, it is important for hedgers to obtain accurate forward-looking estimates of the relative volatility of cash market and futures market prices. A hedger is interested in protecting himself by offsetting adverse movements in cash prices with favourable movements in futures prices. To do this well requires careful analysis of the relationship between different sets of prices through time. Statistical concepts such as regression analysis and bond duration analysis are crucial in predicting such relationships.

Secondly, the trader is interested in whether statistical techniques can be used to help predict the future development of interest rates, exchange rates, interest rate spreads and others. Such techniques may vary from simple moving averages, and time series models used in a form of technical analysis to full-scale econometric models of interest rate and exchange markets with forecasts as an output.

The techniques of correlation analysis and linear regression are the ones most commonly used in statistical and econometric analysis.

Correlation analysis

Correlation analysis is concerned with determining the closeness of the relationship between two time series, which might be interest rates, exchange rates or whatever. Thus if two series generally go up in level at the same time and fall at the same time, they are described as positively correlated. For instance, a monetary economist might expect to see positive correlation between money supply growth and later price growth.

If, on the other hand, two series move completely independently of one another, they will have zero correlation. Two such series might be the monthly total of observed shooting stars and the US balance of payments. Finally there is negative correlation, where two series move inversely—the lows of one series coinciding with the highs of another series and vice-versa.

Measuring the strength of such relationships is done by constructing a correlation coefficient with a range between -1 and $+1$. A correlation coefficient of -1 indicates perfect negative correlation; a coefficient of 0 indicates no relationship; and a correlation coefficient of $+1$ indicates perfect positive correlation. The formula for the correlation coefficient between two series X and Y is given as

$$P = \frac{\text{Covariance } (X, Y)}{\sigma_X \sigma_Y}$$

$$\text{Covariance } (X, Y) = \Sigma(X - \overline{X})(Y - \overline{Y})$$

$$\sigma_X = \sqrt{\Sigma(X - \overline{X})^2}$$

$$\sigma_Y = \sqrt{\Sigma(Y - \overline{Y})^2}$$

$$\overline{X} = \text{arithmetic mean of series X}$$

$$\overline{Y} = \text{arithmetic mean of series Y}$$

σ_X and σ_Y, which are called the standard deviations of X and Y, are measures of dispersion of a series: measures of how wide is the spread of numbers in the series from the arithmetic mean of the series. Below is an example of how to calculate the correlation coefficient for two short series.

$$X = 2, 4, 7, 9, 6$$
$$Y = 3, 5, 5, 4, 3$$

Calculate arithmetic mean of X and Y

$$\overline{X} = \frac{2 + 4 + 7 + 9 + 6}{5} = 5.6$$

$$\overline{Y} = \frac{3 + 5 + 5 + 4 + 3}{5} = 4.0$$

Calculate standard deviation of X and Y

$$\sigma_X = \sqrt{\Sigma(2 - 5.6)^2 + (4 - 5.6)^2 + (7 - 5.6)^2 + (9 - 5.6)^2 + (6 - 5.6)^2}$$
$$= 5.4$$
$$\sigma_Y = \sqrt{\Sigma(3 - 4)^2 + (5 - 4)^2 + (5 - 4)^2 + (3 - 4)^2}$$
$$= 2.0$$

Calculate covariance of X and Y

$$COV(X, Y) = (2 - 5.6)(3 - 4) + (4 - 5.6)(5 - 4) + (7 - 5.6)(5 - 4) + (9 - 5.6)(4 - 4) + (6 - 5.6)(3 - 4)$$
$$= 3.6 - 1.6 + 1.4 - 0.4 = 3$$

$$\text{Correlation coefficient of X and Y} = \frac{3}{5.4 \times 2.0} = 0.2778$$

The correlation coefficient tells us that the two series are positively but very weakly related, and one series would not be much use in hedging another.

Given below are typical correlation relationships for some pairs of interest rates that a hedger might be interested in. Classic cases of high positive correlation involve families of short-term interest rates: for example, the correlation coefficient for sterling time deposits and CD rates in the UK, using month-end data for 1978–81 was 0.9967; the correlation coefficient for US T-bill and CD rates for 1979–80 was 0.9487. In both these cases the two interest rates moved virtually in unison. Exhibits 3.1–3.3 also give correlation coefficients between sterling time deposit rates and short gilts for the period 1978–81, and between time deposit rates and stock market yields for the same period. The degree of correlation falls off quite rapidly: the correlation coefficient is 0.81 for time deposits and short gilts, and only 0.2258 for time deposits and equity yields.

The strength of correlation between two interest rate or price series is vital information in determining whether futures written on one instrument can be used to hedge cash market exposure in another instrument. Thus if we take the three UK correlation coefficients shown in the exhibits, a hedger would probably feel quite happy hedging a CD exposure with a sterling time deposit future, less happy hedging a short gilt portfolio with a sterling time deposit, and certainly would not try hedging a stock market position with time deposit futures.

The would-be hedger should also remember that he is not dependent just on the relationship between different cash market interest rates, but also between the cash market rates and futures prices. Although over time IMM T-bill futures prices, say, would be expected to parallel closely movements in cash T-bill rates, there may be periods when this relationship does not hold with its usual strength. Assume a December date and a cross-hedge between a cash position in bankers' acceptances and a futures position in IMM T-bills: then the general process of establishing whether a good hedge is possible might be as follows:

How to establish a good hedge

1. Examine correlation coefficient between acceptance rates and cash T-bill rates over last few years.
2. Examine stability of relationship through time.
3. Examine correlation coefficients between March, June, September, December T-bill futures and cash T-bills since beginning of trading in each future. Investigate relationship with trading volume and open interest.
4. Examine correlation coefficients for direct relationship of T-bill futures and acceptances.
5. If correlation information appears satisfactory, go ahead with hedge.

Exhibit 3.1: Sterling time deposits and CDs, 1978–81: high correlation

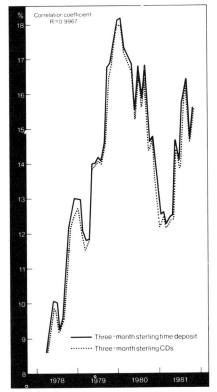

Source: LIFFE

Exhibit 3.2: Sterling time deposits and short gilts, 1978–81: fair correlation

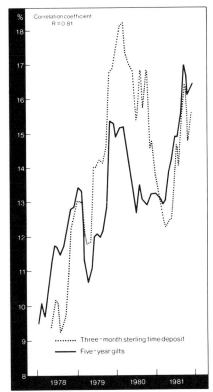

Source: LIFFE

Exhibit 3.3: Sterling time deposits and stock market yields: low correlation

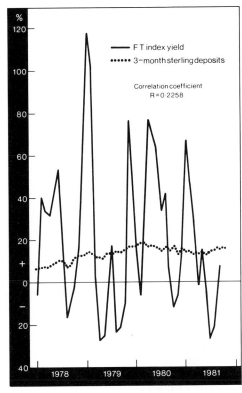

Source: LIFFE

The decision of which time periods to use in constructing correlation coefficients is fairly subjective and partly depends upon the periodicity of the cash market exposure which is to be hedged. Most published correlation coefficients tend to use month-end data based on relating monthly changes in one rate to monthly changes in the other, but end of week and weekly average data could be used if a longer data-run is deemed necessary.

Linear regression

The next stage after establishing the existence of a reasonably strong, stable relationship through correlation analysis is to examine the structure of the relationship with regression analysis. The most common regression technique is known as least squares analysis. In the case of two variables, the method constructs an equation relating one variable, the dependent variable to be explained, to another variable, the independent variable. The resulting linear equation is so chosen to produce the smallest errors between the historical actual values of the series and those estimated by the equation. The easiest way to represent a simple linear regression relationship is in the form of a straight line, with the dependent and independent variables represented on the Y and X axes of a simple graph respectively.

Exhibits 3.1–3.3 displayed correlation relationships between interest rates and yields. However, when examining the relationship between two series, it is often better to draw a scatter diagram to illustrate the relationship. Exhibit 3.4 shows scatter diagrams of one variable against another for sterling deposits against in turn CDs and short-term gilt yields. Least squares regression simply computes the straight line chosen to minimize the sum of squares of deviations of actual data from the equation line. The equation of such a straight line can generally be written as

$$Y = a + b . x$$

In this case, a represents the intercept on the Y-axis in a scatter diagram, and b represents the slope of the regression line, i.e. for a relationship between short gilt rates and sterling time deposit rates the change in the yield on short gilts which corresponds to a 1% change in the sterling deposit rate. Exhibit 3.5 gives an example of such a regression line.

Exhibit 3.4: Scatter diagrams: short-term interest rates

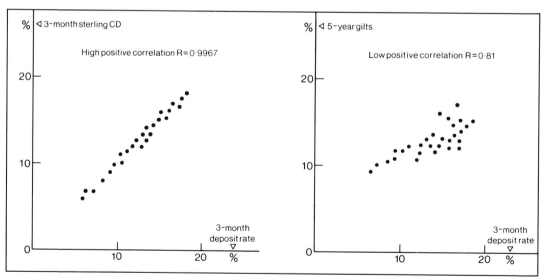

Source: LIFFE

The intercept on the Y-axis is equal to 6.74%; this indicates that the average premium of five-year gilt rates over three-month sterling time deposit rates is 6.74%. The regression coefficient b is 0.47, indicating that a 1% change in the time deposit rate will generally be associated with a 0.47% change in the five-year gilt yield. Other typical cash-cash and

Exhibit 3.5: Least squares regression: five-year gilts on sterling time deposits

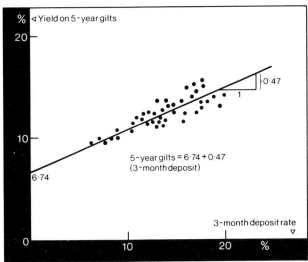

5-year gilts = 6·74 + 0·47 (3-month deposit)

Source: LIFFE

cash-futures linear regression relationships are given below. Cash-cash relationships display consistently stronger correlation figures than cash-futures relationships. This confirms the point that hedging cash positions with futures contracts does not eliminate interest rate or exchange rate risk.

Exhibit 3.6: Typical regression results

Dependent variable (Y)	Explanatory variable (X)	Slope coefficient (b)	Goodness of fit (R^2)
United States			
3-month T-bills	T-bill futures	0.899	0.784
3-month Euro $	T-bill futures	1.243	0.758
United Kingdom			
6-month cash Euro $	3-month cash Euro $	0.934	0.954
Yearling £	3-month cash £ TD	0.690	0.667
3-month Euro $	3-month Euro $ future	0.760	0.890
6-month Euro $	3-month Euro $ future	0.873	0.873
12-month Euro $	3-month Euro $ future	0.870	0.859

Regression of the form:

$$(\text{change in } Y) = a + b \,(\text{change in } X)$$

The slope coefficient (b) indicates the number of units of X required to hedge one unit of Y.

The goodness of fit statistic (R^2) indicates the proportion of the variance of Y which has been explained with X. In hedging terms, it indicates the potential effectiveness of a hedge of Y using X.

With each regression equation we have given values for R^2. This is by far the best-known indicator of the success of a least squares fit. The R^2 figures measures the percentage of the change in the dependent, or Y-variable, in the regression equation which has been caused by changes in the independent or X-variable. Generally the higher the R^2 the better fitted is the equation: R^2 has an upper limit of 1.0 just like the correlation coefficient.

Other statistics often given as part of the output of regression packages are: the standard error of the regression, which is another measure of the goodness of fit; T-statistics for individual variables, which measure the significance of the X-variable in predicting the value of the Y-variable; and the Durbin-Watson statistic, which measures the degree to which the differences between the actual and fitted values of the Y-variables are systematic or non-systematic.[1]

Linear regression and hedge design

The importance of linear regression and regression coefficients in hedge design is that the regression coefficient is a measure of the average relative volatility of two financial instrument yields. Suppose we regressed bankers' acceptance rates in the United States on IMM T-bill futures implied discount yields (a regression of rate changes on rate changes) and determined a regression coefficient of 0.90. This would mean that if T-bill prices rise by 100 basis points, we could expect bankers' acceptance rates to rise by 90 basis points.

This ratio would need to be taken into account in hedging (see Chapter 4). The hedge could involve less T-bill futures face value than the face value of the exposure in bankers' acceptances, because when rates move, the regression relationship tells us acceptance rates move less than T-bill futures implied rates. This is why regression coefficients are a crucial input into hedge design.

There is a further theoretical justification for using the R^2 of the type of regression equation discussed above as a measure of hedge effectiveness, and the regression coefficient as a proxy for the optimal hedge ratio. Generally the optimal hedge is defined as that ratio of futures contracts to cash positions which minimizes the variance of the return to the hedged position. In most hedging models these are defined as:

$$\text{Optimal hedge ratio } b\star = \frac{\sigma_{SF}}{\sigma_F^2}$$

$$\text{Hedge effectiveness} = \frac{\sigma_{SF}^2}{\sigma_S^2 \sigma_F^2}$$

where σ_{SF} = covariance between changes in spot rates or prices and futures rates or prices

σ_F^2 = variance of changes in futures rates or prices

σ_S^2 = variance of changes in spot rates or prices

Good approximations to these two measures are b, the regression coefficient between spot and futures price or rate changes, and the R^2 for the regression.

The use of regression analysis to determine the relative volatility of interest rates on exchange rates is complex. There are various difficulties. For example, what sort of regression analysis should be performed on historical data?

Regression analysis using historical data

1. Historical relationships between two interest rate series may not be stable. Hence *ex post* measures of volatility may not be very good at predicting future relative volatility.
2. Regression relationships between interest rates may not be independent of the level of interest rates. Hence if a major interest rate change has occurred within the recent past, insufficient data may be available since the change to allow appropriate regression equations to be established.
3. Regression relationships between different maturity futures contracts implied interest rates and cash rates may not be identical. Hence hedge design can involve many regression relationships of differing quality.
4. With limited contracts available, for example on LIFFE, it may be difficult to generate enough data to estimate regression relationships between cash rates and a single futures contract through time. On the other hand relationships between cash rates and artificially created continuous futures prices, involving composites of different delivery date futures prices, may have highly unpredictable statistical properties.

The main point is that it is not enough to simply regress cash market rate changes against futures price changes to get a regression coefficient that can be used in setting hedge ratios. Many complex statistical techniques may be required to solve some of the difficulties outlined

---

[1] For an excellent description of linear regression methods and their applications, see N. R. Draper and H. Smith, *Applied Regression Analysis*, John Wiley & Sons, New York (1966).

56

above. Nonetheless, at least with short-term rates, some sort of estimated relationship between cash rates and implied futures rates is essential. For long-term instruments such as gilts, Treasury bonds, GNMAs, and corporate bonds other alternatives are available for comparing cash and futures performance.

B. Conversion factors and duration for long-term interest rate futures

The relationship between financial futures contracts written on such long-run instruments as Treasury bonds in the United States and long-term gilts in the UK and the underlying cash instruments is quite complex. It has already been discussed how many different cash market instruments are deliverable against these futures contracts, and how it is necessary for the exchanges to determine a method of translating the price of a futures contract into an equivalent price for a cash instrument.

This section examines how these conversion factors are derived, and what information they contain about the comparative volatility of cash market prices and futures prices.

LIFFE price factors

To begin with the LIFFE gilt contract: the definition of the price factor is the price per pound nominal value of a stock at which the stock has a gross redemption yield of 12%. Accrued interest at 12% is included in the discounting process, and then accrued interest at the actual rate is subtracted from the price factor. These price factors are calculated as of the first day of the delivery month. How are these factors calculated?

Consider first of all an ordinary yield to maturity on redemption yield calculation ignoring accrued interest.

$$P = \left[\sum_{t=1}^{n} \frac{C/2}{(1 + r)^t} \right] + \frac{100}{(1 + r)^n}$$

where P = market price per £100 nominal of the bond
C/2 = half-yearly interest payment
n = number of half-years to redemption
r = gross redemption yield on a semi-annual basis.

Ignoring accrued interest, what would the price have to be to yield 12% on an annual basis

$$P = \left[\sum_{t=1}^{n} \frac{C/2}{[1 + (0.12/2)]^t} \right] + \frac{100}{[1 + (0.12/2)]^n}$$

$$= \frac{C}{2(0.06)} \left\{ 1 - \frac{1}{(1.06)^n} \right\} + \frac{100}{(1.06)^n}$$

$$= \frac{C}{0.12} \left\{ 1 - \frac{1}{(1.06)^n} \right\} + \frac{100}{(1.06)^n}$$

Adjustments have to be made for accrued interest because the first day of the delivery month does not coincide with interest payment dates on the gilt. The way to do this is to add the price shown above, which determines the price at an interest payment date, to the next coupon payment, and discount the whole sum back to the present at an annual rate of 12%. To get a clean price, subtract the amount of accrued interest on the stock between the previous interest payment date and the settlement date, the first day of the delivery month.

$$P = \frac{1}{(1.06)^{X/182.5}} \left[C^\star + \frac{C}{0.12} \left\{ 1 - \frac{1}{(1.06)^n} \right\} + \frac{100}{(1.06)^n} \right] - \frac{C}{2} \left\{ \frac{Y - X}{182.5} \right\}$$

where $C/2$ = half-yearly interest payments
P = clean price of the gilt
n = number of half-years to redemption from next interest payment date
$C^\star$ = next interest payment, which will usually be $C/2$, but is zero if the stock is ex-dividend
X = number of days from and including the first day of the delivery month up to but excluding the next payment day
Y = number of days after the previous interest payment date up to and including the next payment date

If the stock is ex-dividend on the first day of the delivery month, the final term in the equation above will be $+C/2[(Y - X)/182.5]$ rather than negative.

The price factor or conversion factor is then simply $P/100$. Such conversion factors determine the invoice price for an actual gilt ex delivery. For instance, suppose you decide to deliver Treasury $13\frac{3}{4}\%$ stock against a futures contract. The invoice price would be

$$S = P \times F(T\ 13\tfrac{3}{4}) \times 500 + A(T\ 13\tfrac{3}{4})$$

where S = settlement amount
P = settlement price of the gilt futures contract
F = price factor for Treasury $13\frac{3}{4}$
A = accrued interest on Treasury $13\frac{3}{4}$ since last coupon payment

Suppose we consider a March 1983 contract for the Treasury $13\frac{3}{4}\%$ 2000-03 stock, with interest payment dates 25 January and 25 July. On 1 March, the price factor calculated from the formula above is 1.1268837. There are 34 days between the last payment date of 25 January and 1 March; hence, with a daily accrued interest of £18.8356 there is accrued interest of £640.41 attached to the stock. If the settlement price on the gilt were £96-00, the settlement value on delivery Treasury $13\frac{3}{4}$ 2000-03 would be

$$S = (96\text{-}00 \times 1.1268837 \times 500) + 640.41$$

$$= £54,730.83 \text{ for } £50,000 \text{ nominal delivered}$$

Exhibit 3.7 shows a typical set of gilt price factors put out by LIFFE.

Exhibit 3.7: Twenty-year interest rate contract—price factors and accrued interest
Contract month: March 83

Stock				Price factor	Daily accrued	Initial accrued
Treasury	$15\frac{1}{2}\%$	30 Sept.	1998	1.2446110	21.2329	−636.99
Exchequer	12%	20 Nov.	1998	1.0000623	16.4384	1,643.84
Treasury	$9\frac{1}{2}\%$	15 Jan.	1999	0.8245612	13.0137	572.60
Exchequer	$12\frac{1}{4}\%$	26 March	1999	1.0179052	16.7808	−436.30
Treasury	$10\frac{1}{2}\%$	19 May	1999	0.8939428	14.3836	1,452.74
Treasury	13%	14 July	2000	1.0724969	17.8082	801.37
Treasury	14%	22 May	98-2001	1.1384685	19.1781	1,879.45
Exchequer	12%	22 Jan.	99-2002	1.0001983	16.4384	608.22
Treasury	$13\frac{3}{4}\%$	25 July	2000-03	1.1268837	18.8356	640.41
Treasury	$11\frac{1}{2}\%$	19 March	2001-04	0.9620974	15.7534	−299.32
Funding	$3\frac{1}{2}\%$	14 July	99-2004	0.3504174	4.7945	215.75
Treasury	$12\frac{1}{2}\%$	21 Nov.	2003-05	1.0380064	17.1233	1,695.21
Treasury	8%	5 Oct.	2002-06	0.6882427	10.9589	−394.52
Treasury	$11\frac{1}{4}\%$	22 Jan.	2003-07	0.9806478	16.0959	595.55
Treasury	$13\frac{1}{2}\%$	26 March	2004-08	1.1145726	18.4932	−480.82

Daily accrued: accrued interest per day on $50,000 face value
Price factor: price factor expressed as a fraction of par
Initial accrued: accrued interest on £50,000 face value as of the last day of the month prior to the delivery month
Invoicing formula: invoicing amount = [(settlement price) × (price factor) × 500] + initial accrued + [(daily accrued) × (delivery month)]
Source: LIFFE/Investor Intelligence Systems.

58

CBT price factors

The procedure on the Chicago Board of Trade is similar to the LIFFE gilt, but has been simplified so that new price factors do not need to be calculated for each new delivery month. This is done by invoicing with maturity defined only in complete quarters. Again the first day of the delivery month is used to establish the time to maturity.

For example, a 7% Treasury bond with 25 years, seven months and 10 days to go to maturity would for invoice purposes be deemed to have a maturity of 25 years and six months. Odd periods are always rounded down to the nearest quarter. The Board of Trade then simply calculates what the price of this 25-year six-month bond will be to give an effective yield of 8%. There is no calculation of accrued interest on the bond. Hence although not as accurate as the LIFFE calculation, the CBT price factor system is easier to calculate.

For example, consider the bond described above. The price factor would be calculated simply as

$$P = \frac{7/2}{0.04}\left(1 - \frac{100}{(1.04)^{51}}\right) + \frac{100}{(1.04)^{51}}$$
$$= 89.19$$

Factor = 0.8919

An example of the conversion factors on the CBT is shown in Exhibit 3.8. The simplicity compared with the LIFFE factor tables is evident.

Exhibit 3.8: Conversion factor for invoicing

PRICES TO YIELD 8.000%

TERM	7%	7½%	7¼%	7⅜%	7½%	7⅝%	7¾%	7⅞%
15	.9135	.9243	.9352	.9460	.9568	.9676	.9784	.9892
15-3	.9126	.9235	.9344	.9453	.9562	.9671	.9780	.9889
15-6	.9121	.9231	.9340	.9450	.9560	.9670	.9780	.9890
15-9	.9112	.9222	.9333	.9444	.9555	.9666	.9776	.9887
16	.9106	.9218	.9330	.9441	.9553	.9665	.9777	.9888
16-3	.9098	.9210	.9323	.9435	.9548	.9660	.9773	.9885
16-6	.9093	.9206	.9319	.9433	.9546	.9660	.9773	.9887
16-9	.9084	.9198	.9313	.9427	.9541	.9655	.9770	.9884
17	.9079	.9195	.9310	.9425	.9540	.9655	.9770	.9885
17-3	.9071	.9187	.9303	.9419	.9535	.9651	.9766	.9882
17-6	.9067	.9183	.9300	.9417	.9533	.9650	.9767	.9883
17-9	.9059	.9176	.9294	.9411	.9528	.9646	.9763	.9881
18	.9055	.9173	.9291	.9409	.9527	.9645	.9764	.9882
18-3	.9047	.9166	.9285	.9404	.9522	.9641	.9760	.9879
18-6	.9043	.9163	.9282	.9402	.9521	.9641	.9761	.9880
18-9	.9035	.9156	.9276	.9396	.9517	.9637	.9757	.9878
19	.9032	.9153	.9274	.9395	.9516	.9637	.9758	.9879
19-3	.9024	.9146	.9268	.9390	.9511	.9633	.9755	.9876
19-6	.9021	.9143	.9266	.9388	.9510	.9633	.9755	.9878
19-9	.9014	.9137	.9260	.9383	.9506	.9629	.9752	.9875
20	.9010	.9134	.9258	.9381	.9505	.9629	.9753	.9876
20-3	.9004	.9128	.9252	.9377	.9501	.9625	.9749	.9874
20-6	.9000	.9125	.9250	.9375	.9500	.9625	.9750	.9875
20-9	.8994	.9119	.9245	.9370	.9496	.9621	.9747	.9873
21	.8991	.9117	.9243	.9369	.9495	.9622	.9748	.9874
21-3	.8984	.9111	.9238	.9364	.9491	.9618	.9745	.9871
21-6	.8981	.9109	.9236	.9363	.9491	.9618	.9745	.9873
21-9	.8975	.9103	.9231	.9359	.9487	.9614	.9742	.9870
22	.8973	.9101	.9229	.9358	.9486	.9615	.9743	.9872
22-3	.8967	.9095	.9224	.9353	.9482	.9611	.9740	.9869
22-6	.8964	.9093	.9223	.9352	.9482	.9611	.9741	.9870
22-9	.8958	.9088	.9218	.9348	.9478	.9608	.9738	.9868
23	.8956	.9086	.9217	.9347	.9478	.9608	.9739	.9869
23-3	.8950	.9081	.9212	.9343	.9474	.9605	.9736	.9867
23-6	.8948	.9079	.9211	.9342	.9474	.9605	.9737	.9868
23-9	.8942	.9074	.9206	.9338	.9470	.9602	.9734	.9866
24	.8940	.9073	.9205	.9338	.9470	.9603	.9735	.9868
24-3	.8935	.9068	.9201	.9334	.9466	.9599	.9732	.9865
24-6	.8933	.9066	.9200	.9333	.9466	.9600	.9733	.9867
24-9	.8928	.9061	.9195	.9329	.9463	.9597	.9730	.9864
25	.8926	.9060	.9194	.9329	.9463	.9597	.9731	.9866
25-3	.8921	.9055	.9190	.9325	.9459	.9594	.9729	.9863
25-6	.8919	.9054	.9189	.9324	.9460	.9595	.9730	.9865
25-9	.8914	.9050	.9185	.9321	.9456	.9592	.9727	.9863
26	.8913	.9049	.9184	.9320	.9456	.9592	.9728	.9864
26-3	.8908	.9044	.9180	.9317	.9453	.9589	.9725	.9862
26-6	.8906	.9043	.9180	.9316	.9453	.9590	.9727	.9863
26-9	.8902	.9039	.9176	.9313	.9450	.9587	.9724	.9861
27	.8900	.9038	.9175	.9313	.9450	.9588	.9725	.9863
27-3	.8896	.9034	.9171	.9309	.9447	.9585	.9722	.9860
27-6	.8895	.9033	.9171	.9309	.9447	.9585	.9724	.9862
27-9	.8890	.9029	.9167	.9306	.9444	.9583	.9721	.9860

Reproduced from *Treasury Bond Futures and Treasury Note Futures Conversion Factors*, Pub. No. 765 © 1979, Financial Publishing Co., Boston, MA.

Cheapest to deliver gilts and bonds

What do these conversion or price factors imply? First, the invoice prices of gilts and Treasury bonds are not dependent upon the actual price of gilts and T-bonds in the cash market. The conversion factors assume a completely flat yield curve at 12% and 8% respectively; this may not be the case in the cash market where at various times one observes both upward sloping and downward sloping yield curves.

Differences between cash yields and futures yields could arise from tax considerations, liquidity premiums, risk premiums, or market segmentation. In any case, if there are differences between cash market prices adjusted by the relevant price factor and the futures price, it is evident that some particular gilts or Treasury bonds will be cheaper to deliver than others. The basic concept is what is termed *the cheapest deliverable instrument*. Consider two sets of price information: one on LIFFE and one on the CBT.

LIFFE	Futures price	Price factor	Implied price	Clean* price	Profit from delivery
Treasury 13¾ 2000–03	102-23	1.1274	115-03	116-27	−56/32
Treasury 11½ 2001–04	102-23	0.9619	98-26	103-18	−120/32
Treasury 15.5 1998	102-23	1.2446	127-27	125-21	+70/32

CBT	Futures price	Price factor	Implied price	Clean* price	Profit from delivery
8¾ 2008	79-16	1.079	85-25	85-28	−3/32
9⅛ 2009	79-16	1.1194	89-00	88-30	+2/32
10⅜ 2009	79-16	1.254	99-22	99-28	−6/32

*Clean price is the market price less accrued interest.

Looking at the LIFFE prices, the Treasury 15.5% 1998 is clearly cheaper to deliver than either of the other gilts, since buying in the market and delivering into the futures market creates a cash gain rather than a cash loss. Similarly the 9⅛ 2009 T-bond is the cheapest to deliver on the CBT. In general the cheapest deliverable instrument tends to be the highest coupon gilt or T-bond and/or the one most recently issued. The concept of the cheapest deliverable instrument is widely used in arbitrage in the futures market (*see* Chapter 7).

Because one financial instrument is usually the optimal instrument to deliver, the futures markets in gilts and T-bonds tend to be priced off the cheapest deliverable instrument, i.e. prices in the futures market will generally move in line with prices of the cheapest deliverable instruments, adjusted for the price factor. Other things being equal, we would expect a movement of 4/32nds upwards in the cash 15½% 1998 gilt with a price factor of 1.2446 to be associated with a 3/32nds movement in the price of the future.

Duration

These conversion factors can be used to determine hedge ratios between individual gilt or Treasury bond holdings and gilt or T-bond futures contracts. However, the conversion factors are based on a flat yield curve, and this may not provide an accurate measure of the relative price movements of gilts or bonds of different maturities and coupons. An alternative measure of the comparative responsiveness of prices to yield changes is the duration of a bond. The duration of a bond is a weighted average of the times when payments are made on the bond, with each payment weighted by the proportion of present value contributed by the payment made at the time. Hence the formula for a bond's duration is:

$$D = \sum_{t=1}^{n} \frac{t \cdot (X_t)}{(1 + r)^t} \bigg/ P$$

Where n = number of periods to redemption
X_t = payment on the bond in a particular period
r = yield to maturity
P = market price of the bond

Consider a three-year maturity bond with a coupon yield of 10% and a yield to maturity of 12%, where the market price would be 95-03. The duration would be given by

$$D = \frac{1}{2}\left\{\frac{5}{95\text{--}03}\left[\frac{1}{1.06} + \frac{2}{(1.06)^2} + \frac{3}{(1.06)^3} + \frac{4}{(1.06)^4} + \frac{5}{(1.06)^5} + \frac{6}{(1.06)^6}\right] + \frac{(100)\ \ (6)}{(95\text{--}03)\ (1.06)^6}\right\}$$

= 2.66

The standard duration formula is divided by two because interest payments are made semi-annually.

The useful point about this duration measure is that bonds or indeed bond portfolios of equal duration tend to react similarly to changes in interest rates.

% change in price = Duration × % change in (1 + r)

In other words consider an increase in yield to maturity on the above bond of 0.25%. Then we can determine the % change in (1 + r)

% change in (1 + r) = $\frac{1.1225}{1.12} - 1 = 0.0022$ (or 0.22%)

The change in the price of the bond is given by

% change in price = (−2.66)(0.22%) = −0.585%

And the new bond price is given by

(95-03)(1 − 0.00585) = 94-17

This concept of duration provides another method of calculating optimal ratios between cash and futures positions for use in hedging, spread trading and other practical techniques discussed later in the book.

In all cases the appropriate ratio of a cash position to a futures position can be written

$$\text{Hedge ratio} = \frac{(1 + r_c)(P_s)(D_s)}{(1 + r_s)(P_c)(D_c)} \times C_c$$

Where r_s = yield to maturity on cash bond
P_s = market price of cash bond
D_s = duration of cash bond
r_c = yield to maturity on cheapest to deliver bond
P_c = market price of cheapest to deliver bond
D_c = duration of cheapest to deliver bond
C_c = conversion factor for cheapest to deliver bond

Ratios based on duration measures are likely to be significantly better than those based on conversion factors, and can be estimated just as easily.

C. Futures/cash relationships

Futures prices are determined by the interplay of supply and demand from hedgers, speculators and arbitrageurs. In the absence of arbitrage supply and demand, the equilibrium futures price will only equal the expected spot price if speculators are risk-neutral. If speculators are risk-averse, the futures price can lie above or below the expected spot price, depending on the relative quantities of long hedgers and short hedgers. What about the relationship between the current spot price and the futures price? Speculators essentially try and drive the futures price towards the expected spot price, but do not trade in the cash markets. Hence in a market dominated by speculators, the basis—the difference between the cash price and the futures price—will equal the expected change in the spot price of the cash instrument over the life of the futures contract.

Arbitrage

Arbitrage can be defined as the simultaneous purchase and sale of the same asset in two different markets, to yield a riskless profit. There are two types of arbitrage in interest rate markets. The first type of arbitrage is where the cash instrument on which the future is written is carryable, i.e. the asset can be bought and sold in a spot market and used to make or take delivery on a futures contract.

Consider what a cash and carry arbitrage looks like on a gilt in the UK. Supposing you borrowed money at a fixed rate in the cash market and used it to purchase a gilt: since you would receive the coupon yield on the gilt while you owned it, the net cost of carry would be the interest cost of borrowing less interest earned on the gilt. You will also gain or lose the difference between the cash price of the gilt you purchase and the price you will receive for it when you deliver it into the futures market. This difference between the cash market price of an instrument and the futures market price is known as the basis.

There are, thus, some simple arbitrage strategies for carryable instruments. If the cost of carry is less than the negative of the basis, you will earn an arbitrage profit by buying the cash instrument and selling the futures contract. If the cost of carry is greater than the negative of the basis, you will make an arbitrage profit by buying the futures contract and selling the cash. Futures prices cannot be equilibrium prices if they give investors opportunities to make riskless arbitrage profits, hence, this implies some relationship between spot prices and futures prices.

Even for non-carryable instruments such as Eurodollar or sterling time deposits, another type of arbitrage strategy can be devised. The cash market contains its own prices for instruments in future months in the cash market yield curve.

A three-month interest rate and a six-month rate imply a three-month interest rate commencing in three months time. This is the so-called *forward-forward* rate, found in this simple case from the following formula:

$$\left[\left\{ \frac{1 + \dfrac{\text{6-month rate}}{2}}{1 + \dfrac{\text{3-month rate}}{4}} \right\} - 1 \right] \times 4 = \text{3-month rate starting in 3-months time}$$

Once we have derived such rates, another type of arbitrage is possible. If the forward-forward rate is less than the futures implied rate, buy the future and sell the cash market. If the forward-forward rate is higher than the futures implied rate, sell the future and buy the cash market. Again equilibrium prices should not allow arbitrage profits of this kind.[2]

However, in the futures market, arbitrage profits are not really riskless because of the marking to market principle (described in Chapter 2). Adverse variation margin movements could wipe out potential arbitrage profits, and indeed turn them into losses. Thus, just like speculative demand for futures contracts, arbitrage demand will probably be a function of the size of the arbitrage profit.

If riskless arbitrage is possible, then in the case of a carryable commodity the basis must always be equal to the cost of carry. Similarly, in the case of a non-carryable commodity the futures implied interest rate must always equal the forward-forward rate. Thus, if we assume the spot rate is fixed, then all deferred futures contract prices will be defined by these two arbitrage conditions.

---

[2] There is a lot more to arbitrage transactions than is shown in this simple model. Later in the book we discuss the practicalities of arbitrage trading and illustrate the many difficulties in carrying out arbitrage transactions risklessly.

In a market where both speculators and arbitrageurs exist, the basis is likely to lie somewhere between the balance of the two forces: between the expected change in the spot price and the cost of carry.

When would the basis be expected to be positive, i.e. cash prices to lie above futures prices? There are two inputs which would tend to produce this result: (1) if speculators expect cash prices to fall over the life of the contract; and/or (2) if either the cost of carry is negative—normally associated with a positively sloping yield curve—or, in the case of non-carryable commodities, if the relevant forward-forward rate is higher than the cash market rate. The reverse situation of futures prices lying above cash prices would be expected when either: speculators are expecting prices to rise, or when the cost of carry is positive, or forward-forward rates are lower than cash market rates.

Similar statements can be made about spreads between different futures contracts. Spreads will be positive, i.e. the prices of nearby months greater than deferred months, when either (1) speculators expect prices to fall steadily over the lifetime of all the contracts concerned; or (2) there is a positive cash market yield curve. Spreads will generally be negative when either speculators are expecting steady price rises or there is a negative cash market yield curve.

Strip yield curves

Some of these relationships are worth exploring in more technical detail. How do we tell whether a futures price is cheap or dear? Consider the case of a non-carryable commodity. Using arbitrage arguments of the type outlined above, the argument would suggest that forward-forward rates should equal equivalent futures rates.

A frequent method used to compare these two rates over different futures contracts is the so-called *strip yield curve*. This is simply a synthetic yield curve created from the implied rates embedded in futures prices. This can then be compared with the actual cash yield curve to determine whether cash prices are cheaper than futures prices or vice versa.

This concept can be illustrated simply. Suppose we have the following information.

Cash market yield curve	Future prices (three-month) instrument
3-month R3	3 months to delivery P3
6-month R6	6 months to delivery P6
9-month R9	9 months to delivery P9
12-month R12	12 months to delivery P12
15-month R15	15 months to delivery P15

Strip yield curve

3-month

$$R3$$

6-month

$$\left\{\left[\left(1 + \frac{R3}{4}\right)\left(1 + \frac{(100 - P3)}{4}\right)\right] - 1\right\} \times 2$$

9-month

$$\left\{\left[\left(1 + \frac{R3}{4}\right)\left(1 + \frac{(100 - P3)}{4}\right)\left(1 + \frac{(100 - P6)}{4}\right)\right] - 1\right\} \times 4/3$$

12-month

$$\left\{\left[\left(1 + \frac{R3}{4}\right)\left(1 + \frac{(100 - P3)}{4}\right)\left(1 + \frac{(100 - P6)}{4}\right)\left(1 + \frac{(100 - P9)}{4}\right)\right] - 1\right\}$$

15-month

$$\left\{\left[\left(1 + \frac{R3}{4}\right)\left(1 + \frac{(100 - P3)}{4}\right)\left(1 + \frac{(100 - P6)}{4}\right)\left(1 + \frac{(100 - P9)}{4}\right)\left(1 + \frac{(100 - P12)}{4}\right)\right] - 1\right\} \times 4/5$$

63

If forward-forward rates and futures rates are determined by the arbitrage process, this futures strip yield curve should be identical with the actual cash yield curve.[3] However, in practice this is often not the case. Exhibit 3.9 shows a typical cash market yield curve and a futures strip yield curve.

Exhibit 3.9: Cash and futures yield curves

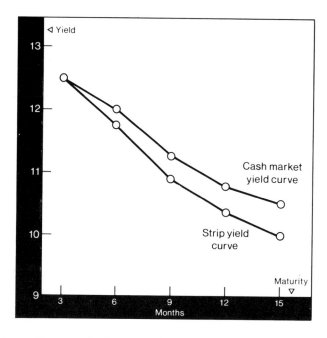

There are significant divergencies between the cash market yield curve and the futures strip yield curve. This apparently would create arbitrage profits because individual forward and futures rates must converge at delivery. Why, then, might there be a discrepancy? First, the process of marking to market makes futures arbitrage transactions risky. Second, the cash market yield curve may reflect liquidity and risk premiums which are not present in the futures yield curve. Third, there may be constraints on institutional investors, including restrictions on the use of the futures markets, which make this arbitrage impossible. Nonetheless the concept of comparing the two yield curves enables us to characterize individual futures prices as relatively dear or relatively cheap.

Implied repo rates

The second major element in cash futures arbitrage is the *implied repo rate*. This applies to carryable commodities. An investor can purchase a cash instrument, finance the position with borrowed money, and cover the rate risk by selling a futures contract. The profitability will depend on the borrowing rate and the implied rate on the cash purchase and futures sale. The borrowing rate at which the whole transaction would break even is the implied repo rate. For example, in a simple gilt cash and carry, the implied repo rate is simply:[4]

$$\text{Current yield on cash gilt} + \left(\frac{[\text{Futures price} - \text{Clean cash price}]}{\text{Clean cash price}} \times \frac{365}{N} \right)$$

where N = number of days to delivery

Just as the futures strip yield curve may be different from the observed cash market yield curve, so the implied repo rate may differ significantly from the actual cost of financing a cash and carry position due to limitations on the arbitrage process.

---

[3] Chapter 8 explores the practical implication of the futures strip yield curve.

[4] The example is deliberately simple. In practice, cash and carry repo rates are quite difficult to calculate since accrued interest has to be included in the calculation. A full treatment of cash and carry arbitrage is contained in Chapter 7.

The basis between a carryable cash instrument and the future can be divided into two parts: the carry basis, which is that price differential which would make the implied repo rate equal the cost of finance, and the value basis, the incremental value of the futures contract over and above the compensation paid by the carry basis to a purchaser of the cash instrument. The value basis is a measure of the cheapness or dearness of a futures contract written on a carryable instrument, and has an important influence on hedging and arbitrage strategies.

Interest parity

A similar arbitrage condition applies in the foreign exchange futures market: the interest rate parity condition. This works on the basis that a three-month investment in sterling, or in dollars at fixed dollar/sterling exchange rates, must earn the same return because they are equally risky. Hence suppose the current $/£ spot exchange rate is 1.6000 and the three-month forward exchange rate is 1.5960. The sterling three-month lending rate is 11.20%. The investor has two choices with £100 to invest.

Alternative 1

Invest £100 for three months at 11.2%

$$\text{Final sum} = 100\left(1 + \frac{0.112}{4}\right) = \text{£}102.80$$

Alternative 2

Change £100 sterling into $160
Invest $160 for 3 month at rate R

$$\text{Final sum} = 160(1 + R/4)$$

Sell $160(1 + R/4)$ forward at 1.5960

$$\text{Total proceeds} = \text{£}100(1.6)(1 + R/4)/(1.5960)$$

Because all the transactions rates are fixed in advance, and assuming the default risk on each investment is identical, the return to the two transactions must be the same.

$$102.80 = 160(1 + R/4)/1.5950$$

Therefore R must equal 9.92%

The difference between the spot and forward exchange rate must always equal the difference between the two interest rates, or arbitrage profits will be available. Hence the interest rate parity condition can be written:

$$\frac{1 + R^\text{£}}{1 + R^\text{\$}} = \frac{\text{\$/£ spot}}{\text{\$/£ forward}}$$

Variations from this relationship, when defined in terms of futures interest rates and exchange rates, are often used as the basis of arbitrage or spread trading (*see* Chapters 6 and 7). The relationship can also be used in hedging to set up artificial interest rate futures contracts which are not currently traded on an exchange.

Chapter 4
Hedging with financial futures contracts: the basic principles

This chapter looks at the hedging uses of financial futures contracts. The conventional division of users of financial futures contracts is into hedgers and speculators, or traders as they are termed in the London markets.

The essence of hedging is the transference of risk, in this case interest or foreign exchange rate risk from the hedger to someone else in the market place. The hedger is primarily worried that adverse changes in rates will harm his earnings, or that even if potential interest rate changes do not harm expected earnings, earnings' volatility will be increased. The central feature of financial futures contracts is that they enable an investor to lock interest or foreign exchange rates now for a transaction to be carried out at some future date. As such they are suitable for hedging the rate risks which face banks, industrial corporations, portfolio managers, and others.

To achieve a suitable transference of risk, however, the hedger will have to choose a hedging instrument whose movements mirror rather closely the price behaviour of the cash position. You would not expect to see a grain exporter hedging his price risk with a futures position in copper or rubber; nor would you expect to see a portfolio manager trying to protect a certificate of deposit position by hedging it with long-term gilt or Treasury bond futures contracts.

Such an approach to hedging is emphasized in the official definition of hedging of the Commodity Futures Trading Commission in the United States, which stresses that a *bona fide* hedge must involve positions in futures contracts which are economically related to the cash position and designed to reduce risks that arise within the normal commercial operations of the company in question.

So, a hedger is a person, or company, who transfers interest or exchange rate risk by temporarily offsetting a position in the cash market with an economically related position in the financial futures market. There are many kinds of potential hedgers. Borrowers of funds can use the futures markets to protect themselves against higher borrowing costs in the future as current loans mature, and to smooth out their pattern of interest payments. Lenders can equally protect themselves against falling interest rates in the future by purchasing financial futures contracts at high current yields. Borrowers and lenders in this sense can include banks making floating rate term loans, corporations borrowing through such loans, and even individuals protecting themselves against higher mortgage rates. Portfolio managers can lock in anticipated prices and yields on financial instruments they plan to purchase in the future, and can protect the asset value of financial assets they already hold against falls in capital value due to rising interest rates. Finally, foreign exchange users such as importers and exporters can use foreign exchange futures as an alternative to the forward market to protect against foreign exchange payment risks and preserve the translation value of their revenue inflows in foreign currencies.

Hedging possibilities will be attractive to many financial and commercial corporations. A certain degree of interest rate risk is part of the normal financial risk of all corporations. Corporations use leverage because they believe in general that the cost of debt will be lower than the rate of return on the money borrowed when invested in the operations of the firm. Since any surplus earnings on debt over and above the interest cost go straight to the shareholders, the use of leverage increases the expected earnings available to shareholders. Shareholders pay for increased expected earnings with increased riskiness of those earnings.

Remove the risk entirely and you effectively remove the higher expected earnings. However, whereas corporations were very willing to accept interest rate risk when rates might vary from 4% to 6% in a year, they are not willing to accept the whole interest rate risk when rates can go from 18% to perhaps 8% in the space of a few months, or when the sterling-dollar exchange rate can move from nearly $2.40 to $1.80, as in the first seven months of 1981. Exhibits 1.1 and 1.2 in Chapter 1 display the interest and exchange rate volatility of the past few years, and against which financial futures allow investors to protect themselves.

The traditional perfect hedge would consist of a cash position in one particular instrument matched by an equal, opposite position in a futures contract written on the same instrument. While this may not be easy to achieve in practice, it serves to introduce a couple of examples of what simple hedges look like.

First, a typical long hedge. A portfolio manager habitually invests in three-month Treasury bills; he believes interest rates are currently at a relatively high level and believes that when he comes to re-invest at the maturity of his current T-bills, he will receive a markedly lower yield. He decides to hedge this risk in the IMM T-bill market. This is a classic long hedge.

Example of assets management: a long hedge

A bank portfolio manager plans to buy $10,000,000 face value of three-month T-bills in six weeks time, and believes T-bill rates are going to decline.

Cash market	Treasury bill futures market (IMM)
2 January: discount yield = 13.0%	2 January: Bank buys $10,000,000 face value of March 90-day T-bills at 86.5 (13.5%)
13 February: Bank purchases $10,000,000 face value of 90-day T-bills at discount yield of 12%. Net cost = $9,700,000	13 February: Bank sells $10,000,000 face value of March 90-day T-bills at 87.5 (12.5%)
Additional cost of T-bill purchase at 12% discount instead of 13%:	Net profit on futures contract equals 100 ticks per contract.
$9,700,000 − $9,675,000 = $25,000	$10 \times 100 \times \$25 = \$25,000$

This is a perfect hedge: rates fell as expected and the portfolio manager had to pay an extra $25,000 to buy the Treasury bills in February. However the futures price moved exactly in parallel with the cash price, and there was a futures gain of $25,000 exactly compensating the portfolio manager for the additional expenditure in the cash market.

A typical short hedge might involve a firm with a floating rate loan, which is worried that rates will have risen by the time of the next rollover date. The firm will try to lock in current interest rates by selling financial futures contracts.

Example of hedging a variable rate loan: a short hedge

A firm has a five-year term loan at a 1% spread over the three-month sterling time deposit rate with three-month rollovers. The treasurer believes rates will rise by the next rollover date in two and a half months time.

Cash market	Sterling deposit futures market (LIFFE)
1 March: Firm plans to roll over £5,000,000 in two and a half months. Current borrowing rate is 14% (13% + 1%)	1 March: Firm sells £5,000,000 face value (20 contracts) of June sterling deposit futures at 86.25 (100 − 13.75)
15 May: Firm borrows £5,000,000 for three months at 16% (15% + 1%)	15 May: Firm buys £5,000,000 sterling deposit futures (June) at 84.25 (100 − 15.75)
Result	**Result**
Borrow £5,000,000 for three months at 14%. Cost = £175,000	Profit per futures contract = 200 ticks
Borrow £5,000,000 for three months at 16%. Cost = £200,000	Cash gain = $20 \times 200 \times £6.25 = £25,000$
Interest expense increase = £25,000	

This is another example of a perfect hedge: the firm's forecast of a rate increase was correct, and they would have ended up having to pay an extra £25,000 in interest. This was compensated for, however, by a £25,000 profit in the futures market. Of course, such hedges are not realistic—we would not always expect to see basis remain constant through time, nor can we always hedge cash positions with futures contracts written on the same financial instruments.

But they do illustrate the basic feature of a hedge strategy—the impact of an adverse change in interest rates is either to give you less interest or return on a loan or an investment, or to make you have to pay more on a borrowing or receive less on the sale of a financial asset. You compensate yourself for this cash or opportunity loss by trying to make offsetting cash gains in the futures market.

The major reason why perfect hedges are not expected to work out so neatly in practice is that basis, or the difference between cash and futures prices, can vary considerably through time. If the basis changes adversely during the life of a hedge, then a portion of the offsetting gain on the futures part of the hedge can be eliminated, making the hedge imperfect.

The perfect short hedge (described above) illustrates this. Consider what would have happened if the three-month sterling deposit futures price on 15 May had been 84.60, i.e. if the difference between the cash and futures had begun to converge as the delivery month approached. This represents an implicit basis change from 75 basis points on 1 March to 40 basis points on 15 May.

The impact on the futures gain would be substantial, reducing it from 200 ticks to 165 ticks per contract. The cash gain would be $20 \times 165 \times £6.25$ or £20,625. The change in basis would mean that the futures gain would cover only 82.5% of the cash market loss—not bad, but by no means a perfect hedge. If basis had moved in the other direction, there would have been a windfall gain on the futures side of the hedge.

Aggressive hedging strategies (discussed later in this chapter) seek to predict these changes in basis to help set the hedge strategy. Nonetheless, it seems that the possibility of basis change, whether it be the basis between cash T-bills and T-bill futures, or between a cash instrument and a futures contract written on a different instrument, will make the choice of a suitable hedge strategy complex.

A. Elements in making the hedge decision

1. Determination of the risk exposure

The first step for any corporation contemplating whether to hedge interest or exchange rate risk is to decide what the level of that risk is. This is not as simple as just considering an individual asset or liability category which the manager is worried about and seeing if it can be hedged.

A company's balance sheet and operating finances contain all sorts of natural hedges; these will have to be carefully identified before any hedging in the financial futures market can be contemplated. Otherwise what appears to the financial manager to be a good hedging decision could actually involve the creation of an open risky position which was not there before. This can be illustrated by looking at a simple balance sheet for a bank.

A bank balance sheet

Liabilities		Assets	
Equity	800	Plants and equipment	300
Certificates of deposit	1,500	Loans	3,000
Deposit accounts	1,200	Treasury bills	1,000
Current accounts	800		
	4,300		4,300

Assumption: 500 of the deposit accounts are interest sensitive; the remaining deposit and current accounts do not respond to interest rate changes.

A bank's net exposed balances by maturity

Maturity (days)	Assets	Liabilities	Net exposed balance	Category
0–90	500	2,000	1,500	Liability
91–180	1,000	0	1,000	Asset
181–270	1,000	0	1,000	Asset
271–365	1,500	0	1,500	Asset
No maturity or non-interest sensitive	300	2,300	2,000	Liability

From the balance sheet of the bank, the management constructs a net exposed balances table. From this table, the interest rate risk that is left after the natural hedges have been taken into consideration is identified. Thus, the interest rate on 2,000 of the liabilities will change in the current quarter, but only 500 of the assets will be re-rated. So, 1,500 of the liabilities are uncovered for one quarter. During the second quarter a further 1,000 of assets will be re-rated but that still leaves 500 of the liabilities uncovered until the third quarter. The conclusion is that there is a net exposed liability balance of 1,500 to refinance: 1,000 will be rolled over once before assets mature, and 500 will be rolled over twice.

A possible hedge using financial futures for this is now evident. The bank could sell 1,500 of short-term interest rate futures with a delivery date near the end of the next quarter, and sell a further 500 of interest rate futures with a delivery date further out. The balance of net exposed positions after hedging would then appear as:

Net exposed balances after hedging

Maturity	Net exposed balance	Asset or liability
0–90	0	—
91–180	0	—
181–270	500	Asset
271–365	1,500	Asset
Non-interest sensitive	2,000	Liability

The hedge is now complete: 2,000 of non-interest sensitive liabilities are matched by 2,000 of assets. All other interest rate exposure has been hedged, although this involves the bank in the elements of basis risk discussed above.

Although this simple example cannot claim to even approximate a real-world bank balance sheet, it illustrates the basic approach to using the financial futures market for hedging. First, natural hedges are identified; then the organization determines whether any net exposed positions can be usefully hedged. Even this simple example shows how use of the market introduces a new element of flexibility into bank portfolio decisions.

In addition to determining net exposed positions in the balance sheet, the organization must also consider additional cash flows in the future. If it expects funds from operations to lead to a significant buildup of cash in the balance sheet over, say, the next two to three quarters, it will want to take that into account in its hedging strategy. The net exposed balances table is a forward-looking, not a static, instrument.

Once a composite net exposed balances table has been constructed for a suitable period into the future, the next step is to determine what the impact of adverse rate changes will be. For this, the organization will need to construct a probability distribution of expected future interest rates. This will provide a mean expected interest rate for various periods into the future, plus a measure of the probability that the interest rate change will be in an adverse direction. Consider, at the beginning of 1983, that the current rate of interest was 13%, such a distribution might look like:

70

Interest rate forecasts: current rate = 13%

1983 (Q2)		1983 (Q3)		1983 (Q4)	
Probability	Rate (%)	Probability	Rate (%)	Probability	Rate (%)
0.1	13	0.1	14	0.3	14
0.2	12	0.1	13	0.3	13
0.4	11	0.6	12	0.2	12
0.2	10	0.1	11	0.1	11
0.1	9	0.1	10	0.1	10
Mean expected rate	11		12		12.6
Probability rate less than 13%	96.6%		78.5%		68.1%
Mean rate contingent on negative rate change	10.8		11.6		11.3

It is assumed that there is an adverse impact upon the corporation's financial position from a fall in interest rates, so that the interest rate table confirms a serious interest rate risk exists. The interest rate information is combined with the net exposed balances table to obtain cash values for the risk.

	1983 (Q2)	1983 (Q3)	1983 (Q4)
Net exposed balance	$15,000,000	$13,400,000	$12,800,000
Probability rate <13%	96.6%	78.5%	68.1%
Cash risk level	($79,695)	($36,817)	($37,046)

The cash risk levels in dollars are found using the following formula:

$$\text{Cash risk} = \left[\begin{array}{c} \text{Current} \\ \text{rate} \end{array} - \begin{array}{c} \text{Mean rate} \\ \text{contingent} \\ \text{on adverse} \\ \text{rate change} \end{array} \right] \times \frac{\text{Number of days' exposure}}{360} \times \begin{array}{c} \text{Probability} \\ \text{of adverse} \\ \text{rate change} \end{array} \times \begin{array}{c} \text{Net exposed} \\ \text{balance} \end{array}$$

It is these dollar figures that need to be compared with the cost of hedging to see whether a hedging strategy is appropriate. To sum up, therefore, the first step in the hedge decision is to work out a net exposed balances table on a pro-forma basis, and then combine this information with an interest rate probability distribution to determine the risk exposure on a cash basis.

2. Decision on whether degree of risk is acceptable

Some degree of risk exposure to interest rates or exchange rates is probably inevitable in the operations of any organization. The question is: when does that risk become unacceptably large? The answer to this question will depend on the risk preferences of senior management.

There are no hard and fast rules on this issue: one management might be prepared to accept the level of risk exposure in 1983 revealed in the numbers above, while another management might not. It is clear that the level of risk should be related to the size of the firm and the capital employed. If the numbers above represented a large proportion of the capital employed in the firm, or a large proportion of shareholders' funds, then a decision to try and hedge the risk would probably be made. Managements should probably set up some sort of maximum percentage of shareholders' funds which they are prepared to accept in terms of interest rate or exchange rate exposure.

3. What hedging alternatives are available and what they cost

A firm examines its risk exposure and concludes that it is too high to be acceptable. It decides to examine hedging alternatives. The first possibility is to simply alter the maturity mismatches in the balance sheet. A firm might react to the mismatch shown in Exhibit 4.1a by moving to a matched book position (Exhibit 4.1b) and thereby increasing the amount of natural hedging. But if the previous structure of the balance sheet existed because it was appropriate for the efficient operation of the company, this step may not be appropriate and will probably involve higher costs. It is unlikely that any major corporation will be able to run a fully matched book for any substantial period of time. However, moves to increase the amount of natural hedging should always be explored before more complex hedging alternatives.

Exhibit 4.1a: Mismatched book

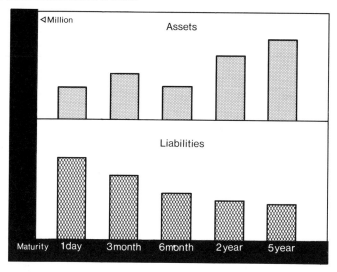

Source: LIFFE

Exhibit 4.1b: Matched book

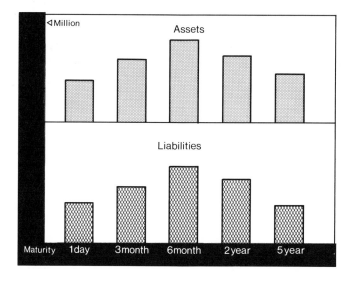

Source: LIFFE

A second alternative is to lock in borrowing and/or lending rates through the forward-forward market. The cash market yield curve implies short-term interest rates at points in the future. For instance, suppose the current three-month Eurodollar rate is R_3 and the six-month rate R_6. Together these rates imply a three-month interest commencing in three months time. The following calculation shows how to derive such a rate:

$$\text{Forward three-month rate} = \left\{ \left[1 + \frac{R_6}{2} \right] \middle/ \left[1 + \frac{R_3}{4} \right] - 1 \right\} \times \frac{360}{90}$$

For instance, if the six-month rate is 12% and the three-month rate is 11.70%, the implied three-month rate in three months time would be:

$$\left[\left(1 + \frac{0.12}{2}\right)\Big/\left(1 + \frac{0.117}{4}\right) - 1\right] \times 4 = 0.1195 \text{ (or 11.95%)}$$

In a simple case where a bank is worried about falling rates and would like to lock in the rate at which it will be able to invest funds in three months' time, say, to the tune of $50 million: it could achieve this by borrowing $50 million for three months at 11.7% and lending $50 million for six months at 12%. This effectively ensures that it will be able to lend $50 million for three months in three months' time at 11.95%. The use of the forward-forward market to lock in future borrowing or lending rates is often advantageous to banks, because they operate on the favourable side of the bid-ask spread. For non-bank corporations, the futures market may provide a better alternative.

A question to be asked is whether the particular interest rate risk can be suitably hedged in the futures market. In the examples of hedges discussed, the financial instrument being hedged was of the same type as the financial futures contract. Quite frequently this will not be the case. Investors may wish to hedge portfolios of corporate bonds or of government bills and bonds for which futures markets do not exist. For instance, the London International Financial Futures Exchange will not initially trade a sterling Treasury bill futures contract. Thus anyone wishing to hedge a Treasury bill position will have to choose one of the other contracts trading in the market.

Hedging one financial instrument with a futures contract on a different underlying instrument is known as cross-hedging, and naturally exposes the hedger to another type of basis risk, because there is no guarantee that interest rates on different financial instruments will always move identically together. The investor will choose to hedge with whichever futures contract has in the past proved most closely correlated with the instrument he is hedging.

The example below illustrates the correlation relationships between some specimen US short-term futures prices and cash market interest rates. The closeness of the relationship between interest rate changes varies rather widely. Sometimes there may be no financial futures trading that is closely enough correlated with the cash instrument to warrant using the financial futures market for hedging. Sometimes there may not be sufficient liquidity in the most ideal futures contract, and a second-best but more liquid contract may have to be used. Finally the corporation may sometimes wish to hedge even if the correlation is very poor, if the level of basis risk is still well below the perceived level of interest rate risk.

Correlations: 1979–81 data* (month-end data)

			R^2
Three-month T-bills	vs	T-bill futures	0.784
Three-month Eurodollar	vs	T-bill futures	0.758
Six-month Eurodollar	vs	Three-month Eurodollar futures	0.954

* Other correlation statistics were shown in Chapter 3.

Important points when choosing a futures contract for hedging

1. Normally choose to hedge with the futures contract most closely correlated with the cash position.
2. But remember correlation can change through time, and past correlations may not be good predictors of future correlation.
3. Make sure the best futures contract possesses sufficient liquidity to put a hedge on in the right volume.
4. Always compare historical variation in basis with historical variation in rates. A badly correlated hedge may be better than none at all.
5. Calculate the transactions and execution costs for the hedge that looks most suitable.

It is impossible to give formal rules of what type of minimum correlation a manager would require before using a financial futures contract. It will depend partly on the ratio of basis risk to interest or exchange rate risk. Nevertheless, most managers would probably be satisfied with correlation coefficients in excess of 0.70.

In establishing the costs of a futures market hedging alternative, the less than perfect correlation should be taken into account as an extra cost, and added to the transactions and execution costs. These costs can then be compared with the risk exposure cash values we have worked out earlier.

4. Deciding how many futures contracts are required for a good hedge (the hedge ratio)

Having chosen a suitable futures hedge vehicle, highly correlated with the cash position and suitably liquid, the next step in the hedge design is to arrive at a decision of the number of futures contracts that are needed to produce a good hedge. This decision involves four basic components.

a. Face value of contracts

The ratio of the cash amount to be hedged to the face value of the underlying contracts must be considered. Other things being equal you would think about hedging £5 million of sterling CDs with 20 sterling time deposit futures of £250,000 face value. You would hedge a $1,000,000 corporate bond position with 10 T-bond futures contracts of $100,000 face value, and so on.

b. Money equivalency

The change in price of a futures contract or a cash instrument for a given interest rate change varies according to the maturity of the instrument. The table below shows the equivalent value of 0.01% interest for typical contract sizes of £250,000 and $1,000,000.

	0.01% of £250,000 (£)	0.01% of $1,000,000 ($)
One year	25.00	100.00
Nine months	18.75	75.00
Six months	12.50	50.00
Three months	6.25	25.00
One month	2.08	8.33

In other words, the price change of a six-month instrument for a 1% change in interest rates will be double that of three-month instruments. This has implications for the hedge. To hedge $1,000,000 of a six-month cash instrument will, other things being equal, require $2,000,000 of a three-month financial futures contract. To hedge $1,000,000 of a one-month cash instrument would only require $333,000 of the same three-month futures contract. The aim is to hedge money equivalency.

c. Regression coefficients

Correlation has been used already as a measure of the stability of the basis between a cash instrument and a financial futures contract. To determine the hedge ratio, we also need to know what change we may expect in the cash instrument for a given change in the futures instrument and vice versa. (Chapter 3 discusses how to derive regression coefficients between cash interest rates and futures prices.)

The rule is: multiply the face value of the cash positions by the regression coefficient between cash rate changes and futures price changes to get the right hedge amount. This only applies to the short-term futures contracts priced on an index basis; determining hedge quantities in the long-term contracts like gilts and T-bond futures requires a different approach.

A simple formula for determining the right number of contracts for a hedge is:

$$\begin{array}{c} \text{Number of} \\ \text{contracts} \\ \text{required} \end{array} = \dfrac{\begin{array}{c}\text{Face value of} \\ \text{cash position}\end{array}}{\begin{array}{c}\text{Face value of} \\ \text{futures contract}\end{array}} \times \begin{array}{c}\text{Money} \\ \text{equivalency}\end{array} \times \begin{array}{c}\text{Regression} \\ \text{coefficient}\end{array}$$

Example

A firm wishes to hedge a $15,000,000 position in six-month commercial paper. Two futures contracts appear to offer sufficient liquidity: IMM 90-day T-bills and IMM 90-day certificates of deposit. The following regression and correlation information is available.

Six-month commercial paper rate $= 0.1020 + 0.967$ (T-bill futures) $R^2 = 0.920$

Six-month commercial paper rate $= 0.0800 + 0.97$ (three-month CD futures) $R^2 = 0.95$

What would a good hedge look like.

Step 1: Choose to hedge with CD futures because of higher correlation.

Step 2: Calculate number of contracts.

$$\text{Number of contracts required} = \frac{\$15,000,000}{\$1,000,000} \times \frac{\$50}{\$25} \times 0.97$$

$$= 29.1$$

Approximately 29 CD futures contracts are required for the hedge.

d. Conversion or price factors

There is another feature of relative price movements that influences the effectiveness of a hedge, which applies to those contracts where a variety of different instruments are deliverable, and the futures price applies to one standardized contract, such as the 20-year 12% gilt on LIFFE, and the 20-year 8% T-bond on the Chicago Board of Trade.

Although the problem of money equivalency does not apply to these long-term contracts, which are priced on a discount basis, the price of a particular instrument being hedged can move at a different rate in response to an interest rate change than the price of the standardized futures contract being used to hedge it. This is the reason for not always choosing to hedge a specific cash position with an equal valued futures position.

The principal of constructing conversion or price factors relating the settlement price of the standard long-term contract to invoice prices for actual contracts at delivery has been discussed in Chapter 3. But, as long as arbitrage pressures exist in the market, the relationship between individual cash prices and the price of the standard gilt should be the same during the life of the contract as at delivery. If this is so, then the conversion factor will be appropriate in deciding how many futures contracts to use in hedging.

$$\begin{array}{c} \text{Number of} \\ \text{contracts} \\ \text{required} \end{array} = \dfrac{\text{Face value of cash position}}{\text{Face value of futures contract}} \times \begin{array}{c}\text{Conversion} \\ \text{factor}\end{array}$$

Example

A portfolio manager holds a portfolio of $15,000,000 face value of $7\frac{5}{8}$% 15 March, 2002–07 T-bonds, on 1 July, 1982. The price factor for a $7\frac{5}{8}$% bond with a maturity of 19 years six months is 0.9633.

$$\text{Number of contracts required} = \frac{\$15,000,000}{\$100,000} \times 0.9633$$

$$= 144.5$$

145 contracts will form a good hedge

There is an important point to note with using conversion factors for deciding on the number of contracts that will produce a good hedge. It assumes that arbitrage trading will bring cash

Treasury bond, gilt or GNMA prices closely in line with the prices implied by the futures prices and the relevant conversion factors. If this does not occur, the hedger may be better advised to use the regression approach to calculating the hedge ratio, even when considering portfolios of long-term instruments. For example he might run a regression of:

Change in price of Treasury 13% 2000 = a + b[Change in gilt futures price]

Whichever of the two—the regression coefficient and the conversion factor—has given the better fit for historical price data will be more suitable for determining hedge size. However, conversion or price factor hedging is dependent on the flat yield curve imposed by the factors. The assumption is that a change in interest rates will affect gilts or T-bonds of different maturities and coupon yields exactly in the manner dictated by the conversion factors. Yet anyone who studies the cash markets for long-term instruments knows that this is not the case: relative bond and gilt volatilities are not independent of the level of interest rates. To handle this problem, two other analytical techniques can be adopted: perturbation analysis and duration analysis.

e. Perturbation analysis

Perturbation analysis examines the changes in the price of the cash instrument and the relevant futures contract for a 1% yield change. For instance, suppose the investor has an exposure in a 15-year 10% T-bond, and would like to hedge this with a T-bond futures position. Suppose the price of the T-bond is 92-24, the price of the T-bond future is 70-20, and the price of the cheapest deliverable T-bond, a 13% 20-year bond, is 107-17. At a price of 92-24 the cash T-bond has a yield to maturity of 11%. Now consider a yield change of 1%, i.e. the yield to maturity rises from 11% to 12%: the price would move from 92-24 to 86-08. To get the equivalent change in the price of the bond future for a 1% yield change, remember that the future will trade off the cheapest-to-deliver bond. At a price of 107-17, the 20-year 13% bond is yielding 12%; thus we consider what happens to the price if yield goes from 12% to 13%, and assume unchanged basis. At a yield of 13% a 20-year 13% bond has a price of 100-00. Hence the price of the cheapest to deliver bond has fallen 7-17.

We now determine what is the equivalent fall in the price of the futures contract by multiplying by the price factor. The price factor for a 20-year 13% bond is 1.4948; hence the implied change in the price of the future is 241/32 ÷ 1.4948 or 161 ticks. We expect the price of the future to fall from 70-20 to 65-19. There is a hedge ratio for a 1% change in yield: a drop in price of the 15-year 10% bond of 6-16 maps into a drop in the futures price of 5-01. Hence the hedge ratio based on a 1% perturbation is 208/161 or 1.29. If the cash exposure is $5 million nominal, the required matching number of futures contracts is 65. This compares with a price factor between a 15-year 10% bond and the standard 20-year 8% T-bond future of 1.173.

Although the use of perturbation analysis is generally better than relying on simple price factors, the hedge ratio will not be independent of the expected interest rate change. For instance, in the case above consider what would have happened if yields moved 2% instead of 1%. At a yield to maturity of 13%, the price of the 15-year 10% bond would fall to 80-13. At a yield to maturity of 14%, the price of the 20-year 13% bond would fall to 93-11, which is equivalent to a futures price of 62-14. Hence the 10% 15-year bond price has fallen by 395 ticks and the bond future by 262 ticks. The implied hedge ratio for full protection against a 2% risk in yield would be 1.508, compared with a 1.29 level for a 1% rise in yield. Thus the hedger will need to add more futures contracts as interest rates increase to maintain the same neutral hedge.

Similarly, on a hedge against falling rates, it would be appropriate to reduce the number of futures contracts as rates fall because the hedge ratio will decline. Nonetheless hedge ratios derived from perturbation analysis seem preferable to using simple price factors.

f. Duration analysis

For reasonable changes in interest rates, the relative duration of bonds can provide yet another type of hedge ratio. Again, consider the three bonds discussed earlier: the 10% 15-year bond at

92-24, the standard 8% 20-year T-bond future at 70-20, and the cheapest deliverable T-bond, 20-year 13%, at 107-17. In each case we can calculate the duration of the bond.

	Yield (%)	Duration
10% 15-year	11	7.81
8% 20-year	11.88	8.58
13% 20-year	12	7.88

What are those measures telling us? Consider the 10% 15-year bond priced at 92-24 with a yield to maturity at 11%. If the yield rises to 12%, which represents a rise of 0.90% in the $(1 + r)$ term, that is from 1.11 to 1.12, we would expect the clean price to decline by 7.03% (7.81×0.90). Similarly if there is a 1% change in yield on the 13% 20-year bond from 1.12 to 1.13 in terms of $(1 + r)$, representing a 0.84% change, the price would be expected to fall by 6.62%. Assuming the pricing of the T-bond future is still done off the 20-year 13% bond, then an appropriate hedge ratio would be the ratio of the duration of the 10% 15-year bond and the 13% 20-year bond adjusted by the price factor of 1.4948 and the prices of the two bonds.

$$\text{Optimal hedge ratio for a cash position in 10\% 15-year bond} = \frac{(1.12)(7.81)(92\text{-}24)}{(1.11)(7.88)(107\text{-}17)} \times 1.4948$$
$$= 1.289$$

Now compare the three hedge ratios: the price factor between the standard 8% 20-year bond and the 10% 15-year bond is 1.173; the perturbation method indicates a 1.29 ratio for a rise of 1% in the yield of both the cash bond held and the cheapest deliverable bond increasing to over 1.50 for a 2% yield rise; and the hedge ratio for equal percentage rises in $(1 + r)$ using duration analysis is 1.29 for a future priced off the cheapest deliverable bond. All such hedge ratios are necessarily approximations in that they need to be adjusted in the light of interest rate changes, and do not take into account the likelihood that yields to maturity of different maturity instruments will react differentially to movements in the overall yield curve.

The best hedge ratio to use will depend upon historical analysis. However, it has been reported[1] that testing of hedge strategies in recent periods for the Treasury bond contract on CBT indicates the hedge effectiveness of a simple conversion factor method was about 84%, the perturbation method around 92.6% and the duration method around 94%, assuming adjustment of hedge ratios in line with changing bond prices and yields to maturity. Thus the duration approach seems simple to handle and may dominate simple price factor hedging.

Recent bond analysis with duration techniques has moved towards the realization that an assumption of equal percentage changes in $(1 + r)$ for different maturity instruments may not be realistic. On average, it appears historically that a shift in the yield curve will generally involve shorter-maturity instruments displaying larger yield changes than longer-maturity instruments. One possible way of introducing this into duration analysis of futures is to assume a constant proportional relationship amongst adjacent forward rate changes. For example with 15–20-year bonds, we could determine from historical data that on average:

% change in one-year implied rate from 16/17 year bonds
$$= \quad k \times \% \text{ change in one-year implied rate (15/16 year bonds)}$$

% change in one-year implied rate from 17/18 year bonds
$$= \quad k \times \% \text{ change in one-year implied rate (16/17 year bonds)}$$

Generally k will be less than 1.0. Once k is established, then the comparable duration equation would be:

$$\% \text{ change in price} = -\sum_{t=1}^{n} \frac{t(X)_t}{(1 + r)^t} \Big/ P \times \frac{1 - k^t}{1 - k} \times \% \text{ change in } (1 + r)$$

The use of this adjustment procedure may increase the accuracy of the hedge ratio.

---

[1] This analysis and results are described in P. Wilkinson and N. Sedergren, "Weighted Hedging Techniques", *Futures World*, 14 October, 1982.

5. What type of hedge should be used?

Once the choice of futures contract has been made, and the number of contracts to hedge the estimated risk exposure has been calculated, the manager is faced with a final choice—which type of hedge to put on. There are basically five types of hedges that are commonly used.

a. One-off hedge

In this type of hedge, one distant contract month is used to hedge the whole cash position through time.

Example

1 January

Risk exposure (rate fall)		Hedge	
1 February	$15,000,000 three-month T-bills	1 January	Buy 42 Sept. T-bills
1 May	$14,000,000 three-month T-bills	1 February	Sell 15 Sept. T-bills
1 August	$13,000,000 three-month T-bills	1 May	Sell 14 Sept. T-bills
		1 August	Sell 13 Sept. T-bills

This is a rather risky type of hedge, because basis tends to be more volatile the bigger the time gap between the cash exposure and the delivery date of the futures contract. Here the gap is quite wide between a February exposure and a September futures contract, so that basis risk could be higher than necessary relative to interest rate risk. This risk would be reduced by using the second type of hedge.

b. Strip hedge

In this hedge, the aim is to match the maturity of the figures instrument into the time-span of the exposure, thereby eliminating much of the extra basis risk.

Example

1 January	Hedge:	1 Jan.	Buy 15 March T-bills
			Buy 14 June T-bills
			Buy 13 September T-bills
		1 Feb.	Sell 15 March T-bills
		1 May	Sell 14 June T-bills
		1 Aug.	Sell 13 September T-bills

Here, each exposure is hedged with an interest rate future with a delivery date just after the exposure date. The one problem with this type of hedge is that it demands putting on contracts for as far out as the exposure to be hedged extends. This may not always be easy if the liquidity in the more distant contracts is not adequate. One way of getting round this is to use a third type of hedge.

c. Rolling strip hedge

This hedge follows the same principle as the strip hedge, but initially puts on the whole hedge amount in the nearby contract to take advantage of its high liquidity. In due course, as liquidity grows in the deferred contracts, some of the nearby contracts are rolled over into the more distant contracts.

Example

1 January	Hedge:	1 Jan.	Buy 42 March T-bills
		1 Feb.	Sell 42 March T-bills
			Buy 27 June T-bills
		1 May	Sell 27 June T-bills
			Buy 13 September T-bills
		1 Aug.	Sell 13 September T-bills

Such a hedge gives most of the basis risk benefits of a strip hedge, while taking advantage of the higher liquidity of the nearby contracts. It is much less risky than the fourth type of hedge.

d. Rolling hedge

This hedge hedges each exposure in turn. That is, a futures position is put on to hedge the first exposure risk: when the first exposure date arrives, a new hedge is put on to hedge the next exposure, and so on. This is not as effective as a strip hedge or a rolling strip hedge, because the deferred risk exposures are not hedged in the short-term.

Example

1 January	Hedge:	1 Jan.	Buy 15 March T-bills
		1 Feb.	Sell 15 March T-bills
			Buy 14 June T-bills
		1 May	Sell 14 June T-bills
			Buy 13 September T-bills
		1 Aug.	Sell 13 September T-bills

Before discussing the fifth rather different type of hedge—the spread hedge—let us examine how each of the above four hedges would have performed for a reasonable set of prices for T-bills and T-bill futures over the hedge period.

Data	T-bill cash discount yield (%)	March T-bill	June T-bill	September T-bill
1 January	14.0	85.50	86.00	86.50
1 February	13.5	86.00	86.50	87.25
1 May	12.5		87.60	88.50
1 August	12.0			88.00

Hedge results	Position	Cash gain or loss
	Cash T-bill exposure	($136,250)
	One-off hedge	$146,875
	Strip hedge	$123,500
	Rolling strip hedge	$110,500
	Rolling hedge	$ 41,000

The most successful hedge has been the one-off hedge because of favourable basis movements; however, such basis movements could just as easily have been the other way. By far the worst hedge, and one which should not be used in these circumstances, is the rolling hedge. The best general purpose hedge for the pure hedger is the strip hedge, liquidity of contracts permitting. Use of the one-off hedge may be appropriate for the more aggressive hedging strategies.

e. Spread hedge

A rather more complex hedge which is widely used in the US markets is the spread hedge. This is based on the fact that a spread between two futures contracts on long-term financial instruments is equivalent to an implied short-term rate between the delivery months: the June–September T-bond spread can be considered as a three-month interest rate for June–September. Hence such a spread provides an alternative means of hedging short-term rates. Before adopting its use the hedger would need to carefully explore the regression and correlation relationships between the T-bond spreads and the cash instruments that were being hedged. The main use of these spreads on the US markets has been in hedging risk exposures quite a long way in the future, since the T-bond contract tends to have greater liquidity further out than the IMM T-bill contract and other short-term contracts. For our example, a spread hedge strategy might look like:

Example

1 January

Hedge structure	March T-bond	June T-bond	September T-bond	December T-bond
1 January	Long 150	Short 10	Short 10	Short 130
1 February	0	Long 140	Short 10	Short 130
1 May		0	Long 130	Short 130
1 August			0	0

Note: This example of hedge is only included for illustrative purposes. It is highly unlikely that the regression coefficient between T-bond spreads and T-bill rates would be 1, so the hedge ratio is not likely to be simply the ratio of the face values as shown above.

In the vast majority of circumstances, a rolling strip hedge is likely to perform as well if not better than a spread hedge, without involving many of the complexities of the spread hedge. Another possible use of spread hedging is to protect a standard hedge against undue basis risk.

6. Assessing the impact of marking to market on hedging

Even after the hedge has been totally devised and its transactions, execution and basis risk costs have been compared favourably with the degree of interest rate exposure, the hedger must assess the degree of risk attached to possible adverse variation margin requirements. Institutions need to be aware that, although they are operating what they see as a fully hedged position, they may be required to put up considerable sums of margin during the life of the hedge. While loan commitments to provide such funds should be readily available, taking into account the actual or opportunity gain on the cash position, this feature of futures hedging can occasionally cause problems for corporations in maintaining the hedged position, and investor policy on this issue needs to be sorted out well in advance.

It would be an unfortunate treasurer who convinced his board of directors of the value of hedging, but did not explain the principle of marking to market, and then suddenly had to come along to explain that he would need to take out a temporary loan of £2 million to hold open his futures position. Use can, however, be made of limit orders to hold down the amount of adverse variation margin demands in hedging strategies.

The basic steps in a simple futures hedging decision

1. Combine net exposed balances and rate probability distributions to determine cash risk level.
2. Compare cash risks with shareholder equity level to make decision to hedge or not.
3. Compare cash market and futures markets alternatives on cost grounds.
4. Use correlations to decide on the most suitable futures contract to hedge with.
5. Combine money equivalences, regression coefficients and conversion factors to determine number of contracts for the best full hedge.
6. Determine the best type of hedge to use.
7. Assess negative variation margin probabilities and set up bank lines accordingly.

So far we have discussed what might be termed the traditional theory of pure hedging—identifying the risk exposure and then putting on an opposite position in the futures market to eliminate as much as possible of the interest rate or exchange rate risk. In practice this type of pure hedging is rather rare. Hedgers may choose to hedge only a certain proportion of their rate exposure, they may use limit orders to take off the hedge at certain points, or they may use their projections of what basis is going to do to help determine their hedging strategy.

These approaches can be grouped under the heading of aggressive hedging strategies.

B. Aggressive hedging strategies

1. Making use of basis relationships

Rather than looking upon basis risk in a negative way—as the necessary price which has to be paid in eliminating interest rate risk—a hedger could be viewed as a basis speculator. This approach leads to an examination of how a hedger can use basis forecasting techniques to improve hedge performance or reduce hedge costs. Any hedger must be fully aware of the factors that influence basis and that lead basis to change over time.

The first important element in using basis relationships to improve hedge performance is that of *convergence*. As a futures contract approaches delivery, the futures price will approach closer to the spot or cash price. Although most of this convergence happens in the last few weeks of a contract's life, and even within the last couple of months of a contract basis can vary widely, it is none the less true that a large negative or positive basis in the months before delivery is bound to be largely eliminated at delivery. Exhibit 4.2 illustrates this basis convergence for sterling deposit contracts traded on LIFFE.

Exhibit 4.2: Convergence for sterling deposit contracts

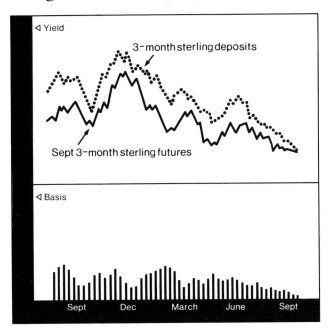

Source: LIFFE

Although convergence is clearly observable in the exhibit, the basis can still show major cyclical variations within even a few months of delivery. The basis varies widely over the life of the contract. In the case of T-bill futures in the United States (the March 1982 contract is shown in Exhibit 4.3); the basis varies from minus 200 basis points to plus 400 basis points. The degree of variation of basis confirms the necessity for the hedger to make an accurate comparison of basis risk and underlying interest rate risk.

The cost of carry relationship will be a major determinant of the futures yield curve: in a positive cost of carry market the futures prices will lie below cash prices, and in a negative cost of carry market futures prices will lie above cash prices. Now consider our two basic types of hedges: the short hedge and the long hedge. A short hedge is long the cash position and short the futures; it will benefit if the basis becomes less negative, but will suffer if the basis becomes less positive.

Example

A hedger is hedging a $1,000,000 risk exposure on 1 May with a short $1,000,000 position in June T-bill futures. Currently the cash rate is 16% and the June futures price is 84.5. Therefore basis is (50) basis points.

> June's futures price moves to 84.20.
> Basis moves to (20) basis points.
> Cash gain on future = 30 × $25 = $750.

By contrast a long hedger, who is effectively short the cash position and long the futures

Exhibit 4.3: Convergence for US T-bill futures

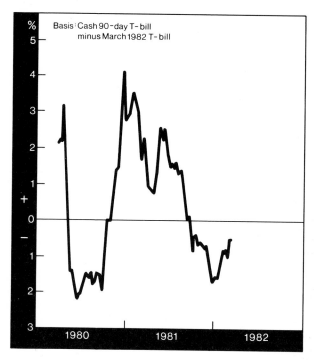

Source: DRI Drifacs Database

position, will benefit if the basis becomes less positive, and suffer if the basis becomes less negative.

Example

A hedger is hedging a $1,000,000 risk exposure on 1 May with a long $1,000,000 position in June T-bill futures. Currently the cash rate is 16% and the June futures price is 83.5. Therefore the basis is 50 basis points.

> June futures price moves to 83.8.
> Basis moves to 20 basis points.
> Cash gain on futures position = 30 × $25 = $750.

Thus the impact of convergence suggests that short hedges will be favoured in negative cost of carry markets, and long hedges will be favoured in positive cost of carry markets. Moreover since we know that convergence is more rapid in the later months of a contract as delivery nears, we know that short hedges in negative cost of carry markets should be put on in months as nearby as possible and long hedges in positive cost of carry markets should also be put on in nearby months.

In contrast, if it is necessary to put on short hedges in positive cost of carry markets and long hedges in negative cost of carry markets, contracts should be as deferred as possible so that the influence of convergence during the life of the hedge is minimized. If it is still felt that convergence will play an adverse role in the efficiency of the hedge, it may be necessary to put on more contracts than indicated by the pure hedge ratio, to compensate for the impact of convergence.

Convergence is not the only determinant of basis change through time. The graphs of basis (Exhibits 4.2 and 4.3) indicate clearly that basis can vary considerably through time. Basis will be determined partly as a function of the cost of carry and partly as a function of the market's expectations about interest rates in the future. Thus, if either the basis looks too far out of line with the cost of carry in either direction, or if the individual hedger's interest rate forecasts differ significantly from those in the market, this could be information useful for forecasting future movements in basis.

Such forecasts enable the hedger to go beyond defensive hedging to generating extra profits through trading on the basis. The hedger will seek to put on his long hedges when the basis

82

looks particularly strong, and his short hedges when the basis looks particularly weak. One important input into decisions of this kind are the basis charts (see Exhibits 4.2 and 4.3); these give the hedger a quick indication of whether the basis is within its normal bounds. Depending on the type of hedge desired, an abnormal basis may indicate a good or a bad time to put on the hedge.

To estimate formally whether a futures price is cheap or dear relative to a cash price, the first step is to draw futures and cash market yield curves. If the futures curve is adjusted by the cost of carry, it should be exactly equal to the cash market yield curve. If it is not, the relative position of the two curves will identify overvalued and undervalued futures contracts. Exhibit 4.4 shows this in practice.

Exhibit 4.4: Cash yield curve versus strip yield curve

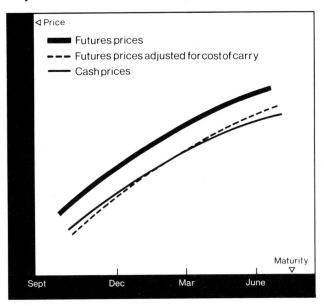

The December futures price adjusted for the cost of carry is cheap relative to that implied by the cash market yield curve. The March contract looks fairly priced, while the June contract appears to be overvalued. Again depending on which type of hedge is being used, an investor might want to choose a futures contract to hedge, according to whether it is over or undervalued in this way.

The aim of basis hedging is, therefore, to combine the basic hedge ratio analysis outlined earlier with timing decisions based on forecasts of basis changes to maximize cash gains from the futures side of the hedge. The end result will, hopefully, be net profits from the set of hedging transactions carried out by the firm. More to the point, a good knowledge of how basis changes through time should enable even pure hedging to become a less risky activity.

Rules for basis hedging

1. When cash prices are below futures prices:
   a. Favour short hedges. Put them on in nearby contracts.
   b. If you must long hedge, do it in distant contracts.
2. When cash prices are above futures prices:
   a. Favour long hedges. Put them on in nearby contracts.
   b. If you must short hedge, do it in distant contracts.
3. Compare cash-futures differences with cost of carry to identify under-valued and over-valued contracts.
4. Hedge with over-valued contracts for short hedges; hedge with under-valued contracts for long hedges.

This type of analysis can help considerably in choosing which particular contracts to hedge with. However, it cannot fully answer the question of timing. A hedger may not wish to put on his hedge, while the proposed contract looks very overvalued in basis terms; on the other hand, the longer he waits to put on his hedge the greater his exposure to a sudden adverse interest rate movement. The hedger will have to be careful in trading off the benefits of hedge timing using basis relationships against the benefits of being hedged as quickly as possible against the interest or exchange rate risk.

Spreads can also be used as a hedge against undue basis risk on a straight hedge. In many cases, the basis between cash and nearby futures positions is highly correlated with the spread or price differential between nearby and deferred futures positions. If this is the case a spread may be a useful hedge against adverse basis change (see Chapter 5 on hedging applications).

2. Making use of limit and stop orders

In contrast to the pure hedger, who theoretically should not care if the futures side of the hedge makes or loses money, many practical hedgers are reluctant to leave the hedge fully on when the cash position is showing a substantial realized or unrealized gain, and often like to take futures markets profits if the interest rate change is out of line with expectations. Similarly, some firms will be willing to accept a certain amount of interest rate risk as part of normal operations, and therefore may wish to trigger the hedge only after a certain amount of interest opportunity loss. This will often involve the use of limit orders in conjunction with the traditional hedging strategies. It is impossible to give formal rules for the use of limit orders in hedging strategies, since this will depend upon the individual risk preferences of management. However, the normal type of system can be represented graphically (see Exhibit 4.5).

Exhibit 4.5: Use of orders with a long hedge

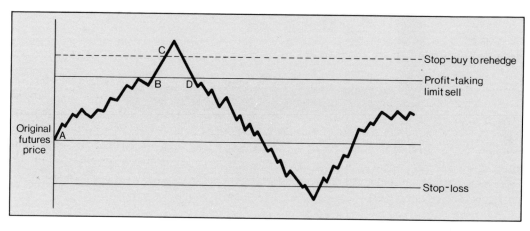

The hedger has decided to put on three limit orders: a lower stop-loss order, a profit-taking sell order, and another higher stop-buy order which will re-institute the hedge if the cash position continues to go bad. In the exhibit, the futures price rose, triggering the profit-taking limit at B. However, the profit continued to rise, re-instituting the hedge at C. Then the price eventually fell to D, at which point the hedge was again removed, giving a net loss on the futures position of the vertical difference between the profit-taking limit and the re-triggering stop-buy. No further orders were triggered during the period shown, and the hedge probably showed a net profit on the futures position over and above that required to meet losses on the cash position.

Thus while there are no systematic rules for the use of specific orders, they can be used to improve the profit potential of a hedging strategy. All hedgers should be familiar with the opportunities presented by the use of these orders.

3. Deciding on the size of hedge

This chapter has concentrated on working out optimal hedge ratios to determine the right number of futures contracts to put on to create the nearly perfect hedge—an approach rarely followed in practice. In most cases hedgers will only hedge a portion of their interest rate exposure. One of the arguments for this has been based upon a portfolio approach to firms' assets and liabilities management. Risk exposure positions unhedged and hedged represent different assets or liabilities with different risk return characteristics, and both may be appropriate in a given optimal portfolio. The argument is that since presumably basis risk and interest rate risk are not perfectly correlated, they may well both have a simultaneous place in a well-diversified portfolio. Further examination of this approach to hedging is beyond the scope of this book, and indeed no significant work has been done to try and operationalize hedging decisions within a portfolio analysis context.

Thus, all we will try to do here is explore some rules-of-thumb which might lead to less than 100% hedging even for a risk-averse hedger who has carried out all the analyses discussed to date and determined that the risk exposure is not acceptable.

a. Accepting some of the risk exposure

One way of accepting a portion of the identified risk exposure is by triggering the hedge with a limit order after some acceptable cash market loss. The alternative approach is to put on a partial hedge which will cover a portion of the risk exposure to a given level of probability.

Consider once again the initial risk exposure table for 1983 (Q2)

Probability	Rate (%)	
0.1	13	Net exposed balance = $15,000,000
0.2	12	Probability rate <13% = 96.6%
0.4	11	Cash risk level = ($79,695)
0.2	10	
0.1	9	
Mean expected rate	11	

This could be treated in a slightly different way. Suppose the hedger was willing to accept a cash risk of $40,000. The hedger knows from his forecast that the minimum interest rate could be 9%. If interest rates go to 9%, his total cash loss would be $150,000; since he is willing to accept $40,000 of that potential loss, to be sure of covering the rest of the loss through hedging he would need to put on a hedge of 73% of the total risk exposure. Some hedgers adopt an even simpler approach and simply hedge a proportion that represents the probability from the interest rate distribution that the interest rate will move in an adverse direction. However, there seems to be no scientific justification for this procedure.

b. Taking the basis forecast into account

The basis hedging approach can also be used to reduce the scale of the hedge. So far we have talked about studying basis to improve hedge profits; equally it can be used to reduce hedge costs by using smaller numbers of contracts.

Example

A hedger wishes to hedge a risk exposure of $20,000,000 six-month T-bills on 30 May. The relevant regression coefficient with three-month June T-bill futures is 0.98. The hedger is worried rates will fall and works to put on a short hedge. The current six-month T-bill discount yield is 13%; the current three-month T-bill discount yield is 12.5%, and the current June T-bill futures price is 88.25.

Step 1: Work out numbers of contracts required:

$$\text{Number of contracts} = \frac{\$20,000,000}{\$1,000,000} \times \frac{\$50}{\$25} \times 0.98 = 39.2$$

Step 2: Hedger forecasts that by 30 May the cash three-month T-bill to June futures T-bill will converge from (75) basis points to (15) basis points.
   If this occurs, profit to futures position for no cash market changes is:

$$\text{Futures gain} = 60 \times 39 \times \$25 = \$58,500$$

85

Step 3: Combine estimated extra profit with interest rate forecasts and reduce required number of contracts. For example, assume maximum adverse interest rate change = 2%.

Required futures gain to hedge 2%	= $200,000
Gain per contract from basis change	= $1,500
Gain per contract from 2% rate change	= $5,000
Number of contracts required	= 30.8 (200,000/6,500)

The forecast profit per contract from the expected convergence is used to reduce the number of contracts needed for a full hedge.

One final point that needs to be brought out in connection with hedging is the tax treatment of unrealized cash market gains or losses. The treatment of tax can have important implications for hedge design (*see* Chapter 9). For instance, supposing the hedge manager had used the methods outlined in the text to determine an optimal hedge of 10 LIFFE sterling time deposit contracts. Consider two results:

Result 1:	Cash position	loss	= £150,000
	Futures position	gain	= £150,000
Result 2:	Cash position	gain	= £150,000
	Futures position	loss	= £150,000

As long as the cash position opportunity gain or loss can be offset against the futures position gain or less for tax purposes, the hedger will not face a tax liability. However, suppose this were not the case, and futures gains were taxed but cash market opportunity gains were not offsettable. At first sight the solution might appear fairly simple: take the tax rate into account in determining the optimal hedge. For instance, if the optimal hedge above were 50 contracts and the firm's tax rate was 50%, the hedge manager should buy 100 contracts.

If result 1 still applied, double the number of contracts would give a profit of £300,000, which after tax at 50% would equate to the same required profit of £150,000 to offset the cash market loss. But what would happen if result 2 applied? The futures position of 100 contracts would show a loss of £300,000 which could not be offset against the cash market gain, which in any case is only £150,000. Hedging in this case would be risky: the optimal hedge, if the hedger's interest rate forecasts are correct, is risky if the forecasts are incorrect. In other words, differential tax treatment of cash market gains and losses and futures markets gains and losses increases the risk of hedging dramatically and may deter many corporations from using the futures markets for hedging.

C. The hedge management process

Once the hedging strategies have been defined and the decision to hedge is made, follow-up hedge management processes are vital. The management process will basically involve three stages:

1. hedge monitoring;
2. hedge adjustment; and
3. hedge evaluation.

1. Hedge monitoring

Management must design an efficient system for monitoring the success or failure of a hedge programme, particularly for management information purposes rather than for accounting and taxation purposes. The following information should always be available in up-to-date form.

(i) **Cash position.** This means not just the original risk exposure levels, but the new risk exposure levels that currently exist. The net opportunity or realized loss or gain to the cash poition must also be identified.

(ii) **Futures position.** The size and profit or loss to the futures position must be clearly identified. The total amount of margin currently assigned to the position should be known, and any net margin financing costs should be projected for appropriate periods.

(iii) **Basis movements.** Profit and losses to the futures position should be sub-divided into those due to overall interest rate movements and those due to basis changes.

(iv) **Financing requirements.** Degree of use of existing financial resources for margin payments should be noted to aid with decisions as to adequacy of resources for continuation of the hedge.

(v) **Fulfilment of forecasts.** Original forecasts for interest rates, exchange rates and basis made in conjunction with the hedge strategy design should be compared with realized data, and any required forecast adjustments carried out.

(vi) **Regression and correlation.** Historical data for correlation and regression used in designing hedge strategy should be compared with period of hedge to date to see if it was appropriate.

2. Hedge adjustment

The hedge monitoring process provides most of the information which is needed to decide to adjust the hedge through its life. Various reasons for hedge adjustment are evident.

(i) **Alterations in risk exposure.** If the cash market sums change, because perhaps cash flows are unexpectedly high or unexpectedly low, the size of the hedge will have to change too. This may involve realizing losses on contracts no longer required for a hedging function.

(ii) **Alterations in risk preferences.** If the management of the firm is changed, or the overall goals of the firm alter, then previous hedging strategies may not be appropriate.

(iii) **Interest rate projections.** The previous analyses suggested that a forward-looking probability distribution of interest rates was vital in determining risk exposure and assessing hedge strategy. Changes in the interest rate forecasts can lead to major changes in the hedging strategy.

(iv) **Basis projections.** If an aggressive hedging strategy has been pursued, and basis has moved in the forecast direction, the situation should be analysed carefully to see if further advantage of basis movements can be gained by switching the hedge to other contracts. For example, a switch from a negative to a positive carry market could lead to major changes in hedging strategy.

(v) **Increasing liquidity.** Nearby contracts may be switched into more distant contracts during the life of the hedge as liquidity in those contracts improves.

(vi) **Up-to-date hedge ratio components.** Changes in regression coefficients as more data becomes available may alter the required number of contracts to match a particular cash position.

3. Hedge evaluation

In essence, the process of hedge evaluation is simply to investigate how good the original hedging strategy was. Hedge efficiency is measured as:

$$\text{Hedge efficiency} = \frac{\text{Gain (loss) on futures position}}{\text{Gain (loss) on cash position}}$$

Even if the hedge was perfectly efficient, we need to see why. The two main inputs into hedge efficiency are:

1. Size of basis changes.
2. Quality of the components of the hedge ratio.

The process of evaluation is therefore two-fold. First, realized basis risk over the life-time of the hedge is compared with interest or exchange rate risk, to see whether the process of exchanging the two risks was a net gain for the firm. Second, the portion of hedge inefficiency not explainable by basis changes is examined to see whether bad regression results or inappropriate conversion factors are the cause. If this is the case, the firm's methods of acquiring regression and conversion data should be re-evaluated. Finally, the realized success and costs of the financial futures hedging strategy should be re-compared with the cash market alternatives to examine whether the right alternative was chosen.

This chapter has concerned itself with exploring the broad principles of hedging in the financial futures market. The next chapter will examine how these techniques can be used by different financial institutions and corporations to improve their financial performance. One point worth mentioning though before leaving the principles of hedging, is the importance of people. The design and implementation of hedging strategy is a complex process, which will only be successfully implemented by a first-class hedging team. Moreover the relationships between the hedging team and senior management must be close, with exact divisions of authority made clear.

Chapter 5
Hedging applications of financial futures

This chapter gives illustrations of the hedging principles described in the previous chapter, and the uses they can be put to in different financial and commercial enterprises. The applications are clearly not an exhaustive list, nor is the variety of potential users. However, the coverage is wide enough to illustrate the main practical applications of the principles of hedging with financial futures.

A. Hedging for a commercial bank

The essence of commercial banking is to borrow at one rate from customers and lend either to the government, through purchases of public sector fixed interest securities, or to other customers at a higher rate of interest. The difference between the cost of borrowing and the average lending rate, less any operating expenses, represents the profitability of the bank. The presence of interest rate risk is obvious: if the cost of borrowing increases while the lending rate remains fixed for a period the profitability of the bank will decline. The profitability of the bank will also decline if the average lending rate falls while the cost of borrowing remains unchanged. The use of financial futures may allow the banker, if he so desires, to lock in borrowing or lending rates to preserve a particularly attractive spread.

Most bank balance sheets contain a large number of natural hedges; for instance, loans with three-month rollovers are often matched against three-month maturity certificates of deposit and/or interbank deposits. These natural hedges must be eliminated by netting out the maturities of the assets and liabilities sides of the balance sheet to arrive at the mismatched position which may need to be hedged.

1. Hedging a balance sheet maturity mismatch

Consider the net exposed balances table of a bank shown in Chapter 4 (*see* p. 70).

Maturity (days)	Net exposed balance ($ million)	Category
0–90	1,500	Liability
91–180	1,000	Asset
181–270	1,000	Asset
271–365	1,500	Asset
No maturity or non-interest sensitive	2,000	Liability

Step 1

1 February   Determine exact rollover dates for assets and liabilities.
$1,500 m of liabilities (90-day certificates of deposit) 1 April
$1,000 m of assets (six-month interbank loans) 1 July
$1,000 m of assets (nine-month loans) 1 October
$1,500 m of assets (12-month loans) 1 January
Current rate on 90-day CDs = 13.5%.

Step 2
Determine hedge structure

Lock in 13.5% CD rate on $1.5 billion 1 April–1 July
Lock in 13.5% CD rate on $500 million 1 July–1 October
Hedge with IMM domestic CD futures—Liquid contract: correlation = 0.97
Regression coefficient = 1.05.

Strip hedge

	Cash CD market	CD futures market
1 Feb.	CD rate = 13.5%	Sell 1,575 June CDs 87.00 Sell 525 September CDs 86.50
1 April	Re-issue $1.5 billion CDs at rate of 14.25%.	Buy 1,575 June CDs 86.30
	Additional cost = 1,500,000,000 × (0.1425–0.135) × $\frac{1}{4}$ = $2.8125 million	Futures profit = 1,575 × $25 × 70 ticks = $2.75625 million
1 July	Re-issue $500 million CDs at 14.5%	Buy 525 September CDs 85.80
	Additional cost = 500,000,000 × (0.145–0.135) × $\frac{1}{4}$ = $1.25 million	Futures profit = 525 × 70 ticks × $25 = $918,750
	Total additional cost = $4.0625 million	Total futures gain = $3.675 million

Step 3
Hedge evaluation

$$\text{Hedge efficiency} = \frac{3.675}{4.0625} \times 100 = 90.5\%$$

	1 February–1 April	1 February–1 July
Change in cash rate	75 bp	100 bp
Implied futures price change from regression coefficient	71 bp	95 bp
Actual futures price change	70 bp	70 bp

Hence an adverse basis change between the cash CD and the September T-bill contract accounts for most of the hedge inefficiency. The appropriateness of using the same regression coefficient to relate the cash CD rate to both the June and September T-bill contracts should be investigated.

This example illustrates most of the practical points of hedging the liabilities side of a bank's balance sheet to lock in a suitable spread in the period before assets are rolled over. However, an alternative method of locking in borrowing rates for three-month money on 1 April and 1 July would be to use the forward-forward interbank market. For example, suppose on 1 February, the following set of interbank borrowing and lending rates was observed:

Interbank rates 1 February

59-day money	$13\frac{5}{8}$–$13\frac{3}{4}$
150-day money	$13\frac{3}{4}$–$13\frac{7}{8}$
242-day money	$13\frac{7}{8}$–14

We can work out the implied borrowing costs for the three-month periods beginning 1 April and 1 July.

$$\text{Borrowing rate 1 April–1 July} = \left[\frac{1 + (0.1375 \times [150/360])}{1 + (0.1375 \times [59/360])} - 1 \right] \times \frac{360}{91}$$

$$= 13.45\% \ (0.1345)$$

$$\text{Borrowing rate 1 July–1 October} = \left[\frac{1 + (0.13875 \times [242/360])}{1 + (0.13875 \times [150/360])} - 1 \right] \times \frac{360}{92}$$

$$= 13.12\% \ (0.1312)$$

In this case, the implied borrowing rates in the so-called strip yield curve are lower than the current cash CD rate, which the bank hoped to lock in by putting on a strip hedge in CD futures. Given that the futures hedge is subject both to basis risk, and to the possibility of adverse variation margin payments, it is likely that the bank would prefer to hedge this exposure in the forward-forward market rather than the futures. Forward-forward hedges are frequently preferred to futures for short hedges for banks, because the bank is able to operate on the advantageous side of the bid-ask spread in the interbank market.

Other points to note with this hedge include the choice of futures contract for hedging. This was an easy choice because the net exposure was in domestic CDs. However, if the borrowing medium had been interbank deposits, the choice would not have been so easy. Then the bank would need to look at the strength of the relationship between the interbank exposure and the available hedging instruments—Eurodollar time deposits, CDs and Treasury bills—to determine the best futures contract to use for hedging.

A second point is that we have assumed the spread between six-month rates (the assets side) and three-month rates (the liabilities side) will remain constant on rollovers at the same time. This may not be the case; a rise in rates may result in a less sharp rise in six-month rates than in three-month rates. Hence at the rollover on 1 July, the rise in income on the six-month loans may be smaller than the loss on the domestic CD futures position. This will introduce more complexity into the choice of how many CD futures to use to hedge the exposure.

The basis between cash CD rates and the September future implied rate went from 0 on 1 February to (30) ticks on 1 July. This may have occurred because of a generally more negative slope of the whole CD futures price curve. For instance the following set of prices and yields is consistent with the figures given in the example:

	Cash CD	June future	September future	December future
1 February	13.50%	87.00 (13.00)	86.50 (13.50)	86.40 (13.60)
1 July	14.50%		85.80 (14.20)	86.00 (14.00)

This is an example of a twist in the yield/price curve. When this occurs the adverse basis movement which we commented on earlier could have been offset by a spread position in the September/December CD futures. For instance, if the bank was worried about an adverse basis change, it could have decided to hedge that by selling the September/December spread. Spread trading is discussed in Chapter 6; however, in this particular case, hedging the basis by selling September futures and buying December futures would result in the following transactions:

1 February	Sell September/December spread	Sell further 525 September CDs at 86.50
		Buy 525 December CDs at 86.40
1 July	Buy back September/December spread	Buy 525 September CDs at 85.80
		Profit = (525 × 70 ticks × $25) = $918,750
		Sell 525 December CDs at 86.00
		Loss = (525 × 40 ticks × $25) = $525,000

Net spread gain = $393,750

This additional spread gain added to the previous futures position gain of $3.675 million gives a total gain of $4.0688 million. Hence the hedge efficiency rises to:

$$\text{Hedge efficiency} = \frac{4.0688}{4.0625} \times 100 = 100.2\%.$$

In this case the process of hedging the basis risk with a spread position improved the efficiency of the hedge to over 100%. The sophisticated hedger should consider introducing spread positions into his hedge portfolio if he is worried about adverse basis risk.

The example is rather simplistic in another way. It assumes we could easily sell in the CD futures market in one day 1,575 June contracts and 525 September contracts. On current volume figures on the IMM, this is unlikely. First, it may be necessary to put all contracts on initially in the June contract month and then roll into the September contract as liquidity builds up. Secondly, it would probably be necessary to carry out the futures transactions over a number of trading days to avoid moving the market significantly against the seller.

2. Hedging an asset purchase

A bank, like any other portfolio manager, may also sometimes wish to hedge the asset side of the balance sheet. A classic example might be a situation where a bank expects a reduction in loan demand at some point in the future; at that point the bank intends to put its excess funds into six-month Treasury bills. The bank is worried that rates will decline before the Treasury bills are purchased, leading to a reduction in potential earnings. Therefore the bank decides to lock in current interest rates.

Example

1 February: The bank plans to purchase $10 million of six-month T-bills on 1 July. It is worried about falling rates. It decides to hedge with IMM T-bill futures. Regression coefficient for rate change between September T-bill futures and cash six-month T-bills is 0.9420.

$$\text{Number of contracts} = \frac{10,000,000}{1,000,000} \times \frac{50}{25} \times 0.9420 = 18.84$$

Cash six-month T-bill market		T-bill futures market	
1 February	Current rate = 12%	1 February	Buy 19 September T-bills at 89.00
1 July	Buy $10,000,000 six-month T-bills maturing 1 January at 11%	1 July	Sell 19 September T-bills at 90.06
	Interest opportunity loss = $50,000		Futures profit = 19 × 106 ticks × $25 = $50,350

The small excess profit produced by this hedge is attributable to the bank's inability to hedge in exactly the right number of contracts. The stated regression coefficient implied a change in the futures price of 106 basis points for a 100 basis point change in cash six-month T-bill rates. This implied change in basis from (100) ticks to (106) ticks actually occurred and benefited the hedger because the hedge had to be in 19 futures contracts rather than the required number of 18.84. Although the inability to hedge in exactly the right proportions benefited the hedger in this case, it does introduce another element of risk into the hedging decision.

3. Offering fixed rate funds

Another major opportunity for banks in the futures market is to use the market to offer fixed rate loans to customers. A typical example might be where a bank intends to lend a customer £5 million at a fixed rate for one year. The loan will be made on 10 March and repaid in full on 10 March the following year. Interest will be paid on the loan quarterly. The loan will be priced at a spread of 100 basis points over the sterling three-month interbank rate. The current set of prices and yields applies on 10 March.

	Cash three-month interbank	June sterling deposit future	September future	December future
Price		(87.50)	(87.25)	(87.00)
Rate	12.00	12.50	12.75	13.00

The first step is to determine the price that can be offered to the customer. The method is to combine the four rates quoted above into an equivalent annual yield, and then quote a rate to the customer 100 basis points above that rate. Because we are directly comparing this with a floating rate loan, the equivalent annual rate is the arithmetic average of the cash rate and the three implied futures rates, i.e. 12.56%. The loan will be quoted at 13.56% (12.56 + 1.00).

92

Stage 1

10 March   1. Borrow sterling interbank funds for 92 days at 12%

$$\text{Total cost} = £5,000,000 \times 0.12 \times \frac{92}{365} = £151,232.88$$

         2. Sell 20 June sterling time deposit futures at 87.50
           Sell 20 September futures at 87.25
           Sell 20 December futures at 87.00

Stage 2

10 June   1. Borrow sterling interbank funds for 92 days at 13.10%

$$\text{Total cost} = £5,000,000 \times 0.1310 \times \frac{92}{365}$$
$$= £165,095.89$$

         2. Buy 20 June sterling deposit futures at 86.80
           Futures gain = 70 (87.50 − 86.80) × 20 × £6.25
$$= £8,750$$

         3. Effective borrowing rate 10 June–10 September

$$= \frac{156,345.89 \ (165,095.89 - 8,750)}{5,000,000} \times \frac{365}{92}$$
$$= 12.41\%$$

Stage 3

10 September   1. Borrow sterling interbank for 91 days at 13.00%

$$\text{Total cost} = £5,000,000 \times 0.13 \times \frac{91}{365} = £162,054.79$$

         2. Buy 20 September futures at 86.98
           Futures gain = 27 (87.25 − 86.98) × 20 × £6.25
$$= £3,375$$

         3. Effective borrowing rate

$$\text{10 September–10 December} = \frac{158,679.79 \ (162,054.79 - 3,375)}{5,000,000} \times \frac{365}{91}$$
$$= 12.73\%$$

Stage 4

10 December   1. Borrow sterling interbank for 90 days at 11.50%

$$\text{Total cost} = £5,000,000 \times 0.115 \times \frac{90}{365}$$
$$= £141,780.82$$

         2. Buy 20 December futures at 88.53
           Futures loss = 153 (87 − 88.53) × 20 × £6.25
$$= £19,125.00$$

         3. Effective borrowing rate $= \dfrac{160,905.82 \ (141,780.82 + 19,125.000)}{5,000,000} = \dfrac{365}{90}$
$$= 13.05\%$$

Actual hedged borrowing cost for bank

$$= \left(12 \times \frac{92}{365}\right) + \left(12.41 \times \frac{92}{365}\right) + \left(12.73 \times \frac{91}{365}\right) + \left(13.05 \times \frac{90}{365}\right)$$
$$= 12.54\%$$

This compares favourably with an estimated borrowing cost of 12.56% originally. Thus apparently the realized spread on the loan is 102 basis points. However, variation margins have to be paid on the futures position. The precise amount of variation margin will depend upon the daily price movements in the futures prices. We cannot simulate daily prices. However, a simple assumption about margin payments will give an idea of the net cost. Assuming the profit or loss to each contract occurs continuously throughout the period, and that both initial and variation margin were financed or earned interest at the average interbank rate for the three-month period concerned:

Margin costs

a. 20 June contracts. Initial margin = 20 × £500 = −£10,000
Average variation margin = £8,750/2 = £4,375

Margin of £5,625 to be financed at 12.55% $\left[\dfrac{12.00 + 13.10}{2} \right]$

Margin cost = £177.94

b. 20 September contracts. Initial margin = −£10,000
Average variation margin = £3,375/2 = £1,687.50

Margin of £8,312.50 to be financed at 12.70 $\left[\dfrac{12.00 + 13.10 + 13.00}{3} \right]$

Margin cost = £532.18

c. 20 December. Initial margin = −£10,000
Average variation margin = −£19,125/2 = −£9,562.50

Margin of £9,562.50 to be financed at 12.40% $\left[\dfrac{12.00 + 13.10 + 13.00 + 11.50}{4} \right]$

Margin cost = £893.37

Combining these total margin costs of £2,537.74 with the figures estimated earlier gives a net borrowing rate of 12.58%, which is now two basis points higher than the original estimate. This assumption about margin costs is rather simplistic, but it does serve to show that banks in offering fixed rate loans do need to carefully consider margin costs in determining the cost of fixed funds obtained via futures market hedging. If the bank were to ignore variation margin payments, it could directly take the cost of initial margin into account by assuming margins were financed at the same rate as the basic borrowing was carried out, and adjust the futures hedge accordingly.

This use of financial futures markets to enable banks to offer fixed rate loans to customers has further potential other than simply providing funds of a fixed maturity at a particular rate. Several US banks have instituted schemes whereby fixed rate funds are made available to customers at specific dates in the future. The schemes broadly fall into two categories.

1. The customer undertakes to borrow a fixed sum at a fixed rate at a future date. This is a classic hedging strategy for the customer, who consequently gives up the opportunity of benefiting from lower interest rates.
2. The bank offers to lend the customer funds at a future date at the market rate existing when the funds are drawn, but in addition guarantees that the rate will not be higher than a certain level. In this case, the customer retains the opportunity of benefiting from lower interest rates.

The first question for a bank wishing to provide these sorts of facilities is: which fixed interest rates will be offered to customers? There are several alternatives.

(a) Current market rates prevailing in the cash market.
(b) Interest rates embedded in current futures prices.
(c) Interest rates implicit in the forward-forward market.
(d) Interest rates determined at the discretion of the borrower.

It is possible for a bank to offer very flexible fixed rates at various future dates and for loans of different maturities. The provision of such flexible fixed rates would necessitate conventional hedging, of the type described in Chapter 4, in the financial futures market, and would expose either the borrower or the lender to basis risk—the risk that interest rates in the cash market will not move exactly in line with futures prices. One would assume that bank customers would probably not be willing to take on this risk, so it would be up to the bank to assume, and to charge an appropriate spread to cover, the basis risk.

The way to avoid basis risk is for the bank to lock in interest rates at a future date directly through the futures market or the forward-forward market. It is easy for banks with direct access to the interbank market to lock in borrowing and lending rates through the forward-forward market. This is by far the easiest way to offer fixed rate money at a future date, and given that a bank will be on the right side of the bid-ask spread, probably the most profitable.

For institutions with restricted access to the forward-forward interbank market, there remains the possibility of offering fixed rate funds at a spread over the rates prevailing in futures market prices. However, to avoid basis risk, funds would need to be offered only for three-month periods commencing on the delivery dates of the relevant short-term interest rate futures contracts. This would put considerable restrictions on the financing alternatives that can be offered to a customer.

Moreover, even to offer such restricted short-term fixed rate financing, the lending institution will still need access to the money market. As illustrated in the example, to lock in a borrowing rate for short-term funds in the futures market, one needs to set up a short position, say in the sterling three-month time deposit futures contract. But to be certain of the implied rate, the short may have to go to physical delivery, since cash settlement in short-term futures contracts on LIFFE is at the discretion of the long. The importance of being able to carry out the transactions on the right side of the bid-ask spread is also evident.

So far, this discussion has been consistent with the simple provision of future funds at a fixed rate of interest. The risk involved in providing merely an interest rate ceiling as mentioned in the second scheme is much greater. If the lender locks in a current interest rate and then promises the borrower to lend at or below this rate, any decline in market rates below the fixed rate will represent a direct cost to the lender. Given the current volatility of interest rates, any lending institution indulging in this type of lending will have to be careful about the type of spread it charges to compensate for this added risk.

If the provision of fixed rate forward finance is provided through the forward-forward market, there does not appear to be any problem of interim payments. However, if funds are to be acquired through the futures market, the holder of the futures position will be marked to market every day in the usual manner. The question then is whether requests for margin payments are passed on to the customer, or absorbed by the lending institution.

4. Providing fixed rate funds in other currencies

For banks, the availability of both interest rate futures contracts and foreign exchange rate futures contracts provides a means for commercial banks to lend funds in currencies other than dollars or sterling at fixed rates in the future. For example, suppose a customer wishes a bank to quote a firm rate for six-month Deutschemark funds in six-months' time. By using the Eurodollar contract quoted on LIFFE or the IMM plus the LIFFE or IMM currency contracts, it is possible to create a proxy Euro-DM hedge.

Example

A customer on 10 December asks the bank to quote a fixed rate for Deutschemark funds for the period 16 March–16 September. The current futures prices on the IMM are:

	March	June	September
$/DM	0.4116	0.4156	0.4192
Eurodollar time deposit	90.23	89.78	89.42

First, the bank works out the swap price—the cost of simultaneously selling dollars at one date and buying them back at a subsequent date for the two periods March–June and June–September.

$$\text{Swap price} = \frac{\$/\text{DM rate (date 1)} - \$/\text{DM rate (date 2)}}{\$/\text{DM rate (date 1)} \times (\text{Number of days}/360)} \times 100$$

$$\text{Swap price } (\$/\text{DM}) \text{ 16 March–16 June} = \frac{0.4116 - 0.4156}{0.4116 - (92/360)} \times 100$$
$$= -3.803\%$$

$$\text{Swap price } (\$/\text{DM}) \text{ 16 June–16 September} = \frac{0.4156 - 0.4192}{0.4156 \times (92/360)} \times 100$$
$$= -3.390\%$$

Given these swap prices, the bank can now determine the borrowing costs of DM funds it can lock in for the March–June period and the June–September period. The transactions would be carried out in the following manner:

10 December

March–June	Buy March DM at 0.4116 Sell June DM at 0.4156 Swap price = −3.803%	June– September	Buy June DM at 0.4156 Sell September DM at 0.4192 Swap price = −3.390%
	Sell March Eurodollar at 90.23		Sell June Eurodollar at 89.78
	Net cost of DM borrowing = 5.97% (9.77 − 3.803)		Net cost of DM borrowing = 6.83% (10.22 − 3.390).

Assuming interest on the DM borrowing is to be paid quarterly and the bank desires a 75 basis point spread, the bank would be able to quote a fixed annual rate for 16 March in December of 7.15%.

Now let us see how this hedge might work out in practice. Assume the following sets of prices apply on 16 March and 16 June.

	Cash DM three-month Euro-rate	$/DM swap price March–June	$/DM swap price June–September	March Eurodollar	June Eurodollar
16 March	7.01%	−2.90%	—	90.10	—
16 June	7.40%	—	−2.60%	—	90.00

Now let us examine the actual borrowing costs on the two dates

16 March	Buy March Eurodollar at 90.10 Gain = 0.13%	16 June	Buy June Eurodollar at 90.00 Loss = 0.22%

	Unwind March/June DM
	spread
	  Bought at swap price of
	  (3.803%)
	  Sold at swap price of (2.90%)
	  Gain = 0.903%
			Unwind June/September DM
			spread
			  Bought at swap price of
			  (3.390%)
			  Sold at swap price of (2.60%)
			  Gain = 0.79%

	Combined gain = 1.033%		Combined gain = 0.57%
	Cash Euro-DM rate = 7.01%		Cash Euro-DM rate = 7.40%
	Net borrowing of DM funds = 5.977% (7.01 − 1.033)		Net borrowing cost of DM funds = 6.83% (7.40 − 0.57)

Thus the net effective cost of borrowing DM funds to provide the fixed rate funds to the customer was identical to the cost originally estimated. This is because basis risk is virtually eliminated by the closeness of the lending date to the delivery dates of the IMM Eurodollar contract, and the maintenance of the interest rate parity condition discussed in Chapter 3.

Although these assumptions may not always hold, and adverse variation margin payments may be necessary, it is apparent that the financial futures markets may provide commercial banks with opportunities for fixed rate lending in currencies other than those in which interest rate futures contracts are denominated.

This discussion of the hedging applications of financial futures for commercial bank operations has necessarily been illustrative rather than comprehensive. Nonetheless it suffices to indicate the myriad of hedging uses the financial futures market presents for the major commercial banks. The financial futures market provides a mean of altering the net maturity of a bank's assets/liabilities position. It is an invaluable aid to 'gapping' in the conventional banking parlance. Banks are enabled to hedge prospective issuances of certificates of deposit, or to lock in rates at which subsequent investments in T-bills or commercial paper will take place. The futures market provides an additional means by which banks can provide fixed rate funds either at once or at a future date to commercial customers.

B. Hedging by portfolio managers

The financial futures market provides virtually unlimited opportunities for portfolio managers to tailor the returns on existing portfolios, or to lock in rates on anticipated sales or purchases of assets. This section gives a representative selection of these strategies using various of the financial futures contracts described earlier. The distinction between hedging applications of financial futures and the investment applications (described in Chapter 8) is to a certain extent artificial and the types of transaction overlap considerably.

1. A simple hedge

A classic simple hedge for a portfolio manager is to lock in an interest rate or yield on an anticipated purchase of securities. For instance, consider a portfolio manager in the UK who is intending to purchase a particular gilt-edged stock at a later date. If he is worried that gilt interest rates will rise prior to the purchase date, he can lock in the effective price of the gilt by hedging the anticipated purchase with gilt futures contracts on LIFFE.

Example

It is 30 March. The manager of a gilt portfolio intends to purchase £1,000,000 nominal of Treasury 15.5% 1998 gilt stock at the end of July. The price of this gilt is 108-14 giving a current yield to maturity of 13.94%. Being worried about falling interest rates he decides to hedge the prospective purchase in the futures market.

The number of contracts for full hedge is found by:

$$\text{Face value} \times \text{Money equivalency} \times \text{Conversion factor}$$

$$\frac{£1,000,000}{£50,000} \times 1 \times 1.242 = 24.84$$

The conversion table of LIFFE indicates that 1.242 times as many standardized 20-year 12% gilt futures are required as actual Treasury 15.5% 1998s. To simplify this example further, the gilt cash market prices exclude accrued interest.

Cash market	Futures market
30 March	30 March
Expect to purchase £1,000,000 nominal of Treasury 15.5% 1998 on 30 July	Buy 25 September gilt futures at 87–02
Current market price is 108-14. Yield to maturity 13.94%	
Market value of gilt = £1,084,375	
Price is equivalent to 87-10 for LIFFE standard gilt	

Basis = + 8 ticks

(example continued on p. 98)

Cash market	**Futures market**
30 July	30 July
Buy £1,000,000 nominal of Treasury 15.5% 1998 at 114-20	Sell 25 September gilt futures at 92-18
Yield to maturity = 13%	
Market value of gilt = £1,146,250	
Price is equivalent to 92-09 for LIFFE standard gilt	

$$\text{Basis} = -9 \text{ Ticks}$$

Gilt purchase costs an additional £61,875	Futures profit = 25 contracts × 176 ticks (92-18 − 87-02) × £15.625 = £68,750

The effectiveness of this hedge was as high as 111%. The change in basis from a positive 8 ticks to a negative 9 ticks favoured the long hedger. If the hedger has reason to believe the basis will move in a favourable direction, this fact can be used in hedge design. For example, in the above case the investor will realize that the basis of 8 ticks will be eliminated by the end of August, assuming the futures market is pricing itself off the cheapest deliverable gilt, which is almost certainly the Treasury 15.5% 1998 described in the example. Transactions costs would lead one to expect the standard gilt in the delivery month to trade at a premium over the equivalent parity price (obtained from the conversion table) for the cheapest deliverable gilt.

Assuming, however, that the investor believed the basis would move from +8 ticks to zero by the end of July as the process of convergence occurred. The investor knows that convergence during the life of the hedge is forecast to produce a cash gain per contract of £125. A neutral hedger would put on the hedge for a lesser amount than the 25 contract shown above. To determine the optimal hedge *ex post* it is necessary to see how many contracts would have been required to produce the equivalent profit on the futures position to that loss on the cash position, assuming the basis only moved from +8 to zero.

$$\text{Futures gain per contract} = £15{,}625 \times 167 \text{ ticks } (92\text{-}09 - 87\text{-}02)$$

$$= £2{,}609.38$$

$$\textit{Ex post} \text{ perfect hedge} = £61{,}875/£2{,}609.38 = 23.71$$

Depending upon the maximum level of adverse interest rate change the investor was forecasting, the hedger could have afforded to purchase only 24 rather than 25 contracts to produce a good hedge.

There is always an alternative strategy available to a portfolio manager in these hedges of prospective asset purchases. In the above case, the manager could simply have purchased the asset immediately by borrowing short-term funds. The current price of the gilt is locked in with certainty, but there is a cost of borrowing between 30 March and 30 July. On the other hand, accrued interest on the Treasury 15.5% 1998 will be gained by the investor over the same period. Careful comparison of the respective costs of hedging in the futures market and/or borrowing funds and purchasing assets immediately need to be made by the prospective hedger. In most cases, it is quite likely to be the case that simple direct purchase of the asset may be the favoured strategy.

2. A portfolio hedge

A second and more common use of futures hedging for portfolio managers is to lock in the current value of an asset portfolio without the necessity of actually selling the assets concerned. There may be several reasons for this: a portfolio manager may hold assets with market values below original cost and not wish to realize the capital loss, and he may believe dumping large quantities of assets on the market may adversely affect the price against him. Interest rate futures and stock index futures provide a means of temporarily insulating portions of a portfolio against general adverse movements without trading in the assets of the portfolio directly.

Bond portfolio hedging

A pension fund holds three gilt-edged stocks: £200 million nominal of Treasury 10.5% 1999, £100 million nominal of Treasury 13% 2000, and £70 million nominal of Exchequer 12% 1999–2002. The following data is available. The date is 25 March.

Stock	Market price	June conversion value	September conversion value
Treasury 10.5% 1999	94–00	0.8922	0.8925
Treasury 13% 2000	110–16	1.0738	1.0726
Exchequer 12% 1999–2002	102–20	1.0006	0.9997

June gilt futures price = 104–00
September gilt futures price = 103–04.

The pension fund is worried that interest rates will rise between now and August, and wishes to insulate 40% of the gilt portfolio from general interest rate movements.

Stage 1
Determine basis between parity prices of stock held and gilt futures prices. (Parity price = Cash gilt price ÷ Conversion factor.) We assume gilt prices given are clean prices; in practice, the investor would need to factor out accrued interest in this calculation.

June
Parity price of Treasury 10.5%	=	105–11	Basis =	43 ticks
Parity price of Treasury 13%	=	102–29	Basis =	−35 ticks
Parity price of Exchequer 12%	=	102–18	Basis =	−46 ticks

September
Parity price of Treasury 10.5%	=	105–10	Basis =	70 ticks
Parity price of Treasury 13%	=	103–01	Basis =	−3 ticks
Parity price of Exchequer 12%	=	102–21	Basis =	−15 ticks

Stage 2
Compute value weighted parity price for portfolio, and basis at each futures price. Values are determined as individual gilt parity prices times nominal portfolio holdings.

June
Treasury 10.5% value	=	£200,000,000 nominal at 105–11
	=	£210,687,500
Treasury 13% value	=	£100,000,000 nominal at 102–29
	=	£102,906,250
Exchequer 12% value	=	£70,000,000 nominal at 102–18
	=	£71,793,750.
Total portfolio value	=	£385,387.500

Weighted parity price of portfolio: June futures basis:

$$(105\text{-}11)\,\frac{210{,}687{,}500}{385{,}387{,}500} + (102\text{-}29)\,\frac{102{,}906{,}250}{385{,}387{,}500} + (102\text{-}18)\,\frac{71{,}793{,}750}{385{,}387{,}500}$$
$$= 104\text{-}06$$
$$\text{Basis} = +6 \text{ ticks}$$

September
Treasury 10.5% value	=	£200,000,000 nominal at 105–10
	=	£210,062,500
Treasury 13% value	=	£100,000,000 nominal at 103–01
	=	£103,031,250
Exchequer 12% value	=	£70,000,000 nominal at 102–21
	=	£71,859,375
Total portfolio value	=	£384,953,125

Weighted parity price of portfolio: September futures basis:

$$(105\text{-}10)\left(\frac{210,062,500}{384,953,125}\right) + (103\text{-}01)\left(\frac{103,031,250}{384,953,125}\right) + (102\text{-}21)\left(\frac{71,859,375}{384,859,375}\right)$$

$$= 104\text{-}07$$

$$\text{Basis} = +35 \text{ ticks}$$

Remember that the market value of the portfolio on 25 March is:

$$(94\text{-}00)\,(2,000,000) + (110\text{-}16)\,(1,000,000) + (102\text{-}20)\,(700,000)$$

$$= £370,337,500$$

Stage 3

Decide on appropriate futures contract for hedging.

Since this is a short hedge, i.e. long cash and short the futures contract, the portfolio manager will effectively be long the basis after the hedge is put on. The portfolio manager cannot be certain that the positive basis shown will disappear entirely at delivery, since none of the gilts held is the cheapest deliverable stock from which it is generally assumed the futures contract is priced. However, it seems most likely that the basis between the aggregate portfolio parity price and the September contract will decline over the life of the hedge. Hence the investor concludes that his purpose will best be served by a piled-up roll hedge rather than a strip hedge. To hedge rates through the end of August, he will initially hedge with the June contract, which he rolls into the September contract at the end of May or at a nearer point if there is a favourable basis move. Because the basis between the weighted parity price and the June futures price is so small, there does not appear to be any compelling call to overhedge or underhedge. However, this may be called for if the adverse basis between the cash position and the September futures price persists at the end of May.

The decision is to hedge initially with the June contract.

Stage 4

Determination of number of contracts for hedge

For full hedge
    £200 million of Treasury $10\frac{1}{2}$%

$$\text{Number of contracts} = \frac{200,000,000}{50,000} \times 0.8922$$

$$= 3568.8$$

£100 million of Treasury 13%

$$\text{Number of contracts} = \frac{100,000,000}{50,000} \times 1.0738$$

$$= 2147.6$$

£70 million of Exchequer 12%

$$\text{Number of contracts} = \frac{70,000,000}{50,000} \times 1.0006$$

$$= 1400.84$$

For 40% hedge as desired

$$\text{Number of June contracts} = 0.4\,[3,568.8 + 2,147.6 + 1,400.84]$$

$$= 2,846.9 \text{ contracts}$$

Hence an appropriate hedge to fit in with the portfolio manager's desire to insulate 40% of his gilt portfolio from general interest rate movements would involve the sale of 2,847 June gilt futures on LIFFE. Given the fact that LIFFE has only been trading for a limited period of time, it is unlikely that the manager would be able to deal in this sort of volume. However, this is not the case for an equivalent portfolio holding of Treasury bonds in the United States. Currently the Chicago Board of Trade Treasury bond contract which trades in $100,000 nominal units has frequently traded over 200,000 contracts in a day. A hedge of the size estimated above could be absorbed without too much difficulty over two or three days in such a market. Nonetheless, given the relatively small size of the LIFFE gilt futures and CBT Treasury bond contract, hedges of significant size against portfolio positions will involve a substantial number of contracts.

Let us follow this hedge through with some assumed prices for end–May to study the nature of the decision about rolling the contracts into the September month:

29 May

Market price (clean prices)

Treasury $10\frac{1}{2}$%	90–21
Treasury 13%	108–18
Exchequer 12%	101–09
June gilt future	101–10
September gilt future	100–20

Cash position

$$\text{Portfolio value} = (90\text{–}21)\,(2{,}000{,}000) + (108\text{–}18)\,(1{,}000{,}000) + (101\text{–}09)\,(700{,}000)$$

$$= £360{,}771{,}880$$

Portfolio has declined in value by £9,565,620.

Futures position

$$\text{Futures gain} = 2{,}847 \text{ contracts} \times £15.625 \text{ per tick} \times 86 \text{ ticks}$$

$$= £3{,}825{,}656.30$$

Since a futures hedge was designed to be 40% of the portfolio, a perfect hedge would involve a future gain of

$$(0.40)\,(£9{,}565{,}620) = £3{,}826{,}248$$

Hence hedge efficiency period 25 March–29 May is

$$\text{Efficiency} = \frac{3{,}825{,}656.30}{3{,}826{,}248} = 99.99\%$$

Now consider what would have happened if the hedge for this period had been put on in the September contract.

$$\text{Futures gain} = 2{,}847 \text{ contracts} \times £15.625 \text{ per tick} \times 78 \text{ ticks}$$

$$= £3{,}469{,}781.30$$

$$\text{Hedge efficiency} = \frac{3{,}469{,}781.30}{3{,}826{,}248} = 90.68\%$$

Although the hedge was still largely successful, the expected adverse basis movement between the cash value weighted parity price and the September contract made it significantly less efficient than the hedge with the June contracts. Since the estimated value weighted parity price of the cash portfolio on a September futures basis on 29 May has fallen to 101-14, it is apparent that the cash September futures basis has moved adversely from +35 ticks on 25 March to +26 ticks on 29 May.

Although in this case we determined the number of contracts to optimally hedge each individual gilt using the conversion on price factor, it would have been equally easy to use the perturbation method described in Chapter 4, comparing the effects of a 1% change in the yield of each individual stock with that of the standardized 12% 20-year gilt future. Alternatively, we could calculate the duration of each individual gilt in the portfolio, and estimate hedge ratios from the ratio of the duration of the individual stocks to that of the cheapest deliverable gilt—the Treasury 15½% 1998—adjusted by the conversion factor of the cheapest deliverable gilt.

Moving on to consider the rolling over of the hedge on 29 May, the pension fund manager has to take two basic issues into consideration. First, does he wish to continue to hedge the 40% of the total portfolio: has the actual increase in rates and decreases in gilt prices that has occurred been as large as he feared. If so, he may alter his forecast of subsequent interest rate movements, and consequently reduce or eliminate his hedge. But if he believes rates could rise further, he determines to continue to hedge 40% of his portfolio. Now the hedge will have to be in the September contract; and he would look at contracts even further out (for the sake of simplicity this example ignores that possibility).

In hedging with September contracts, the manager must take into account the possibility that the current positive basis of +26 ticks will decline further between 29 May and the end of August. Let us assume he expects it to converge to the basis observed for the June contract with the cash portfolio on 29 May. The value weighted parity price on a June futures contract basis for the cash gilt portfolio on 29 May was 101–13, giving a basis of +3 ticks. Let us further assume the portfolio to September contract basis on the 30 August will be the same, i.e. the basis will decline from +26 ticks on 29 May to +3 ticks on 30 August. This means that even if the general level of interest rates does not change, each September futures contract will show a significant loss.

$$\text{Contract loss} = 23 \text{ ticks} \times \pounds15.625 \text{ per tick}$$

$$= \pounds359.375$$

The optimal level of a 40% hedge, ignoring this potential adverse basis movement, is:

$$40\% \text{ ex ante optimal hedge} = \left[\left(\frac{200,000,000}{50,000} \right)(0.8925) + \left(\frac{100,000,000}{50,000} \right)(1.0726) \right.$$
$$\left. + \left(\frac{70,000,000}{50,000} \right)(0.9997) \right] \times 0.4$$
$$= 2,845.9 \text{ contracts}$$

Now consider the potential loss of 23 ticks per contract. The hedger is unprotected against a decline in the value weighted parity price of his cash portfolio of this amount. There is nothing he can do about this if prices decline in general by this amount or less. If the gilt futures price rises by 23 ticks due to general price trends and falls by 23 ticks because of adverse basis movements, the hedge is neutralized and the cash position is unprotected.

On the other hand, if prices in the futures market were to rise by more than 23 ticks due to general price trends, the hedger can offset his expected losses due to basis changes by putting on more contracts. However, in this case the structure of the hedge becomes a function of the pension fund manager's interest rate forecast, and this introduces new risk elements into the hedging decision. Examine this type of decision on 29 May where the manager makes the following forecast for gilt prices, but still only wishes to hedge 40% of his portfolio.

Forecast for 30 August

Probability	Treasury 10½%	Treasury 13%	Exchequer 12%
0.10	86–00	105–16	92–24
0.20	86–16	106–00	100–00
0.30	87–00	106–16	100–16
0.30	87–16	106–24	100–24
0.10	88–00	107–00	101–00
Mean price	87–02	106–14	100–14
Equivalent parity price	97–18	99–08	100–15

102

$$\text{Portfolio parity price} = (97\text{-}18)\left(\frac{195,125,000}{364,843,750}\right) + (99\text{-}08)\left(\frac{99,250,000}{364,843,750}\right)$$

$$+ (100\text{-}15)\left(\frac{70,468,750}{364,843,750}\right)$$

$$= 98\text{-}18$$

To compensate for this decline in the portfolio parity price, each futures contract must show a price rise of 80 ticks, equivalent to the difference between the portfolio parity price 101–14 on 29 May and the expected parity price of 98–18 calculated above. In fact, however, because of the potential adverse basis movement of 23 ticks, we would expect a 80 tick loss in the cash position price to be matched by just a 57 tick gain in the futures price. We can thus work out how many futures contracts per cash position we need to put to produce a neutral hedge:

$$\text{Number of futures contract per single cash position} = \frac{80 \text{ ticks}}{57 \text{ ticks}}$$

$$= 1.40$$

Since the optimal hedge ignoring adverse basis movements has been calculated as 2,846 contracts, we now have our final hedge to be put on in September contracts on 29 May, contingent upon the pension fund manager's forecast of future gilt prices.

$$40\% \text{ hedge} = 2,846 \text{ contract} \times 1.4$$

$$= 3,984 \text{ contracts}$$

This number of contracts will constitute a perfect hedge if, and only if, the forecast change in the portfolio parity price occurs, and the adverse basis movement is also as predicted. However, it is a riskier hedge strategy than a simple hedge. This can be seen if we consider what will happen if gilt prices actually rise rather than fall. Not only will the futures position decline because of the adverse basis movements, but the ratio of basic losses on the futures position to that of the cash portfolio will also be in the ratio 1.4 to 1.0. Moreover, the hedge is neutral only if the exact change in prices forecast occurs; otherwise the hedger will find himself under or over-hedged.

Although very simplified, this example of portfolio hedging brings out the major points. Long-term interest rate futures contracts can be used to insulate parts or all of an asset portfolio from general market movements. However, the construction of such hedges is relatively complex, and they need to be monitored carefully on a continuous basis to check that conversion factors are adequately mapping the relative price movements of cash gilt or Treasury bond holdings, and that basis trends are taken into account in adjusting the size of the hedge.

Points to note for portfolio hedging

1. Number of contracts to hedge each asset is determined from its conversion factor with the standardized futures contract, or by perturbation or duration analysis.
2. Examine the basis between the weighted portfolio parity price and the different futures contract prices in determining which contract to use.
3. Study the behaviour of the basis through time and adjust your hedge accordingly.
4. Weighting a hedge to overcome adverse convergence of cash and futures prices demands a forecast of future prices, and is more risky than a straight hedge.

---

3. Hedging with stock index futures

Rather similar principles apply to hedges by portfolio managers using the comparatively recent innovation of stock index futures. The main institutional use of these futures is to allow fund managers to adjust the systematic risk of equity portfolios. The risk of an equity portfolio is generally divided into two types—systematic risk and non-systematic risk.

Non-systematic risk is that risk which is individual to a specific firm or stock, and which can therefore be eliminated by diversification. Such diversification cannot completely eliminate risk, however, since there are economic, political and social events which can impact upon the prices of stocks generally. The price variability associated with such general or global events can not be diversified away and is called market or systematic risk.[1]

Stock index futures provide a means for the portfolio manager to adjust his level of systematic risk. This is because the Standard and Poor's index, on which the IOM index future is written, is based on the performance of a very large number of shares, and hence has negligible non-systematic risk. Thus, if a portfolio manager sells stock index futures in the same dollar amount as his own stock portfolio, he should theoretically eliminate systematic risk entirely. The systematic risk of an equity portfolio is measured by the weighted "beta" of the portfolio. Beta is a measure of the relative expected movement in a specific share price in response to a movement in the overall index. Ignoring, for simplicity, the question of dividends, a stock having a beta of 2.00 implies that for a 10% rise in the S + P index, you would expect the individual stock to rise by 20%. Similarly for a 10% fall in the value of the index, the stock would be expected to decline by 20%. Thus, if a portfolio manager expects the stock market to rise, he would favour high beta securities; if he expects the market to fall, he would like to keep the beta of his portfolio as low as possible.

Betas for individual stocks are published by many brokerage firms both in the UK and the United States, and by those exchanges trading stock index futures.

To calculate the weighted portfolio beta, a fund manager will determine a composite beta consisting of the individual betas weighted by the market values of the individual stocks in the portfolio. Thus, consider the following small portfolio:

Stock	Price	Holding	Beta	Market value
ABC	$80	400,000	1.15	$32,000,000
XYZ	$25	625,000	0.94	$15,625,000
DDD	$104	250,000	1.36	$26,000,000

Market value of portfolio = $73,625,000

$$\text{Weighted portfolio beta} = (1.15)\left(\frac{32,000,000}{76,625,000}\right) + (0.94)\left(\frac{15,625,000}{73,625,000}\right) + (1.36)\left(\frac{26,000,000}{73,625,000}\right)$$
$$= 1.16$$

Suppose the choice of these stocks is a careful long-term programme. Further suppose that liquidation is not possible in a falling market, because this is an all-equity fund. If the fund manager is worried about an overall fall in stock prices in the short-term, his strategy could be to establish a short hedge by selling stock index futures against his portfolio. We will assume the current level of the S + P index is 122.20, and the futures prices are observed on 6 July:

$$\text{September S + P future} = 121.80$$
$$\text{December S + P future} = 121.70$$
$$\text{March} \quad \text{S + P future} = 121.70$$

Since this is a short hedge, a positive basis is adverse to the hedger because of possible convergence. If the portfolio manager wishes to hedge the portfolio only between 6 July and the end of September, he decides to use the March contract, hoping that convergence will be small over the next three months for that contract. If the beta of his portfolio was 1.00, as measured relative to the Standard + Poor's 500 stock index, virtually all the risk would be eliminated by selling an equal dollar amount of futures contracts:

$$\text{March futures price} = 121.70$$
$$\text{Dollar value} = 121.70 \times £500 = \$60,850$$
$$\text{Optimal hedge for a portfolio beta of } 1.00 = \frac{\$73,625,000}{\$60,850} = 1,209.9 \text{ contracts}$$

In the case of our portfolio, however, the beta is 1.16, so that we have to weight the number of contracts accordingly.

Optimal hedge for a portfolio beta of 1.16 = (1,209.9) × (1.16) = 1,403.5 contracts

[1] For a discussion of systematic risk, beta analysis and portfolio diversification techniques, see, for example, W. F. Sharpe, *Investments*, Prentice-Hall, 2nd edition, (1982).

Hence a suitable short hedge for this portfolio would be 1,404 contracts sold.

Assuming that the market fell by 10% during the period 6 July to the end of August, while the S + P March index future fell by 9.80% to 109.75; there was a small amount of the convergence the portfolio manager was worried about. On 30 August the following prices were observed:

Stock	Price	Holding	Beta	Market value	% stock price change
ABC	$72.8	400,000	1.15	$29,120,000	−9.00
XYZ	$22.75	625,000	0.94	$14,218,750	−9.00
DDD	$83.20	250,000	1.36	$20,800,000	−20.00

$$\text{Market value of portfolio} = \$64,138,750$$

$$\text{Cash position loss} = \$9,486,250$$

$$\text{Futures position gain: } 1,404 \text{ contracts} \times \$25 \text{ per tick} \times 239 \text{ ticks} \left(\frac{121.70 - 109.75}{0.05}\right)$$

$$= \$8,388,900$$

$$\text{Hedge efficiency} = \frac{\$8,388,900}{\$9,486,250} = 88.5\%$$

The hedge, although relatively successful, was not perfect. In contrast to interest rate futures contracts, there are other reasons for this than just adverse basis movements. In this case, part of the hedge inefficiency is due to adverse basis developments: the cash S + P index fell by 10% from 122.20 to 109.98, the March S + P futures contract fell by only 9.8% from 121.70 to 109.75. In addition, however, the betas for the individual shares were not good predictors of the actual *ex post* reactions of the individual share prices to market movements, particularly for company DDD. This could have arisen because of two causes.

First, the shares could have been reacting to additional inputs, other than the general market movements, which were specific to those shares—they are displaying unsystematic risk. We would not expect the hedge to offset this sort of loss, because it is a hedge designed specifically to neutralize systematic not non-systematic risk.

There is also a second possibility: that the estimated betas were not good predictors of the relationship between the individual share and the market over the period in question. The *ex post* betas differed significantly from the *ex ante* betas.

The process of estimating stock and portfolio betas is a complex one, but the degree of success of a hedge with stock index futures will depend crucially on the validity of the betas used in determining the size of the hedge as predictors of actual betas over the life of the hedge. Thus, stock index futures hedges involve two risks: basis risk and beta forecasting risk.

In this example, the portfolio beta varies with time as the relative market value of individual stock holdings varies. For instance on 30 August, the portfolio beta would be (assuming the betas of individual stocks are unchanged):

$$(1.15)\left(\frac{29,120,000}{64,138,750}\right) + (0.94)\left(\frac{14,218,750}{64,138,750}\right) + (1.36)\left(\frac{20,800,000}{64,138,750}\right)$$

$$= 1.17$$

Although this is not a large change, it does mean that if the portfolio manager wishes the hedge to remain on, he must adjust the number of contracts.

$$\text{Optimal hedge for portfolio beta of } 1.17 = \frac{\$64,138,750}{\$54,875 \ (109.75 \times 500)} \times 1.17$$

$$= 1,367.5 \text{ contracts}$$

Hence the number of contracts in the hedge can be reduced by 60.

1. Number of contracts for hedge is ratio of dollar value of portfolio and dollar value of futures contract times portfolio beta.
2. Examine basis between current index level and index futures prices in determining which contract to use.
3. Portfolio betas and dollar value of index change through time and hedge should be adjusted accordingly.
4. Success of hedge depends on how good your beta estimates are.

4. Locking in stock prices with index futures

Stock market index futures can also be used to attempt to lock in buying or selling prices for stocks or groups of stocks at a later date. Quite frequently a portfolio manager will know that he will have to liquidate a portion of his equity holdings at some future date to meet a demand for cash, or he may anticipate an inflow of cash at a particular time in the future which he will use to purchase a stock or group of stocks. In the former case, a short hedge with stock index futures will eliminate a proportion of the risk that the stock prices will fall before the liquidation occurs. In the latter, a long hedge will offset a rise in stock prices before the purchase occurs.

Example

A fund manager anticipates receiving $10 million cash inflow on 30 May. It is now 10 March. He will use the money to increase the proportion of his portfolio devoted to the oil industry. A portfolio of oil industry shares has a beta of 1.10 with the S + P 500 index. Current values of the index are:

	Spot	March	June	September
S + P 500	140.20	140.10	139.40	139.20

Stage 1

Choice of contract: This is a long hedge. Because the basis is positive, convergence favours the hedger. Hence, the fund manager will hedge using the nearest available contract: the June contract.

Stage 2

$$\text{Number of contracts: } \frac{\$10,000,000 \times 1.10}{\$69,700 \ (139.40 \times 500)} = 157.8 \text{ contracts}$$

Fund manager buys 158 June S + P futures contracts.

Stage 3

30 May

Cash market

The stock market has risen by 10%, but since OPEC raised the oil price by $4 a barrel in April, oil sector shares have risen by 22%. Therefore to buy the same portfolio of shares that would cost $10,000,000 on 10 March now costs fund manager $12,200,000.

$$\text{Cash opportunity loss} = \$2,200,000$$

Futures market

S + P 500 index spot rose by 10% from 140.20 to 154.22. Basis for June contract was reduced from 16 ticks (140.20–139.40)/0.05 to 2 ticks (154.22–154.10)/0.05 as futures price rose to 154.10.

$$\text{Futures gain} = 158 \text{ contracts} \times \$25 \text{ per tick} \times 294 \text{ ticks} \left(\frac{154.10-139.40}{0.05}\right)$$

$$= \$1,161,300$$

Hedge efficiency = 52.8%

Although the hedge efficiency was improved by the favourable basis movement, it could not offset the impact of the oil price rise, which caused oil shares to rise well above that amount predicted by the oil sector beta. Nonetheless, for a typical oil share priced at $100, that would have cost $122 to buy on 30 May, the futures hedge succeeded in reducing the effective cost of that share to $110.39.

In practice the fund manager would wish to consider alternatives to this strategy. He could borrow funds short-term and purchase oil shares immediately. Another alternative in the stock market is to buy call options on a portfolio of oil shares to lock in purchase prices. Although the analysis of option strategies is not dealt with in this book, any investor should be aware that the use of options is often an alternative to futures for hedging. The role of the options alternative will increase as options on fixed interest rate instruments and even on financial futures are introduced on major exchanges.

Stock index futures may also play an important role for specialists on the New York and other US stock exchanges, and for jobbers in the UK if and when an FT index futures contract is introduced. Any market maker has a constant need to hedge inventory positions. This is particularly the case in the US where stock exchange specialists are restricted from trading options on stocks in which they are specialists. Hedge strategies in these non-diversified portfolios follow similar principles to the first portfolio example given above.

Hedging for portfolio managers

1. Interest rate and stock index futures can be used to lock in purchase prices for intended bond or stock acquisitions at a later date through long hedging.
2. Interest rate and stock index futures can be used to lock in sale prices for intended bond or stock divestitures at a later date through short hedging.
3. Futures can be used to insulate part or all of a portfolio from overall interest rate or stock market movements by short hedging.

C. Hedging for a corporation

The principles of using financial futures for hedging by a commercial corporation are identical to those illustrated for commercial banks and pension fund managers. Short hedges can be used to lock in rates at which funds can be borrowed; long hedges can be used to lock in rates at which funds can be invested. In addition, for corporations involved in international trans-actions, the futures market in foreign exchange provides an alternative hedging mechanism for locking in future exchange rates to the forward market.

There are two caveats to this similarity. First, many of the interest rate risks with which corporations are concerned are frequently in instruments where no direct futures contract is available. Hence cross-hedging is more frequent and the estimation of relationships between cash instruments and available futures contracts more important. Second, the cash flow forecasts of corporations are frequently more uncertain and risky than those of financial institutions, so that the question of what proportion of expected cash flows should be hedged becomes of major importance.

Three examples of corporate hedging with financial futures will bring out the essential points.

1. Example of hedging expected cash flows

A corporation has the following expected net cash flows; the current date is 31 December:

31 January	$5,000,000
28 February	$2,500,000
31 March	$3,000,000
30 April	$6,000,000
31 May	$2,500,000
30 June	$3,250,000

Current cash in the balance sheet is $16,000,000. The company invests all surplus cash in one-month interbank deposits. Interest on one-month deposits is repatriated to the company's parent abroad.

The corporation wishes to lock in current one-month deposit rates on expected cash positions. The current one-month rate is 11.0%. Available IMM Eurodollar time deposit and domestic CD futures prices are:

| | Eurodollar | | CD | |
	Price	Open interest	Price	Open interest
March	88.28	12,260	89.10	11,250
June	88.40	5,750	89.20	4,571
September	88.62	3,200	89.43	2,216
December	89.10	520	90.00	402

The following regression relationships are also available:

$$\text{One-month deposit} = -0.582 + 1.10 \,(\text{three-month Eurodollar futures})$$

$$R^2 = 0.932$$

$$\text{One-month deposit} = 0.456 + 1.05 \,(\text{domestic CD futures})$$

$$R^2 = 0.762$$

Stage 1
Determine the monthly cash exposure (millions)

31 January	28 February	31 March	30 April	31 May	30 June
21.0	23.5	26.5	20.5	23.0	26.25

Stage 2
Determine number of contracts for full hedge.

(a) Which future: Comparing the R^2 of relationship between one-month deposit rates and respectively Eurodollar futures and domestic CD futures strongly suggests hedging with the Eurodollar future.

(b) Number of contracts:

$$\text{Face value} \times \text{Money equivalency} \times \text{Regression coefficient}$$

$$31 \text{ January} = \frac{21,000,000}{1,000,000} \times \frac{\text{one month}}{\text{three months}} \times 1.10 = 7.7$$

$$28 \text{ February} = 23.5 \times \tfrac{1}{3} \times 1.10 = 8.6$$

$$31 \text{ March} = 26.5 \times \tfrac{1}{3} \times 1.10 = 9.7$$

$$30 \text{ April} = 20.5 \times \tfrac{1}{3} \times 1.10 = 7.5$$

$$31 \text{ May} = 23.0 \times \tfrac{1}{3} \times 1.10 = 8.4$$

$$30 \text{ June} = 26.25 \times \tfrac{1}{3} \times 1.10 = 9.6$$

Stage 3
Determine what type of hedge: roll, piled-up roll, strip, etc. There is an opportunity for aggressive hedging here. The basis for all contracts except December is strongly positive; hence, convergence will favour the long hedger.

Decision: to put on all contracts in the March future, and roll the March, April, May and June hedges into the June contract at the end of February.

Stage 4
For full hedge of expected cash flows against expected falls in interest rates, buy 52 March Eurodollar futures contracts at 80.28.

Now let us consider possible outcomes for the hedge position at the end of January and the end of February.

31 January
Cash flow forecasts unchanged
One-month deposit rate = 10.3%
March future 89.30
June future 89.35

(1) Cash flow interest opportunity loss = $21,000,000 × (0.110 − 0.103) × 1/12
$$= \$12,250$$

(2) Sell 9 futures to close January hedge

$$\text{Realized futures gain} = 9 \text{ contracts} \times \$25 \text{ per tick}$$
$$\times \$102 \text{ ticks (89.30–88.28)}$$
$$= \$22,950$$

$$\text{Hedge efficiency} = \$22,950/\$12,250 = 187.4\%$$

The very favourable convergence and its impact upon basis has resulted in a substantial profit to the hedge strategy.

(3) Running profit on remaining contracts

$$\text{Gain} = 43 \text{ contracts} \times \$25 \text{ per tick}$$
$$\times 102 \text{ ticks (89.30 − 88.28)}$$
$$= \$109,650$$

At this point the hedge must re-evaluate his interest rate forecast. Rates in the one-month cash market have fallen by 70 basis points: does the hedger think rates will go lower? If he does, he will want to keep on the hedge; if he believes they have fallen as far as is likely, he may want to take part or all of it off. We assume for the time being the decision is to continue to hedge.

28 February
February cash flow is actually $3,000,000
New cash flow forecasts are:

31 March	30 April	31 May	30 June
2,000,000	−7,000,000	1,500,000	3,000,000

One-month deposit rate = 12.5%
March future 87.30
June future 87.25

(1) Cash flow interest = $18,000,000 × (0.125 − 0.11) × 1/12
$$= \$22,500$$

(2) Sell nine futures to close February hedge

$$\text{Realized futures loss} = 9 \text{ contracts} \times \$25 \text{ per tick} \times 98 \text{ ticks (88.28–87.30)}$$
$$= \$22,050$$

Here the hedge is almost perfect but rather fortuitously. The corporation was overhedged, since the February cash flow came in well under forecast, but this was compensated by the favourable effects of convergence on the March contracts.

(3) Running loss on remaining contracts

$$\text{Loss} = 34 \text{ contracts} \times \$25 \text{ per tick} \times 98 \text{ ticks (88.28 − 87.30)}$$
$$= \$83,300$$

The corporation now has two decisions to make. First, has its views on interest rates changed: does it expect interest rates to fall back again after their recent rise, or does it expect the rise to continue. The forecast will determine whether to continue to hedge or not. Secondly, the marked change in the firm's cash flow forecasts means that the size of a full hedge has now altered. This is the new exposure.

Date	Exposure	Hedge
31 March	20,000,000	7.3
30 April	13,000,000	4.8
31 May	14,500,000	5.3
30 June	17,500,000	6.4

The full hedge now calls for 24 June contracts, i.e. 12 of the existing contracts in the March future should be closed out rather than rolled into June contracts.

$$\text{Realized loss on 12 March contracts} = 12 \times 25 \times 98$$
$$= \$29,400$$

The incorrect cash flow forecasting has resulted in a substantial realized loss unrelated to basic movements in one-month interest rates on cash investments. This brings out an important point for corporations hedging expected cash flows with futures positions. Incorrect cash flow forecasts can result in very substantial windfall gains or losses depending on the accuracy of the corporation's overall interest rate forecasts. In many cases, the corporation may choose not to hedge the mean expected cash flow forecast, but rather that portion of cash flow which it is absolutely certain to receive. This is equivalent to the corporation hedging only a portion of expected cash flows.

Hedging expected cash flow investment rates

1. Always take into account your confidence in your cash flow forecasts in determining what proportion to hedge.
2. Good regression estimates and correlations are vital in corporate cross-hedging.
3. Always look at cash/ futures basis in designing hedging strategies. Remember for cross-hedging, basis is two things: the futures price relative to equivalent price of the instrument it is written on; and the cash instrument equivalent price relative to the cash rate being hedged.
4. Constantly update your interest rate forecasts and adjust your hedge accordingly.

Another use of futures hedging for corporations is to hedge against increases in interest rates payable on variable rate loans. Long-term fixed rate bank lending has become a thing of the past with the increased volatility of money market interest rates, and virtually all bank term loans are variable rate loans with the interest rate adjusted to market rates at regular intervals called rollover dates. Rollover intervals are most frequently three months or six months although other periods are possible.

Futures contracts can be used by corporations to lock in the interest rates at these rollover rates, effectively converting the variable rate bank loan into a fixed rate loan again. A numerical example of this technique is not necessary, because for the corporation it is simply a mirror image of the procedure illustrated in section A for a commercial bank using the futures market to lock in a fixed borrowing rate for a customer, except that in this case, the corporate borrower carries out the relevant futures transactions directly.

In fact, given that access to the interbank forward-forward market is not easy for corporate customers, and certainly not on the right side of the bid-ask spread, corporations are more likely to be seen using futures to lock future borrowing rates than banks to lock in future lending rates.

2. Example of foreign exchange hedges

Corporations may use foreign exchange futures as substitutes for the forward market in currencies.

1 March: A UK firm is planning to import chemicals worth $4 million from the United States on 1 June. The current exchange rate is $1.6149 to the pound; the three-month forward rate is 1.6065; and the June LIFFE $/£ futures price is $1.6090.

Consider a futures hedge:

Cash market	**Futures market**
1 March	1 March
Spot rate is $1.6149	Sell 99 June sterling futures at $1.6090
$4,000,000 = £2,476,933.60	(£25,000 units)
	Contracts' value = £2,475,000
	= $3,982,275 at $1.6090/£
1 June	1 June
Spot rate is $1.56	Buy 99 June sterling futures at $1.5560
Buy $4,000,000 which costs £2,564,102.60	Contracts' value = $3,851,100
Opportunity loss = £87,169.00	Futures gain = $131,175
	Which at $1.56 = £84,086.54

$$\text{Hedge efficiency} = \frac{£84,086.54}{£87,169.00} = 96.5\%$$

This was a successful hedge: a net translation loss of £3,082.46 compares with an opportunity loss of $87,169.00 if the position had been left unhedged. There were two elements in the hedge's modest inefficiency. First, there was an adverse change in the basis—this was a short hedge, i.e. long in the cash market and short in the futures market. Since the basis went from a positive 59 ticks (1.6149 − 1.6090)/0.0001 on 1 March to only +40 ticks (1.56 − 1.556)/0.0001 on 1 June, each contract showed a net loss due to basis change of nine ticks or $47.50, representing a total cash loss of £3,014.42 (99 contracts × $47.50 ÷ 1.5600). Thus the hedger might have considered hedging with a more deferred futures contract where convergence might be less.

The other minor element in hedge inefficiency illustrates an important point where hedging is done with futures contracts as opposed to forward contracts. The standardized nature of the LIFFE and IMM foreign exchange contracts often makes it impossible to hedge exactly the desired cash exposure. For instance, in the case above the exposure was exactly $4,000,000, but the dollar amount of the futures hedge on 1 March was only $3,982,275; i.e. there was a net dollar exposure of $17,725.00 left unhedged. This produced a small further opportunity loss to the hedge strategy as the spot sterling rate declined over the period.

It is interesting in this case to compare the rate actually obtained through the futures market with that which could have been obtained through the forward market. To do this, the futures rate needs to be adjusted for transactions costs and the adverse change in the basis.

Forward:	$4,000,000 at $1.6065/£	=	£2,468,884.80
Futures:	$4,000,000 at $1.5600/£	=	£2,564,102.60
	Add transactions costs of £30 per contract	=	£2,970 (99 × 30)
	Less futures gain	=	£84,086.54
	Net cost	=	£2,482,986.10

$$\text{Implied futures exchange rate} = \$1.6110 \left(\frac{4,000,000}{2,482,986.10} \right)$$

Despite the adverse basis move and the transactions cost of purchasing futures, the effective exchange rate at $1.6110 was 0.0045 cents better than that available in the forward market.

In addition, while the profitable futures position was open, the firm may have been earning interest on surplus variation margin. However, this is not the whole story. The firm would have run the risk of having to put up additional variation margin if the pound had strengthened. There would also probably have been interest costs in putting up initial margins. On the other hand, by using futures the firm would not use up bank credit lines, as it would have done through operating in the forward market.

Thus, the decision whether to use foreign exchange futures or the foreign exchange forward market will depend upon a hedger's careful assessment of costs and risks. For example, the extra 0.0045 cents per pound on offer in the example may not be sufficient to compensate for the risk of adverse margin requirements for many corporations. Moreover, for very large corporations who are able to demand extremely fine forward rates from banks, the heavy transactions costs associated with the relatively small size of currently traded foreign exchange futures contracts may make futures trading uneconomic compared with forward trading. In forward trading it is also easy to match the exact cash exposure with the hedger's forward commitment.

Nonetheless, there are advantages to using the futures market, particularly for the smaller corporation. It is frequently more difficult to unwind a forward position when it is deemed no longer necessary by the hedger. The smaller corporation will not get as good forward rates as the larger corporation from the commercial banks, particularly if the transaction is in small size, say less than $1 million or equivalent. In such cases, the futures market which quotes the same identical rate to all customers may be an acceptable alternative. On the whole, the foreign exchange futures market would not provide much competition for the forward market for large multinational corporations. The smaller corporation and individual may well, on the other hand, find implied rates in futures keener than those in the forward market. In any case, it is always worth hedgers comparing implied rates in both markets before a decision is taken on which market to use.

3. Example of hedging a corporate bond issue

A corporation wishes to borrow long-term funds through the debenture market at a subsequent date to finance a capital project, but likes the look of current interest rates. Since the exposure is in a long-term instrument, the appropriate hedging vehicle is clearly the LIFFE gilt contract. Let us assume that the corporation intends to issue £25,000,000 of 15-year bonds in 12 months time. Current coupon rates on debentures of this quality and maturity are 12%. The company decides to hedge the bond issue on LIFFE. The date is 1 March.

1. Determine present value of a 1% rise in bond rates for corporation.

$$\text{Nominal cost} = £25,000,000 \times 0.01 \times 15 \text{ years} = £3,750,000$$

Present value of an extra £125,000 interest per half-year for 30 years with a 10% annual discount rate = £1,921,556.40

2. Determine cheapest deliverable gilt
Currently Treasury 15.5% 1998
Conversion factor = 1.2446

3. Determine regression coefficient between 20-year government stock yields and equivalent grade 15-year corporate bonds.

15-year corporate bond yield = 1.460 + 0.95 (20-year government bond yield)

4. Determine futures price change for a 1% yield change.
Current price of LIFFE March future 103-10 (11.572%)
For LIFFE standardized gilt, yield of 12.572% implies price of 95-27.

$$1\% \text{ increase in yield} = \text{Price fall of 239 ticks}$$

5. Determine number of contracts for hedge:

$$\frac{£1,921,556.40}{239 \times £15.625} \times 0.95 = 488.8 \text{ contracts sold}$$

Result: 1 March following year

Cash market
Corporate bond rate = 13.5%
Present value of additional
 interest = £2,882,334.60

Futures market
Buy 489 contracts at 92-14 (13.072%)
Profit = 348 ticks × 489 contracts × £15.625
 = £2,658,937.5

$$\text{Hedge efficiency} = \frac{£2,658,937.50}{£2,882,334.60} = 92.3\%$$

Although this is a good hedge for the corporate bond issuer, it is by no means perfect. This is despite the fact that the rise in the interest rate on the corporate bond issue is exactly equal to that of the rise in yield to maturity on the gilt contract.

This result occurs because, although there is a linear relationship between the present value of additional interest on the corporate bond and an interest rate change, there is not a linear relationship between the yield to maturity of the gilt contract and its price. Thus the rise in the gilt yield to maturity from 11.572% to 12.572% produced a price change of 239 ticks, but the yield change from 12.572% to 13.072% produced a price change of only 109 ticks. Moreover, the relationship is not even symmetrical around a particular starting point.

A decline in yield to maturity from 11.572% to 10.572% would cause the gilt price to rise by 261 ticks. In the case above, therefore, to produce a better hedge, one would have needed to adjust the size of the hedge as the interest rate and yield to maturity rose by 1% and beyond. In addition, since the interest rate change and the yield to maturity moved in exact parallel, the regression coefficient shown earlier was not a good predictor of interest rate relationships over the hedge period.

Another possibility is to take into account the general assumption that the gilt contract will trade off the cheapest deliverable gilt, which is the Treasury 15.5% 1998, adjusted by a conversion factor. The assumption that conversion factors will always describe relative price movements regardless of yield is not always valid. Hence a 1% change in yield of the Treasury 15.5% may not produce a price change 1.2446 times the price change that would occur in a 20-year 12% gilt for a 1% yield change. The procedure in this case is to determine the price change that will be produced in the Treasury 15.5% at its current price. This divided by the conversion factor will give the equivalent price change in the standard gilt, which can then be divided into the present value of the interest opportunity loss to produce the appropriate hedge.

This is an example of perturbation hedging. Tests using price data on the Chicago Board of Trade for Treasury bonds suggests it may be somewhat better than conversion factor hedging even for Treasury bond portfolios.

Another more precise way of formulating the hedge would be to use the duration approach. Suppose we assume the cheapest to deliver gilt, the Treasury $15\frac{1}{2}$% 1998, is trading at 128-16, implying a redemption yield of 12.17. This in turn implies a duration of 7.43. To determine the hedge:

1. Implied percentage change in (1 + redemption yield)

$$= [(1.13/1.12) - 1] \times 100 = 0.89\%$$

2. Implied percentage change in (1 + redemption yield) for cheapest to deliver gilt assuming regression coefficient of 0.95 = 0.85%

3. Implied price change of cheapest to deliver gilt

$$= (128\text{-}16) \, (0.0085) \, (7.43)$$
$$= 8\text{-}04$$

4. Implied price change in gilt futures contract

$$\frac{8\text{-}04}{1.2446} = 6\text{-}17$$

5. Equivalent value of futures price change

$$209 \text{ ticks} \times £15.625 \text{ per tick} = £3,265.625$$

6. Optimal hedge

$$\frac{£1,921,556.40}{£3,265.625} = 588 \text{ contracts}$$

7. Result: 1 March following year

Cash market

Corporate bond rate = 13.5%
Present value of additional
    interest = £2,882,334.60

Futures market

Sell 588 contracts at 103–10
Buy 588 contracts at 92–14
Profit = 348 ticks × 588 contracts × £15.625
    = £3,197.250

8. Hedge efficiency = $\dfrac{£3,197,250}{£2,882,334.60}$ = 110.9%

Thus although it is relatively easy to design a hedge to protect against a specific forecast interest rate change, the hedger needs to be aware that if interest rates change by a different amount, then even if the exact relationship between corporate interest rates and gilt yields is maintained, the hedge will be imperfect. In particular, in the case shown above, if the futures position were showing a loss and there was a saving in interest expense on the corporate bond, the company would find itself involved in a net cash outflow over the life of the hedge.

In addition to the various hedging possibilities for commercial corporations described here using financial futures, many of the examples shown for commercial banks and portfolio managers are also applicable to corporate customers (*see* sections A and B). Firms can hedge seasonal cash flows, lock in rates on intended short-term investments, and lock in rates at which they will issue commercial paper at future dates. In these circumstances, it is somewhat surprising that commercial hedging usage of the Chicago futures markets has been relatively limited. This may change in the future.

D. Underwriting applications of financial futures

Equity and bond underwriters frequently have to take a temporary cash position in fixed interest or equity securities. In the United States, both government securities and corporate stocks and fixed interest securities are most often issued through underwriters. An underwriter purchases newly issued securities from a corporation or government, usually at a fixed price and then resells the securities to investors. Alternatively, the underwriters may guarantee to acquire the whole of an issue from the issuers at a fixed price, if insufficient investors are prepared to purchase the issue at that price. In the former case, underwriter earnings are the difference between the price the underwriter pays for the issue and the proceeds of the resale. In the latter case, more frequent in the UK, the underwriters would be paid an agreed fee for their underwriting guarantee. In either case, in the period between the date at which the issue price is fixed and the price at which the stock is sold on to the market, the underwriters face a risk that the issue will decline substantially in value.

With large issues, such as the recent issue of Britoil shares in the UK, the underwriting risks can be very large. The concessions or fees received by underwriters can be wiped out and large financial losses incurred if there is a sharp price drop before the shares or bonds can be sold to the market.

Dealers in the United States who take such risks with Treasury bond auctions, domestic and Eurobond placements, and stock issues have increasingly tended to hedge all or part of their risk in the financial futures market. Below is a typical example of this type of hedging.

Underwriting a stock issue

On 5 April, the Fitz Investment Corporation underwrites a $50,000,000 issue of XYZ common stock, beta = 1.0, at $50 per share. Current market price is $52 a share.
June S + P 100 index future = 155.00

5 April

Hedges 50% of underwriting liability:

$$\text{Number of contracts} = \frac{\$25,000,000}{\$77,500 \ (500 \times 155.00)} = 322.6$$

Sells 323 contracts at 155.00

7 April
Issue is 40% subscribed at $50.50 per share
S + P 500 June future = 151.15.

$$\text{Underwriting opportunity loss on 40\% subscription} = \left(\frac{\$20,000,000}{\$50}\right)(\$1.50)$$

$$= \$600,000$$

Buys (323) (0.4) or 129 contracts at 151.15:

$$\text{Futures profit} = 129 \text{ contracts} \times \$25 \text{ per tick} \times 77 \text{ ticks} \left(\frac{155.00 - 151.15}{0.05}\right)$$

$$= \$248,325$$

9 April
Market trading of issue begins
Market price = 48.25
S + P index future 144.00

$$\text{Underwriting opportunity loss on remaining 60\%} = \left(\frac{\$30,000,000}{\$50}\right)(52.00 - 48.25)$$

$$= \$2,250,000$$

Buys remaining 194 contracts at 144.00:

$$\text{Futures profit} = 194 \text{ contracts} \times \$25 \text{ per tick} \times 220 \text{ ticks} \left(\frac{155.00 - 144.00}{0.05}\right)$$

$$= \$1,067,000$$

Taking into account that the intention was to hedge 50% of underwriting risk:

$$\text{Hedge efficiency} = \frac{\$248,325 + \$1,067,000}{(0.5)(\$600,000 + \$2,250,000)}$$

$$= \frac{\$1,315,325}{\$1,425,000} = 92.3\%$$

Hedging away the systematic risk of the stock produced a 92.3% efficient hedge. Unsystematic risk elements plus possible adverse movements in basis will ensure that the hedge is rarely perfect. However, the underwriter is probably quite happy with the hedge shown.

Hedging corporate or government bonds will follow similar principles, save that in the case of corporate bonds the structure of the hedge will be determined by the value of the regression coefficient between changes in the price of similar grade corporate bonds and changes in the price of the Treasury bond or LIFFE gilt contract, and in the case of Treasury bond issues by the relevant conversion factor between the newly issued bond and standard 20-year 8% Treasury bond future, or equivalent perturbation or duration measures.

This ability to hedge underwriting risk should improve the efficiency of the new issue market in all forms of fixed interest and equity securities. Even so, it is likely that the hedging process would be improved still further by the provision of financial futures contracts written on domestic corporate bond indices and Eurobond indices. Several exchanges including LIFFE, the CBT and Intex are contemplating contracts of this kind.

E. Mortgage hedging with financial futures

In the United States, the provision of mortgages, both for private housebuyers, and for builders and property developers, has tended to involve mainly fixed rate loans as opposed to the variable rate loans more common in the UK and Europe. This method of issuing fixed rate long-term loans and funding them with short-term funds has led to a whole new set of risks which can be hedged in the financial futures market, particularly the GNMA market. The

GNMA futures market provides a means for bankers to hedge mortgage values for sales occurring in the future, and indeed provides an alternative method of making those sales.

For instance, a mortgage banker who is in the process of accumulating a pool for the purpose of originating a GNMA encounters various potential delays. First, there will generally be a 60–90 day lag between applications for mortgages and completion of the loans. Second, it may take some time to build up a suitable loan portfolio. Since the rate on the mortgage is generally fixed at some point significantly before the closing date on each loan, changes in mortgage interest rates can have a substantial impact on the resale value of the mortgages in the GNMA pool. This in turn can have a major impact upon the profitability and cash flow of the mortgage banker. The banker can avoid this risk by hedging the anticipated transactions in the GNMA futures market. Then any loss incurred in selling the mortgage pool at a discount from the purchase price will be compensated for by corresponding profits in the GNMA futures market. The design of the hedge will follow the basic principles outlined earlier. In addition a holder of a long position in conventional mortgages could also hedge with a short position in GNMA futures, although the correlation between conventional mortgage rates and GNMA future implied rates will probably not be as close as that between cash GNMA prices and GNMA futures prices.

The mortgage banker would probably also wish to compare the GNMA futures hedge with alternative hedging strategies. Mortgages can be sold directly to a private investor or through the Federal National Mortgage Association auctions. If operating through the GNMA market seems preferable, the pool originator has the alternative of selling the GNMA securities directly at a fixed price through either the GNMA standby market or the GNMA pass-through forward market. Any hedge by a GNMA pool originator in the GNMA futures must be carefully compared with all these alternatives before a final hedging decision is made.[2]

A mortgage banker could also actually use the GNMA futures market to make delivery of a mortgage pool if this should prove economical. Similarly, GNMA futures contracts can often be used to recover the costs of standby commitments previously paid.

Another use of GNMA futures for hedging is for builders constructing housing developments. To ensure ready availability of mortgage funds, builders will often enter into arrangements with thrift institutions which will, in exchange for a commitment fee, undertake to provide a fixed dollar amount of mortgage funds within a specific time period. Frequently these funds would be provided at the market rate at the time of the mortgage closing. However, the builder, in order to sell his houses easily, may be keen to assure home-buyers that their mortgage rates will not exceed a certain level. One method he has for achieving this is through a short hedge in the GNMA futures market. A typical example is given below.

Example

1 June
  Thirty-year conventional mortgage rates are 10.75%.
  A thrift commitment for $5 million of mortgage funds for one year costs 0.75% for market rate mortgages equal to $37,500.00.
  Builder wishes to guarantee mortgage rates no higher than 11.50%

Hedging strategy design

1. If conventional mortgage rates rise to 11.25%, the builder will hedge $2.5 million of the commitment in the GNMA futures market.
2. If mortgage rates rise to 11.5%, builder will hedge a further $2.5 million in the GNMA futures market.
3. Positions will be offset if a sale occurs and buyer obtains a mortgage from the thrift or when rates fall back below 11.25%.

The question of coupon slippage comes into this hedge. Higher coupon instruments will show a bigger dollar change in value than low coupon instruments. Hence a larger futures

---

[2] For an excellent description of the detailed techniques of mortgage bank operations in GNMA futures, see E. W. Schwartz, *How to use Interest Rate Futures*, Dow-Jones, 1979.

hedge will be needed to hedge a 12% instrument than an 8% instrument. The amount of coupon slippage depends upon the coupon, the overall level of interest rates and the maturity of the security. In this case, the builder is trying to hedge a conventional mortgage interest rate change with a futures price change. For the sake of simplicity, however, it is assumed that regression relationships are determined by using current yields rather than yields to maturity.

Numbers of contracts

At 11.5% assume the thrift will require payment of 2% per 0.25% annual interest for mortgage interest reduction.

Cost of insulating each 1% interest over 11.5% = \$400,000

June (following year) GNMA contracts = 66-21 (12.00 current yield)
1% rise in current yield = equivalent GNMA price of 61-17

Futures gain when current yield moves from 12% to 13%
= 164 ticks × \$31.25 per tick = \$5,125

Δ Conventional mortgage rate = 1.00 Δ GNMA futures current yield

Number of contracts for hedge of 1% (11.5 → 12.5) interest rate change

$$= \frac{400,000}{\$5,125} = 78.05 \text{ contracts}$$

But futures gain when current yield
moves from 13% to 14% = 140 ticks (61-17 − 67-05) × \$31.25 per tick = \$4,375

Number of contracts for hedge of 1% (12.5 → 13.5) rate change $= \dfrac{400,000}{\$4,375} = 91.4$ contracts

Hence size of hedge will increase with each jump in conventional mortgage rate over 11.5%.

Hedging results

1 June: Builder buys commitment described above. Cost = \$37,500

1 October: Mortgage rates rise to 11.26%
              Builder sells 39 June GNMA contracts at 65-30

1 December: Mortgage rates rise to 11.60%
              Builder sells 39 more June GNMA contracts at 64-00

1 March: Closing takes place on \$1.4 million of mortgage. Rate = 11.40%.
              Builder closes out 22 contracts at 64-08
              Futures profit = 22 contracts × \$31.25 per tick × 54 ticks (65-30 − 64-08)
                          = \$37,125

1 May: Closing takes place on remaining \$3.6 million of mortgages. Market
                  rate = 12.00%
              Builder closes out remaining 56 June GNMA contracts at 62-16.

Futures profit (a) 17 contracts × \$31.25 × 110 ticks (65-30 − 62-16)
                              = \$58,437
                   (b) 39 contracts × \$31.25 × 48 ticks (64-00 − 62-16)
                              = \$58,500

Total cumulative futures profit = \$154,062.5
Cost of compensating thrift for ½% mortgage interest = (0.04) (\$3,600,000)
                                                    = \$144,000

Hedge efficiency = 154,062.5/144,000 = 107%

This was a very successful hedge by the builder—indeed the excess profit on the hedge actually covered a proportion of the original commitment fee demanded by the thrift institution. The choice of 78 contracts as a hedge was designed to protect the builder against a 1% rise in interest rates. Since the actual rise was only $\frac{1}{2}$% by the end of the hedge period, the builder was overhedged and therefore reaped a windfall gain. On the other hand this overhedging might have affected him adversely in the other direction had he not originally decided to remove the hedge if interest rates went back through 11.25%. The windfall gain to overhedging in this case concealed the fact that the assumed regression coefficient of 1.00 between conventional mortgage rate changes and changes in the current yield on the standard GNMA contract was not a good predictor of relative changes. In fact, empirical evidence suggests that for significant periods of time, conventional mortgage rates and GNMA yields are not closely correlated. Any builder hedging conventional mortgages with GNMA futures must take this additional basis risk into account.

F. Conclusions

This chapter has, through the use of numerous examples, tried to give a flavour of the type of hedging that different institutions can use in the financial futures market. Although some examples were quite complex, they do not compare with the actual complexities of real-life hedging, and the difficulties of setting up a hedging programme. For example, except in isolated cases, the examples have omitted commission costs and margin costs. The cost of initial margin and commissions has to be included in the cost of a hedging strategy. Normally this is done by adjusting the observed futures price to determine an effective futures price (*see* the foreign exchange futures hedge example, p. 110).

Variation margin risk is more difficult to handle. It may be ignored altogether by assuming that futures prices are just as likely to move in one way or another, or simulations can be run on different assumptions about futures price changes to examine the impact of alternative variation margin scenarios on hedge profitability. But the importance of the adverse interest rate or exchange rate forecast on which the hedge decision is based must be remembered. If that forecast is fulfilled and the futures side of the hedge is profitable, as in most of the examples discussed to a greater or lesser degree, additional profits will accrue to the hedge via surplus variation margin payments.

This chapter has dealt only with a limited survey of some hedge possibilities in a few types of institutions. The list of institutions or people which could hedge with financial futures is extremely long: among ones not discussed are savings and loan institutions in the United States, building societies in the UK, investment banks, jobbers, commodity dealers, insurance companies, etc. The use of financial futures for hedging is an area that is only beginning to be explored, and there should be a considerable extension of commercial, as opposed to speculative, usage of these markets in the years to come.

Chapter 6
Trading and speculating in financial futures

This chapter looks at the techniques and strategies that can be adopted by investors who are not so much interested in hedging interest rate and foreign exchange rate risk, as taking on such risks in the hope of substantial profits. Such investors in financial futures markets are generally known as speculators in the United States and traders in the United Kingdom. They operate in the financial futures markets because they believe they can forecast movements in absolute or relative interest and foreign exchange rates better than the rest of the market.

Traders generally take on the interest or foreign exchange rate risk which hedgers are trying to get rid of; and they expect to be paid for their trouble in doing this. There should, therefore, be a net transfer of funds from hedgers to traders on the financial futures exchanges. Traders in financial futures should on average make money, though presumably good or efficient speculators will make more money than bad or inefficient speculators.

The essential characteristic of a trader in financial futures is that he is taking a view on the future evolution of rates, either because he believes he can forecast better than the market, or because he believes two or more futures and/or cash prices are out of line. He could be taking a view on the overall level of rates, called *open position trading*; he could be taking a view on the evolution of the relationship between two different futures prices, called *spread trading*; or he could be looking to profit from price discrepancies and inconsistencies, called *arbitrage trading*. The various traders will also differ in their timing of futures market transactions. Some traders will be in and out of the market minute by minute or even second by second, and are generally known as scalpers. Some traders will be willing to hold positions longer but never overnight and are known as day traders. Finally there are those traders who will hold positions for much longer, perhaps for days, weeks or even months. The length of time for which an individual trader takes a view may be highly variable, but different traders tend to specialize in a particular duration.

No matter what view the trader takes or in what time-frame he operates, he must be aware that he is dealing in volatile, high-risk instruments, and his trading strategy must reflect this fact. A trader cannot expect to make money on every trade. Some trades will go right and some will go wrong; the question is whether the sum of a trader's positions makes profits over some appropriate time period. A key input into the profitability of financial futures trading is the extreme volatility of interest and foreign exchange rates, characteristic of modern financial markets. Combined with the high leverage that is provided by the financial futures market, and the principle of marking to market, this rate volatility means that big changes are possible in a trader's financial position over very short periods.

It is worth restating the sort of leverage that is available with financial futures. An initial margin of only $1,000 is required to set up a long position of $1,000,000 in Eurodollar time deposit rates by buying one futures contract on LIFFE. The tick size for Eurodollar deposit futures is $25. So, if the futures price rises by 50 basis points, reflecting a fall in short-term interest rates, the trader's position will show a profit of $1,250 (50 × $25), i.e. the trader has made a positive return of over 100% on his original capital investment of $1,000. But volatility can work the other way as well—not only profits are credited to the trader's account daily, but losses as well. If rates had risen by 50 points and prices fallen, the trader would have had to deposit variation margin of $1,250, reflecting the loss of over 100% of his capital. A trader will have to be extremely careful in deciding how much finance to devote to financial futures trading, and how long to continue to run a futures position which is losing money.

The efficient trader will also need to be aware of all the basic concepts of financial futures operations. He needs to be aware of the tick sizes for different contracts, to be able to work out quickly the profitability of his trades. He needs to know the different classes of orders that can be used on the exchanges, and how to use all the different techniques of fundamental and technical analysis to help him assess correctly the outlook for the market.

A. Open position trading

When a trader initiates a plain open position in a financial futures contract, he is backing his opinion that interest rates or exchange rates implicit in financial futures prices are going to move in a particular direction. If a trader believes interest rates are going to rise, which in turn means futures prices are going to fall, a short position in futures should be established. Similarly, if it is believed that interest rates are going to fall, then a long position in the futures contract would be established.

Example
A trader on 1 June believes short-term interest rates will fall and sells one September sterling time deposit future on LIFFE at a price of 88.5 (100-11.5)

Date	Action	Futures price	Initial margin	Variation margin	Profit
1.6.83	Sell 1 contract	88.5	−£500	0	0
2.6.83	Hold	89.0	—	−£312.50	−£312.50
3.6.83	Hold	88.75	—	+£156.25	−£156.25
4.6.83	Hold	88.30	—	+£281.25	+£125.00
7.6.83	Hold	88.15	—	+£ 93.75	+£218.75
8.6.83	Buy 1 contract	88.00	+£500	+£ 93.75	+£312.50

The trader sold short a three-month sterling futures contract because he thought rates were going to go up, putting up an initial margin of £500. At first, rates fell, pushing futures prices up, and the trader had to put up variation margin of £312.50 on 2 June to cover the losses on his futures position. By 8 June, however, the position was showing a profit of 50 basis points or £312.50, so he closed out the position by buying a September sterling futures contract. At that point, the original initial margin of £500 would also be paid back to the trader.

When would a trader be likely to set up an open position of this kind? The most likely situation is when the trader takes a view different to the general view that is held in the market. A classic example of open position trading is the establishment of a financial futures position just before the announcement of important economic statistics. A large volume of futures trading in the United States tends to occur around the publication of the weekly money supply figures.

Example

Friday 16 November, 2:00pm
The Federal Reserve will announce the change in M2 later in the day. The market consensus is for a rise of about $1 billion. As a trader, you feel the rise will be much higher than the market expects, and that after the announcement rates will rise sharply. You decide to sell 10 Treasury bond contracts (December) on the Chicago Board of Trade at the current price of 74-00, with a stop-loss buy order at 75-00.

Friday 16 November, 5:00pm
The money supply figures showed a drop of $1 billion—well below market expectations.

Monday 19 November
The CBT Treasury bond December future opened sharply up at 74-30 and prices traded quickly up to 75-10. The stop-loss was triggered at 75-00 at which price 10 contracts were sold.

Result of open position trade
Short 10 contracts at 74-00
Buy 10 contracts at 75-00

Ticks lost = 32
Cash loss = 10 × 32 × $31.25 = $10,000

The trader's rate forecast was in the wrong direction, and he lost 32 ticks on each Treasury bond contract. His limit order probably reduced his potential losses; if the market traded quickly up from 74–30 to 75–10, he might not have been able to get out at 75–00 unless his order was already with the market.

A given change in interest rates also leads to a much bigger change in the price of the Treasury bond contracts than for short-term contracts.

The longer the maturity of the underlying instrument, the more risky is an open financial futures position.

The secret of good position trading, though, must lie in the trader's ability to accurately forecast interest and/or foreign exchange rates. As much as anything, the position trader needs a feel for the market which can only be developed with experience. Particularly important to the position trader is an appropriate use of limit and stop orders. The first rule of position trading remains the old adage:

Cut your losses and run your profits.

In the example above a stop-loss buy order at 75–00 and a profit-taking sell limit order at 71–16 would look like good trading: a stop-loss order at 76–00 and a profit-taking order at 73–00 would be stupid.

B. Spread trading

A less risky form of trading is spread trading—the simultaneous purchase and sale of related financial futures. Here, the trader takes a view on the relationship between two futures prices; such a position will generally display less volatility than a pure open position and will, in the case of trading in spreads on a single contract type, incur significantly lower margin requirements. It is probably the most common type of financial futures trading in the United States.

Before discussing different types of spread trading, a few definitions are necessary. A spread is the purchase of one futures contract and the simultaneous sale of a different but related futures contract.

Example

2 January: Buy one March three-month sterling time deposit future at 86–00
                Sell one June three-month sterling time deposit future at 85–00

The size of the spread which the trader is buying or selling is simply the nearby futures price minus the further out or deferred futures price.

Example

2 January	March futures price = 86.00
	June futures price = 85–00
	Spread = 86.00 − 85.00 = 100 basis points or ticks
3 January	March futures price = 85.00
	June futures price = 83.50
	Spread = 85.00 − 83.50 = 150 basis points or ticks

This example also serves to show how the trader expects to benefit from spread trading. Suppose that on 2 January the trader purchased the nearby contract and sold the deferred contract, termed *buying the spread*.

Example

2 January	Buy one March contract 86.00	Sell one June contract 85.00
3 January	Sell one March contract 85.00	Buy one June contract 83.50
Gain/loss	−100 ticks	+ 150 ticks

Net gain: 50 ticks × £6.25 = £312.50

The trader bought the spread (also sometimes called putting on a bull spread) and made a profit of £312.50 when the spread strengthened (became more positive). If the trader had done the opposite—sold the nearby futures contract and purchased the deferred futures contract, called *selling the spread*—he would have lost money as the spread strengthened. Traders who sell the spread make money when the spread weakens (becomes less positive). Knowledge of how you gain or lose from spread positions as the spread strengthens and weakens is essential for the spread trader.

Rules for successful spread trading

1. Buy the spread when you expect it to strengthen:
   - i.e. (a) become more positive;
   - (b) become less negative.
2. Sell the spread when you expect it to weaken:
   - i.e. (a) become more negative;
   - (b) become less positive.

The secret to successful spread trading is the ability to recognize when the differential between two futures prices has got out of line with its equilibrium value. To help him determine this, the spread trader will need to use the techniques of fundamental and technical analysis (*see* Appendix 3).

Fundamental analysis concentrates on two important inputs into the determination of basis (cash prices minus futures prices) and spreads (nearby futures prices minus deferred futures prices). First, we know that open position trading—by traders taking a view on futures interest rates—will make the difference between two prices a function of how much the market expects interest rates will change between one futures month and another. If the trader has a different view than the market of how rates will move, he could put on a spread. The second fundamental input places an upper limit on what the spread should be. The difference between a cash and futures price, or between two futures prices, should not exceed the cost of carry, i.e. the net cost of purchasing an instrument at one date and delivering the instrument against a futures contract at a later date.

A spread trader will be watching those fundamental variables that impact upon future interest rates to see if they seem consistent with the spreads observable in the futures market. The same will apply to traders interested in spreads in foreign exchange rates. Exchange rate discounts or premiums must be consistent with the pattern of interest rates in the futures market; if they are not, spread trading may be advantageous. Technical analysis will also be useful to the spread trader for it attempts to predict the future of a time series from its own past. It could be applied to a series of spreads through time, as easily as to a series of actual interest rates or exchange rates.

Intra-contract spreading

This type of spread trading, known as *straddle trading* on LIFFE, involves purchasing and selling different maturities of the same futures contract on the same exchange. For instance, you could buy a straddle by the purchase of a June three-month sterling deposit future and the sale of a December sterling deposit future, or by the purchase of a September T-bill future on the IMM and the sale of a December future.

The spread trader will be looking for a change in the relationship between two futures prices. He is not interested in overall movements in interest rates and foreign exchange rates. If a nearby sterling futures contract is priced at 86·00 and the deferred contract at 85·00, and the prices then move to 84.00 and 83.00 respectively, the spread remains unchanged and the spread trader does not make money.

In intra-contract spreading, the concept of the cost of carry becomes extremely important. We have already said that it is a major input into basis and spreads. Ignoring expectational effects, we know that in equilibrium the net yield on a position should equal the cost of financing that position. If financing costs exceed the interest yield, the investor should be compensated by a negative spread between nearby and distant futures prices. This is known as a *negative cost of carry* situation. If financing costs are less than the interest yield, the cost of carry is said to be positive, and nearby futures prices will be higher than deferred futures prices.

Below is an example where a trader believes short-term financing costs will rise in the future, i.e. he believes the cost of carry will become more positive. Since this implies a more negatively sloped T-bill prices line, he decides to sell the spread.

Example

5 January   IMM T-bill futures prices—March 88.00
                                June   87.50

Forecast: Cost of carry to rise; deferred futures prices to fall relative to nearby futures.

Action: Buy the spread—Buy one March future 88.00
                        Sell one June future   87.50
                        Spread = 88.00 − 87.50 = 50 basis points

20 January   IMM T-bill futures prices—March 87.30
                                  June   86.48

Action: Sell the spread—Sell one March future 87.30
                        Buy one June future   86.48
                        Spread = 87.30 − 86.48 = 82 basis points

                   Profit to the spread trade = 32 ticks × $25 = $800

Things went right for the spread trader. The forecast that financing costs would rise was correct, the T-bill futures line became steeper, and selling the spread was a profitable transaction yielding $800. Moreover the trader notes that he realized a profit regardless of the fact that the overall level of rates rose and the general level of futures prices fell between 5 January and 20 January.

These same cost of carry arguments apply to longer-term instruments such as Treasury bonds and LIFFE gilt contracts. This is because the spreads between LIFFE gilt futures correspond to a three-month sterling interest rate. Suppose a trader purchased a June LIFFE gilt futures contract and sold a September contract. If he took delivery on the contract in June, and held the gilt to redeliver in September, he would earn on his position the running yield on the contract plus or minus any spread between the two contracts. The futures prices contain an implicit short-term interest rate for the June–September period. The example below shows how to calculate such an implicit rate.

Example

LIFFE gilt futures prices: June 89-09   September 89-16

Step 1: Calculate yield equivalent of spread of 7/32 on annual basis

$$\text{Yield} = \left[\frac{7/32}{89\ 9/32} \right] \times \frac{365}{91} = 0.99\%$$

Step 2: Calculate running yield on June gilt future

$$\text{Yield} = 12\% \times \frac{100}{89\ 9/32} = 13.49\%$$

Step 3: Add together running yield and spread yield to get implicit three-month rate

$$\text{Implicit rate} = 13.49 + 0.99 = 14.48\%$$

If a trader believes that this short-term rate looks too high compared with his forecast of future short-term rates, and he believes the overall level of gilt futures prices will not alter, he would expect the spread to narrow. He should therefore sell the spread.

Example

10 April   Sell the spread —Sell one June gilt contract 89-09
                        Buy one Sept. gilt contract 80-16
                        Spread = 7/32

17 April   Buy the spread—Buy one June gilt contract 91-00
                        Sell one June gilt contract 91-08
                        Spread = 8/32

                   Loss on spread trade = 1/32 = −£15.625

The trader made a small loss on the spread trade; but the implicit three-month sterling rate for the new futures prices of 91 and 91-08 is 14.29%, i.e. the trader forecast the direction of short-term rates correctly but lost on the trade. This is because he forgot to take into account that a change in the June futures price alters the running yield on the gilt-edged stock, so that a higher spread differential is required to produce an equivalent implicit short-term rate. He could get round this problem by buying more September contracts than he sells June contracts—a process known as *tailing*. However, the general conclusion must be that spread trading on cost of carry forecasts is best carried out using the short end of the futures markets.

Rules for cost of carry spread trading

1. If you expect the cost of carry to become more positive or less negative, buy the spread.
2. If you expect the cost of carry to become less positive or more negative, sell the spread.

In spread trading, the trader also needs to be aware that futures contracts prices often behave erratically as the delivery date gets nearer. It is usually recommended not to put on or hold on to spread positions where the nearby contract is very near its delivery date.

Intra-contract spreading in foreign exchange rate futures is based on very similar principles to interest rate spreading. The interest parity theorem (discussed in Chapter 3) held that the differential between two exchange rates at two different time periods must equal the difference between domestic and foreign interest rates over the period. The example below shows how this information could be used to justify a spread trade.

Example

You observe the following futures price on LIFFE.

	Sterling deposit futures	Eurodollar deposit futures	$/£ foreign exchange futures
June	88.00	84.53	2.1825
September	87.50	84.47	2.2105

Analysis

$$\text{Ratio: } \frac{\text{September FX rate}}{\text{June FX rate}} = \frac{1 + \text{June Eurodollar rate on a 3-month basis}}{1 + \text{June sterling rate on a 3-month basis}}$$

$$\text{June 3-month Eurodollar rate} = 15.47 \times \frac{91}{360} = 3.91\%$$

$$\text{June 3-month sterling rate} = 12.00 \times \frac{91}{365} = 2.99\%$$

$$\text{Implied September FX rate} = 2.1825 \times \frac{1.0391}{1.0299} = 2.2020$$

$$\text{Implicit spread from interest rate comparison} = 2.1825 - 2.2020$$

$$= (0.0195)$$

$$\text{Actual spread} = 2.1825 - 2.2105 = (0.0280)$$

Conclusion

Spread is too heavily negative. Buy the spread.

The basic aim in intra-contract spreading is to predict how the spread is going to move. The trader looks at fundamental and technical forecasts for the spread. He examines prices in other futures markets to see if they provide him with additional information. He looks at average, minimum and maximum spreads of the same type in the past to see if the current spread looks right. And in the end he must back his judgement by opening a spread position.

Exhibit 6.1 shows the evolution of a couple of typical straddles on the IMM over the course of 1982: December 1982 T-bills minus March 1983 T-bills; and December CDs minus March CDs. The first point to make is that spreads are quite volatile: the T-bill spread moved from zero in the latter half of June to nearly 400 basis points at the beginning of August, falling back to only 20 basis points later in the month. A trader who was able to trade a bull spread from bottom to top and then switch into a bear spread from top to bottom would show a profit of $19,500 on an initial investment of only $400. There is also some useful information for hedgers: T-bill spreads are consistently larger than CD spreads, though the differences become smaller with time. This tendency could play a part in basis hedging strategies. The lesson, however, is that spread trading is still a high-risk strategy; spreads do move a great deal through time. On the other hand, the rewards to a spread trader who could pick some or all of the turning points in T-bill and CD spreads in 1982 would have been very large.

Exhibit 6.1: Behaviour of straddles through time

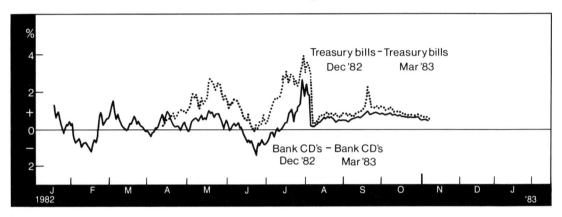

Source: Eurocharts

Inter-contract spreading

This is a more complicated type of spread trading, involving the simultaneous purchase and sale of futures contracts written on different underlying financial instruments on either the same or different futures exchanges. For instance, a classic inter-contract spread on LIFFE would be to purchase a June sterling deposit future and sell a Eurodollar deposit future, or on the IMM to purchase a three-month T-bill contract and sell a 90-day domestic CD contract. An inter-contract spread on different exchanges might involve purchasing a June Eurodollar deposit contract on LIFFE and selling a June domestic CD contract on the IMM.

The considerations in setting up spreads of this kind are more complex than for simple intra-contract spreads. Consider the first spread mentioned—a Eurodollar deposit/sterling deposit spread on LIFFE. A trader might put on such a spread if he believed sterling rates were going to rise relative to dollar rates. He would buy the Eurodollar contract and sell the sterling contract.

Example

7 January

	March	June	September
Eurodollar deposit future	91.13	90.81	90.53
Sterling deposit future	90.05	89.97	89.91

Spot exchange rate = $1.6100

The trader is going to buy Eurodollar futures and sell sterling futures; to insulate himself from overall interest rate movements, he needs to weight the quantities of the two contracts appropriately. If both rates rise 50 basis points, he wants his sterling deposit futures profits to exactly match his Eurodollar deposit futures loss.

$$50 \text{ ticks loss on Eurodollar} = 50 \times \$25 = \$1,250$$
$$50 \text{ ticks gain on sterling} = 50 \times £6.25 = £312.50$$

125

At current £/$ spot rate £312.50 = $503.125.

Hence sell the sterling deposit/Eurodollar spread for March in proportion one Eurodollar to 2.48 (1250/503.125) sterling contracts.

Sell five sterling deposit March contracts at 90.05

Buy two Eurodollar deposit March contracts at 91.13

On 14 January the trader observes the following prices.

	March	June	September
Eurodollar deposit	91.23	90.88	90.56
Sterling deposit	89.52	89.64	89.54

Spot $/£ spot exchange rate = 1.5830

The trader unwinds his inter-contract spread.

Buy five sterling deposit contracts at 89.52

$$\text{Profit} = 5 \times 53 \text{ ticks} \times £6.25$$
$$= £1,656.25$$

Sell two Eurodollar deposit contract at 91.23

$$\text{Profit} = 10 \text{ ticks} \times \$25 = \$250$$

$$\text{Total \$ profit} = \$(1,656.25)(1.5830) + \$250$$
$$= \$2,871.84$$

This is what happens to the spread: it was −108 ticks (90.05 − 91.13) and by 14 January had moved to −171 ticks. Hence the expected dollar return is 2 contracts × 63 ticks × $25 per tick = $3,150.00. The difference between the expected gain and the actual gain, which is quite minor in this case, is due to the fact that exchange rates moved against the trader. The profits or losses on one side of the spread are denominated in dollars: the profits or losses on the other leg of the spread are in sterling. Hence exchange rate changes could potentially wipe out profits on the interest rate spread even if the trader's view is correct. Spreads of this type are actually combinations of interest rate spreads and open positions in foreign exchange rates. In addition, the standard size of the contracts makes it almost impossible to perfectly match the Eurodollar and sterling futures positions. For instance, the perfect proportion was 1:2.48 but a spread in proportion 1:2.5 had to be put on. Thus although traders can use inter-contract spreads to speculate on relative movements in dollar interest rates and sterling interest rates, the additional risks to the strategy should be carefully evaluated.

Spreads between similar short-term instrument futures are more straightforward. There is no exchange risk, and a trader would put on such a spread if he believed, for example, dollar rates on two similar instruments were out of line.

Example

27 April	IMM domestic CD future	IMM Eurodollar deposit future	Inter-contract spread (basis points)
June	85.93	85.30	63
September	85.89	85.51	38
December	85.88	85.54	34

Action: The trader concludes the inter-contract spread for June is too heavily positive. He sells the inter-contract spread.

Sell one June CD future	85.93
Buy one June Eurodollar future	85.30

4 May	Domestic CD future	Eurodollar deposit future	Inter-contract spread
June	85.72	85.14	58
September	85.74	85.33	41
December	85.74	85.36	38

126

Initial spread   = 63
Final spread   = 58
Gain = 5 ticks × $25 = $125

Exhibits 6.2 and 6.3 illustrate typical inter-contract spreads on short-term instruments in 1982. Exhibit 6.2 shows the December T-bill minus the December CD on the IMM; Exhibit 6.3 shows the December CD minus the December Eurodollar contract also on the IMM. These spreads are not generally as volatile as intra-contract spreads or straddles if both contracts relate to the same delivery month. Neither do they follow the same cycles; indeed many spread traders use systems based on one spread acting as a leading indicator for another. In the exhibits we observe that the 1982 peak for the CD/Eurodollar spread occurred several days before the peak for the T-bill/CD spread. If a trader established that as a fairly consistent relationship through time, it could prove very profitable.

Exhibit 6.2: Behaviour of T-bill/CD inter-contract spread through time

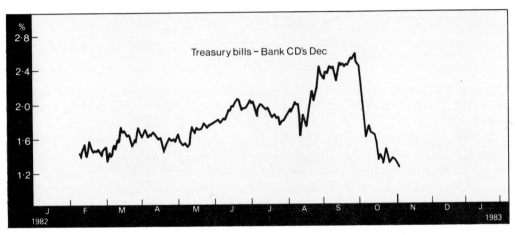

Source: Eurocharts

Exhibit 6.3: Behaviour of CD/Eurodollar inter-contract spread through time

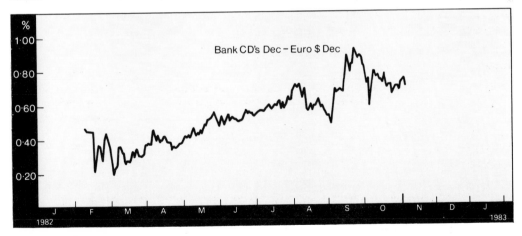

Source: Eurocharts

Another common type of inter-contract spreading in the markets is that between Ginnie Mae futures and Treasury bond futures on the Chicago Board of Trade. This is a spread between two long-term government-guaranteed securities of the same standard yield but different standard maturity. The CBT Ginnie Mae contract is assumed to have a maturity of $12\frac{1}{2}$ years, while the Treasury bond has a 20-year maturity. Inter-contract spreads in long-term instrument futures will not be possible on LIFFE until a medium or short-term gilt futures contract is introduced.

Unlike intra-contract spreads, which tend to reflect cost of carry expectations, spreads between Ginnie Mae futures and Treasury bond futures for a given contract month reflect the shape of the cash yield curve for long-term maturity instruments. Such spreads will react both to changes in the shape or slope of the cash yield curve and parallel shifts in the yield curve with the shape remaining unaltered.

Consider first upward or downward parallel shifts in the yield curve. An equal change in interest rates or yields will affect the prices of different maturity fixed interest instruments differently. The longer the maturity of the instrument, the larger the impact on price of a 1% change in the yield. Thus if the whole yield curve rises, i.e. futures prices fall, Treasury bond futures prices would be expected to fall by more than Ginnie Mae futures prices. Correspondingly if the yield curve shifts downwards, Treasury bond futures prices will rise faster than Ginnie Mae futures. Thus, the following spreading rules apply (though by convention the spread is defined relative to the Treasury bond contract, i.e. buying a Treasury bond future and selling a Ginnie Mae future is a bull spread):

Spread rules
1. If expecting a parallel downward yield curve shift, buy the T-bond/GNMA spread.
2. If expecting a parallel upward yield curve shift, sell the T-bond/GNMA spread.

The trader is taking advantage of the different money equivalency of the two contracts. Below is an example for an upward parallel yield curve shift and a downward parallel yield curve shift.

Example

Initial position: June GNMA futures price 96-03
                 Equivalent yield 8.5%

                 June Treasury bond futures price 90-25
                 Equivalent yield 9.0%

Alternative 1
Upward parallel yield curve shift.

	GNMA	**T-bond**
Yield	8.75%	9.25%
Futures price	94-12	88-23
Price change	−55 ticks	−66 ticks

Alternative 2
Downward parallel yield curve shift

	GNMA	**T-bond**
Yield	8.25%	8.75%
Futures price	97-28	92-31
Price change	+57 ticks	+70 ticks

If the trader had put on a bull spread, and alternative 2 had occurred, he would have made a net gain on the spread of 13 ticks of $406.25. If he expected alternative 1, and had put on a bear spread, he would have made a net gain of 11 ticks or $343.75.

Described above is a type of spread trading geared to expectations of the yield curve shifting, i.e. changes in the overall level of interest rates. It could be argued that if you expect interest rates to shift in this fashion, you would be better off with a straight open position in T-bonds. The more common aim of this type of spreading is to take advantages of changes in the shape or slope of the yield curve—the aim is to make money when 20-year rates rise or fall relative to $12\frac{1}{2}$-year rates. Changes in the shape of the yield curve may occur because of changes in investor expectations, or because of temporary supply-demand imbalances in the two markets. Differences in the supply of and demand for the two types of instrument will change their interest rates relative to one another. The classic three cases often quoted in US publications on the financial futures markets are:

128

(a) Additional supplies of T-bonds relative to Ginnie Maes during the Treasury quarterly refunding dates.

(b) Changes in housing starts will indicate more or less supplies of Ginnie Maes relative to T-bonds in the future.

(c) Corporate bond funding programmes impact on the T-bond market, rather than the Ginnie Mae market.

If the trader is forecasting a change in the shape of the yield curve, he will wish to insulate his trading profit from parallel shifts in the yield curve as described above. He will want to put on a spread whose value does not alter as the overall yield shifts. This means that he must adjust the numbers of contracts in the spread to compensate for differences in money equivalency. To do this he must find a conversion factor between T-bond and Ginnie Maes, like those for deliverable bonds and gilts. The approximate conversion factor for a $12\frac{1}{2}$-year 8% instrument and a 20-year 8% is somewhere around 1.3, i.e. 10 Treasury bonds will change in price by as much as 13 GNMA certificates. Such a weighted spread will serve to protect spread profits from most if not all of an adverse shift in the overall yield curve.

Example

1 July: Current futures prices

	GNMA	**T-bond**
September	96-03 (8.5%)	90-25 (9.0%)

Action: Housing starts have fallen dramatically; you believe the supply of Ginnie Maes relative to T-bonds will also fall, so you sell the T-bond/Ginnie Mae spread.

Alternative 1			*Alternative 2*		
1 July	Sell 13 T-bond futures	90-25	1 July	Sell 13 T-bond futures	90-25
	Buy 13 GNMA futures	96-03		Buy 13 GNMA futures	96-03
	Spread = (170 ticks)			Spread = (170 ticks)	
20 July	T-bond price	90-25 (9.00%)	20 July	T-bond price	92-03 (8.85%)
	GNMA price	97-28 (8.25%)		GNMA price	98-30 (8.10%)
	Spread = (277 ticks)			Spread = (219 ticks)	

A drop in GNMA rates relative to an unchanged T-bond rate gives a profit of 13 × 57 × $31.25 or $23,156.25 to selling the spread.

The same change in relative rates, but plus a 0.15% downward parallel shift in the yield curve reduces the profit to 13 × 49 × $31.25 or $19,906.25.

Now sell spread in proportion: 13 GNMAs to 10 T-bonds

GNMA	Buy 13 at 96-03	T-bond	Sell 10 at 90-25
	Sell 13 at 98-30		Buy 10 at 92-03
	Gain 13 × 91 × $31.25		Loss 10 × 42 × $31.25
	= $36,968,75		= $13,125.00

Net gain on weighted hedge = $23,843.75

The net profit to the weighted spread is very much closer to the profit realized by alternative 1, when there is no parallel shift in the yield curve, than is the profit on the unweighted hedge in the case when there is a parallel shift. The difference arises because a conversion value of 1.3 is only approximate.

In some circumstances a trader may deliberately choose to put on an unweighted spread. For example, he is convinced both that the slope of the yield curve is going to decrease, as in the example above, and that the overall yield curve is going to shift upwards. An unweighted bear T-bond/Ginnie Mae spread would then have two profit possibilities: one, from the change in the slope of the yield curve; and another, from the parallel shift. A trader may also introduce a time spread element into an inter-contract spread, for instance, by buying a September GNMA futures contract and selling a March T-bond contract. However, each additional complexity adds risk, which must always be taken into account in trading these types of spreads.

The recent T-bond/Ginnie Mae spread history is an excellent object lesson for traders who rely on historical patterns and ignore fundamental shifts in market structure. Exhibit 6.4 shows the history of the T-bond/Ginnie Mae March spread during 1982 and early 1983. A spread trader relying on historical highs, lows and averages of this type of spread might have been very tempted to sell the spread as it reached 96/32nds towards the middle of September. At first it would have proved a good trade—there was a downward reduction in the spread. This might have given him confidence to sell even more spreads, when the spread once again went through the 96/32nds level. This time, however, the trader would have looked on in horror as the spread rose almost uninterruptedly in the space of a month to a peak of nine whole points or 288/32nds. The lesson is that a change in tax rules plus a major shift in investor perception of the quality of the two instruments, plus the overall downward movement in rates, made nonsense of historical relationships. A fundamental trader would not have made this mistake; he would have expected the spread to widen from current levels as the overall yield curve moved downwards.

Exhibit 6.4: Behaviour of T-bond/GNMA inter-contract spread through time

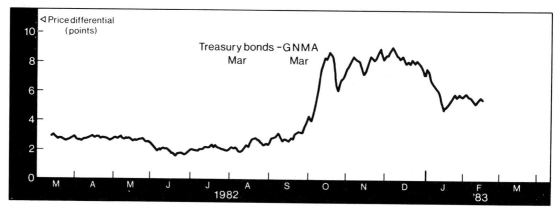

Source: Eurocharts

Another type of speculation on yield curve changes might be to set up spreads between very short-term financial futures such as T-bills or sterling or Eurodollar deposits, and long-term instruments such as gilts or T-bonds. This type of spread can be illustrated with a LIFFE example.

If a trader believes long rates are going to rise relative to short rates, then it is likely that implied yields in the long gilt contract will rise relative to short-term interest rates embedded in the sterling time deposit futures prices. It would seem appropriate for the trader to take advantage of this by putting on an inter-contract spread between sterling deposit futures and gilt futures. For instance, suppose the March gilt future was priced at 104-14, implying a yield to maturity of 11.43%, and the March sterling deposit future was priced at 91.26. If long rates are going to rise relative to short rates, the trader would want to put on a bull spread by buying the deposit future and selling the gilt future.

However, the problem of weighting such a spread to insulate the trader from overall movements in the yield curve, rather than alterations in its slope, is quite complex. The problem arises because the reaction of the gilt futures price to a change in the yield to maturity is not linear, whereas the movement in price per interest rate change for short-term interest rate futures price on an index basis is linear. We can illustrate this by observing price-yield combinations for sterling deposit futures and gilt futures starting at the prices shown earlier.

Sterling deposit future

Yield	7.74	8.24	8.74	9.24	9.74
Price	92.26	91.76	91.26	90.76	90.26
Ticks change	+100	+50	—	−50	−100

Gilt future

Yield	10.43	10.93	11.43	11.93	12.43
Price	113-03	108-20	104-14	100-17	96-27
Ticks change	+277	+134	—	−125	−243

130

It might be argued that these are not equal percentage rises in interest rates; that sterling deposit rates moving from 8.74% to 9.24% is a rise of 5.7% [(9.24 − 8.74)/8.74] × 100 whereas the rise in gilt yields is only 4.4% [(11.93 − 11.43)/11.43] × 100. However, the relationship is not linear in either case, so it seems easier to work with basis point rises to bring out the problems of this type of spread trading.

What the numbers shown are saying is: the weighting to protect against a 100 basis point rise in overall rates on a bull spread would be given by 243 × £15.625/100 × £6.25 = 6.075, i.e. one gilt contract matches into approximately six sterling deposit contracts; however, to protect against a fall in interest rates of 100 basis points, the spread weighting would have to be 277 × £15.625/100 × £6.25 = 6.925 or approximately 7.

What all this means is that the spread weighting will need to be adjusted as interest rates change to preserve the insulation of the spread profit from movements in overall interest rates while taking advantage of relative movements in long-term rates. The way this is done is by using the concept in bond pricing called duration (see Chapter 3).

Duration can be used to determine the appropriate weighting for a sterling deposit/gilt futures hedge.

$$\text{Number of deposit futures to hedge one gilt contract} = \frac{P_g (32)\,(£15.625)\,(D)}{P_s (100)\,(£6.25)}$$

where P_g = gilt futures price

P_s = sterling deposit futures price

D = duration of the gilt future

(32) = number of ticks per percentage point for gilt contracts

(100) = number of ticks per percentage point for sterling contracts

$\dfrac{15.625}{6.25}$ = ratio of tick values

For instance, if we take the situation where the gilt future is priced at 104-14 and the sterling deposit future at 91.26, the spread ratio would be

$$\frac{(104\text{-}14)\,(32)\,(15.625)\,(D)}{(91.26)\,(100)\,(6.25)} = 0.916 \times \text{duration}$$

The spread ratio will change constantly as the ratio of the two futures prices change and the duration changes, and the spread trader will buy or sell contracts to keep the ratio correct. In this way, a weighted inter-contract spread can be used to speculate on changes in the cash market yield curve.

Butterfly spreading

Another fairly complex spreading strategy is butterfly spreading. As in spread trading, where the trader takes a view on the evolution of the difference between two futures prices or rates, so in butterfly spreading the trader takes a view on the relationship of two spreads. In technical parlance, a trader who buys or sells a butterfly spread is buying or selling a *spread of spreads*. The trading strategy is the same as in spread trading: you buy a butterfly if you think the nearby spread (wing) is going to strengthen (become more positive or less negative) relative to the distant spread (wing). A butterfly spread consists of a bull and bear spread using a common middle contract.

The most common usage of the butterfly is when one contract looks out of line with the contracts in the delivery months on either side, but you are not sure whether the anomaly will be eliminated by the inner contract moving towards the other two or vice-versa.

Example

1 March LIFFE gilt futures prices

June	September	December
88-05	89-00	91-20

The gilt price line clearly has a bump in it. The September contract appears relatively overvalued, or more precisely the June–September spread of (27) ticks looks small relative to the September–December spread of (84) ticks. The trader would probably conclude that the nearby spread is likely to become more negative relative to the deferred spread; therefore he decides to sell the butterfly spread.

Example

Sell	One June contract	88-05	June/Sept. spread = (27)
Buy	One Sept. contract	89-00	
Buy	One Sept. contract	89-00	Sept./Dec. spread = (84)
Sell	One Dec. contract	91-20	

Butterfly spread = (27) − (84) = 57 ticks

15 March	**June**	**September**	**December**
	90-00	91-10	93-12

June/Sept. spread = (42)   Sept./Dec. spread = (66)

Butterfly spread = (42) − (66) = 24 ticks

Profit from selling the butterfly = 57 − 24 = 33 ticks.

Net cash gain = 33 × £15.625 = £515.625

The use of the butterfly is when the trader spots a spread which looks out of line with other spreads, but is not sure which is the one that is wrong. If he just buys a spread thinking it will move towards another one, he could be caught out if both spreads moved adversely in the same direction. The solution is to buy the spread that looks relatively too small and sell the one that looks relatively too big, i.e. to put on a butterfly. This insulates the trader from the impact of overall rather than relative spread movements.

Pseudo-butterfly spreads can also be put on between different contracts. Returning to the inter-contract spread between IMM Domestic CD and Eurodollar futures:

	Domestic CD	**Eurodollar**	**Spread**
June	85.93	85.30	63 bp
September	85.89	85.51	38 bp
December	85.88	85.54	34 bp

bp—basis points

Previously the trader decided to sell the June CD–June Euro spread. This was a risky strategy because it might have been the September and December spreads that were out of line. A less risky strategy could have been to sell the June CD/Euro spread and buy the September CD/Euro spread. This would look something like a butterfly spread, although it could not be classed as a true butterfly because it lacks the common middle contract, and is not carried out in just a single futures contract. Butterfly spreads where there is no common middle contract, such as long a June–September spread and short a December–March spread in a particular futures contract, are called condor spreads. Because the spread illustrated is between two different contracts, it could be called a pseudo-condor.

Example

Sell	One IMM CD June future	85.93	Spread = 63 ticks
Buy	One IMM Euro June future	85.30	
Buy	One IMM CD Sept. future	85.89	Spread = 38 ticks
Sell	One IMM Euro Sept. future	85.51	

4 May	June CD/Euro spread	= 58 bp
	Sept. CD/Euro spread	= 41 bp

Initial pseudo-condor spread 63 − 38 = 25 ticks

Final pseudo-condor spread = 58 − 41 = 17 ticks

Gain from selling pseudo-condor = 8 ticks or $200

The net gain is $200 as compared with the straight inter-contract spread of $125, and the spread position was much less risky.

These pseudo-condor spreads between two different financial futures can be looked at in another way.

Example

| Sell | One IMM CD June future | } CD straddle = 4 ticks |
| Buy | One IMM CD Sept. future | |

| Buy | One June Euro future | } Euro straddle = (21) ticks |
| Sell | One Sept. Euro future | |

4 May	CD straddle	= (2) ticks
	Euro straddle	= (19) ticks
	Total gain = (6 + 2) ticks = 8 ticks or $200	

A pseudo-condor spread essentially involves taking a view that a spread in one financial futures market is out of line with a spread in another market. Such spread trading between different three-month instruments is common in US markets, and is encouraged by the much lower commission costs applicable to straddle trading.

Summing up spreading

The basic strategies for spreading have been described, but a few general points about spread trading should be made. First, it is important in spread trading that both legs of the spread be put on and taken off simultaneously. If you put on one leg in one time period and the other leg later, then you simply have an open futures position with all the attendant risks for however long the gap between the two transactions lasts. Similarly both legs of the spread should be taken off simultaneously, again to avoid the risks of carrying an open position for a short period of time. The reduced margins generally charged for intra-contract spread trading are mostly only operational if both legs of the spread are put on simultaneously. If a would-be spread trader is not present on the floor of the exchange to be able to put on the legs simultaneously, he would be wise to operate through a spread broker. A spread broker will quote a client a fixed price differential between two futures contracts, taking on the risk himself of putting on the actual futures contracts at the right price. The use of spread brokers makes spread trading easy for non-members of the exchanges.

Finally, the spread trader should be aware that though spread positions are generally less risky than open position, they are still high leverage, high risk positions. Just as with open position trading, the spreader will need to carefully assess the amount of risk capital he wishes to commit to spread trading. He will also need to decide when to cut his losses on particular trades. However, the direct use of limit orders to close spread positions is very difficult, since it is very unlikely that both orders, one for each leg of the spread, would be triggered simultaneously. Hence if only a single limit order is triggered, closing one of the legs, the trader would be back in the open position situation discussed above. Some spread brokers are generally willing to accept a limit order defined on the spread rather than the underlying contracts, and this solves the problem. Otherwise a spread trader needs to keep in close touch with the market to be sure to unwind his position at the appropriate time.

C. The timing of trading

So far trading has been discussed in terms of different strategies such as open position trading, spreading and arbitrage trading. Another breakdown that is often used is to classify traders by the time-frame of their operations. Three categories are normally used.

Scalpers

Scalpers are the major source of liquidity in the financial futures markets. They will trade the market in and out, second by second and minute by minute. As such they must clearly be present in the trading pit—a scalper cannot operate off the trading floor. His basic aim is to profit from very small price fluctuations over very short spaces of time—possibly as little as two or three tick movements in price. A scalper may expect to realize a large number of small profits and losses on the many transactions undertaken during the day as he tries constantly to exploit market situations. To benefit from such small movements, a scalper clearly needs to be a member of the exchange, for the payment of commissions would rapidly eliminate scalping profits.

The basic aim of the scalper is to take advantage of temporary imbalances in the market: incoming purchase orders often cause a temporary rise in market prices while sales cause a temporary fall. A scalper will be willing to accommodate a seller one or two ticks below the equilibrium price, on the assumption that he will gain these one or two ticks when a buy order pushes the market back up again. The danger is that the market will move against him while he is holding an open position; a scalper's losing positions need to be closed out almost immediately. An even greater danger is a sudden dramatic move in prices while he holds an open position: one big loss can wipe out a lot of small one or two tick gains. It is thus essential for the scalper to monitor order inflows to the floor very carefully, avoid illiquid contracts and particularly avoid putting on trades immediately prior to news announcements of interest to the market. A scalper will also take into account the general direction of market movements, and he would be less willing to accommodate a buyer in a market that seemed to be trending upwards. A scalper will generally stay with a winning position until the price direction changes and then liquidate the position immediately.

The readiness of the scalper to take on perhaps 100 brief open positions during a trading period for a few ticks' potential profit provides the essential liquidity for hedgers and bigger traders to put on their required positions at minimum cost. A scalper may be a spread trader seeking to take advantage of temporary shifts in basis relationships between different futures contracts. The essential point, however, is that this type of trading is bound to involve a lot of losing positions. The test of a good scalper is whether his overall book at the end of a trading period shows a good profit.

Day traders

Day traders are essentially long duration traders with fewer nerves. They may be involved in position trading, spread trading or arbitrage, but they will not allow a position to remain open while the market is closed. Thus they avoid the danger of major adverse price movements in reaction to new information while the position is still open overnight. It is difficult for the day trader, however, to take full advantage of arbitrage and spread trading, because anomalies in the futures price relationships may take several days or weeks to work themselves out. Certainly a day trader who is not an exchange member and who is paying commissions could not, because running an arbitrage position on a daily basis would involve paying a new set of commissions each day. Day trading is best left to exchange members, who take a slightly longer view of price trends than the scalper.

Just as with scalpers, day traders need to be ruthless in assessing when the market is moving against them and closing out their positions quickly. When trading off the floor, the use of stop-loss orders is clearly appropriate. Often day traders take advantage of large overhangs of buy or sell orders (often limit orders) to determine their trading strategy.

Longer duration traders

A classic definition of a long duration trader, who could in this context be a straight position trader or an arbitrage trader, is a person who seeks to profit from changes in supply and demand relationships in the futures markets over a period of days, weeks or even months. Given the longer time-period of trading, it is not strictly necessary for such a trader to be a member of the exchange, since brokerage commissions can be amortized over a longer period and a larger expected profit, while market timing is not as critical as it is for scalpers and day traders. An open position trader will use most, if not all, of the strategies outlined in this chapter, and will make use in particular of technical and fundamental analysis in settling up his positions.

D. A strategy of trading

A trader has to understand the concepts in trading financial futures, the different types of trading strategies, and the different time horizons available. But in the end a good trader needs to adopt an overall strategy adapted to his particular requirements and stick to it, regardless of temptation. Such a strategy would sensibly involve four stages.

1. Specialization

It is simply not possible for a trader to keep track of all the profit opportunities that can arise in financial futures markets. A trader is well advised to specialize in one particular area of trading, and learn all there is to know about the order types, the strategies, and the analytical and forecasting methods that are suitable for his type of trading. The objectives of the trader should be clearly established and committed to writing.

2. Good management of profits and losses

One of the most important rules in all commodity trading, including financial futures, is to set an appropriate limit on losses. Before any position is taken, the maximum permissible loss on the position should be determined, and that limit must be decided in advance and stuck to by the use of limit orders if possible. A trader who does not rigorously follow a policy of preset loss limits will probably not survive in the market-place very long. On the other hand, a good trader does not close out profits on a position too soon. One way of handling the problem is to raise stop-loss orders into take-profit orders as the profit to a position increases. But a good trader will take a profit if it looks as if the market has turned. The market is littered with the losses of those traders who held on to profitable positions that had turned around for too long. Good profit and loss planning is essential to an efficient trader.

3. Appropriate use of risk capital

A trader or trading firm must be aware that financial futures trading is inherently risky. The risk falls into two parts: first, the risk of an overall loss: second, the risk that though the trader's forecast is eventually correct, interim price fluctuations can involve big variation margin payments. The trader therefore needs to decide: (1) how much of his risk capital to devote to financial futures trading; and (2) how much of the sum devoted to financial futures trading should be allocated to initial margin payments and how much held back for possible variation margin payments. Although such decisions will depend on the risk preferences of the individual trader, they should be taken carefully and stuck to. The trader should beware of committing more risk capital to the futures markets than previously intended simply to try and recover previous losses.

4. Measurement of return in relation to capital

The bottom line of trading is whether the trader is earning an appropriate return on capital invested over a given period of time. Once the amount of risk capital devoted to financial trading has been established, effective returns to trading can be determined. If these are not sufficient to compensate for the additional risk of futures trading, trading techniques must be improved, or the trading effort should be discontinued.

E. Monitoring and controlling trading performance

All futures market traders, in addition to developing an appropriate trading strategy, will need to monitor trading performance and ensure that trading activity within a firm is carried out with a recognized system of limits.

For scalpers and day traders, such limits include restrictions on the funds at an individual trader's or dealer's disposal, and overall limits on the number of contracts that may be open at any single point in time. Some restrictions on the amount of activity may also be appropriate.

In addition, appropriate stop-loss orders need to be incorporated into any position trading strategy. Overall limits on contract numbers will generally be higher for spread trading than for open position trading.

The levels of activity at which limits are set will vary depending on assessment and attitude towards risk. These may change over time and procedures should be established to review and adjust limits as appropriate on a regular basis. Limits should be applied to minimize risks, while not imposing undue constraints on a trader's ability to maximize profits through operation in the market. The level of limits will be influenced by the size of the organization, the experience of the trading operation, the current volatility of prices, and the level of understanding of financial futures trading.

Limits, however, are effective only if timely comparisons are available of actual positions against the determined limits. In a market where prices can change very rapidly, there will be a need for trading staff to monitor positions and activity on a minute by minute basis. Formal reporting systems to management of open positions against limits will also need to be established, probably on a daily basis. Such daily formal reporting should also include information on profitability from trading operations, including information on realized gains and losses on positions closed out, unrealized gains and losses on open contracts, transactions and financing costs, and overhead costs.

The aim should always be to check that trading profitability is in line with the overall strategy discussed earlier. Profits from trading need to be measured against targets or budgets drawn up in line with the overall trading strategy.

Finally it is worth stressing that there is no substitute for practice when learning about financial futures trading. The techniques in this chapter can be applied to simulated trading, to see if good trading rules can be developed. In the end, however, a trader will have to carry out some actual transactions to see what trading involves. Moreover, like poker, learning to trade financial futures will probably involve losing some money initially—payment for the teaching, in fact. However, although financial futures do have more complex features than other futures or cash contracts, the potential gains to sensible trading look large.

Chapter 7
Arbitrage with financial futures

The type of trading in financial futures discussed so far has involved the deliberate taking on of risky positions, whether they be open positions or spread positions, in the hope of significant profits. The third type of trading is arbitrage trading—trading to take advantages of temporary price or rate anomalies in the financial futures market.

The term arbitrage is used here in a slightly different way than in many of the commodity textbooks. Market professionals often refer to any type of inter-contract or inter-market spread as arbitrage. In this book, arbitrage is used in its original meaning: the earning of riskless profits, or very nearly riskless profits, by the simultaneous purchase and sale of the same asset at two different prices.

A classical example of arbitrage would be the purchase of oranges at one price in part of a fruit market, and their sale at a higher price in another part of the market. Such simple arbitrages will be rare in the open outcry, centralized trading characteristic of financial futures markets, although opportunities may occasionally transpire in a very active, crowded trading pit. More often, however, arbitrage will depend on the construction of artificial financial instruments and the comparison of prices with prices in the cash or futures markets.

This chapter analyses trading techniques to take advantage of arbitrage opportunities. However, no trading technique involving the holding of financial futures positions can ever really be totally riskless. The principle of marking to market always means that even if the profit is certain at the time delivery is reached, negative variation margins could be called at any point during the time the futures position is open, and the cost of financing variation margins will offset any arbitrage profit to the transaction.

In addition, many of the arbitrage trading techniques described are extremely complex and involve simultaneous access to the futures market and various interbank and money markets. The scale of transactions needed to produce matched positions is often extremely large.

The easiest way to illustrate arbitrage techniques is to use the time-security grid. A typical one is shown in Exhibit 7.1. It simply graphs different securities up the Y-axis and different futures months along the X-axis. Any potential arbitrage using futures can be expressed as a

Exhibit 7.1: The time/security grid

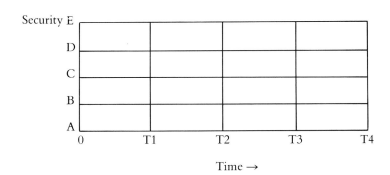

Time →

closed loop within such a grid. The exhibits in this chapter will use the following key:

Horizontal rightward pointing arrow: investment.
Horizontal leftward pointing arrow: borrowing.
Vertical arrows: exchange of one asset for another.

Below is an example of how to use this grid to display a simple arbitrage, involving the simultaneous purchase and sale of Eurodollar futures, sterling deposit futures and foreign exchange futures on LIFFE.

Imagine it is 10 July. A trader is looking ahead to the three-month period September–December. He locks in a three-month borrowing rate for three-month Eurodollars by selling a September Eurodollar time deposit future. He also locks in an exchange rate at which he can turn these dollars into sterling by buying a dollar-sterling foreign exchange future, and an investment rate for the sterling by purchasing a September sterling deposit future. Finally he locks in the rate at which he will change his sterling back into dollars in December, when his time deposit matures, by selling a December dollar-sterling foreign exchange future. In Exhibit 7.2, the dollar borrowing is represented by the upper leftward pointing arrow, the sterling lending by the lower rightward pointing arrow, and the two exchanges of one currency for another are represented by the vertical arrows. It is easy to see how the arbitrage is represented by a closed loop on the time-security grid.

Consider why this is an arbitrage. The trader borrows one dollar, converts the dollar into sterling, invests the sterling, and then changes the proceeds into dollars to repay the dollar borrowing. If all the transactions are carried out at fixed rates, and the trader ends up with a net dollar gain, this is a clear arbitrage profit.

To use the time-security grid to work out whether profitable arbitrages exist, start with one unit of currency somewhere on the loop, and follow it round at the appropriate transactions prices and determine whether it has increased by the time you return to your starting position. If the ratio of the final amount to the initial amount is greater than one, there is an arbitrage profit.

Exhibit 7.2: An example of a closed arbitrage

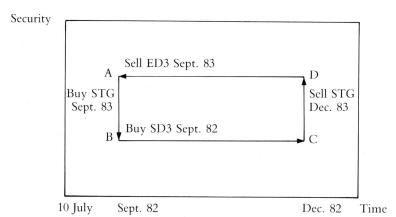

ED3—Three-month Eurodollar time deposit futures contract
STG—Dollar sterling foreign exchange futures contract
SD3—Three-month sterling time deposit futures contract

Let us follow through the example with a set of transactions prices. On 10 July the following set of prices are observed:

	Sterling deposit future	Eurodollar deposit future	$/£ future
September	86.50	85.60	1.7985
December	86.40	85.60	1.8049

Imagine we begin with $1 at A: borrowed at 14.4% (100-85.60):

Transaction 1: AB $1 changed into £0.556

Transaction 2: BC   £0.556 invested at 13.5% (100 − 86.5) for 91 days

$$= £0.556 \times \left(1 + \left[0.135 \times \frac{91}{365}\right]\right) = £0.5747$$

Transaction 3: CD   £0.5747 changed into $ at 1.8049 = $1.0373

Transaction 4: DA   Repayment of $1 loan cost $= \$1 \times \left\{1 + \left[0.144 \times \frac{91}{360}\right]\right\} = \$1.0364$

$$\text{Arbitrage ratio} = 1.0008 \, (= 1.0373/1.0364)$$

Since the arbitrage ratio is greater than one, an arbitrage riskless profit appears to be available. The actual size of the profit will depend on the size of the initial position. If we dealt in one Eurodollar futures contract: we would start with $1 million and our potential profit would be:

$$\text{Profit} = \$1,000,800 - \$1,000,000 = \$800$$

Finally, in assessing these arbitrages, it is often useful to explore the sensitivity of the arbitrage profit to changes in the transaction rates. This is done by calculating the change in the transaction rate which would be necessary to eliminate the arbitrage profit. Consider the arbitrage ratio of 1.0008; what change in the sterling time deposit future implied lending rate would be necessary to reduce it to 1.0000. This would be calculated by dividing the difference between the arbitrage ratio and unity by the fraction of a year for which the money is invested.

$$\text{Sterling deposit} = [1.0008 - 1.0000] \Big/ \frac{91}{365} \times 10,000 = 32 \text{ basis points}$$

The sterling deposit rate would need to drop from 13.5% to 13.18% before the arbitrage profit would disappear. Similar sensitivities for the other three transactions rates are:

(A) Eurodollar deposit rate $= -[1.0008 - 1.0000] \Big/ \frac{91}{360} \times 10,000 = (32)$ basis points

(B) June $/£ rate $= -[1.0008 - 1.000]1.7985 \times 10,000 = (14)$ ticks

(C) Sept. $/£ rate $= [1.0008 - 1.000]1.8049 \times 10,000 = 14$ ticks

Calculating these sensitivities is important in successful arbitrage trading because it is not generally possible to actually carry out futures transactions at observed prices. Hence, an arbitrage where the sensitivities are relatively large is more likely to be successfully implemented, for prices can alter significantly from observed prices before the arbitrage is eliminated.

The second essential element that has to be taken into account is the potential cost of financing initial margin and potential variation margin. Since an almost market rate of interest is paid on initial margin by the clearing system on most, if not all, US exchanges, initial margin costs are small. In fact, on LIFFE in its first months of trading, the ICCH did not pay interest on any margin funds; hence arbitrage costs were higher than in the United States. Further, no interest is paid on negative variation margin by any of the exchanges, though investors do have the advantage of the use of positive variation margin payments. It is always possible in arbitrage trades, where the profit margin is usually relatively small, that adverse variation margin payments and the cost of financing them could wipe out the arbitrage profit. Any arbitrageur will also want to examine the sensitivity of profits to overall interest or exchange rate changes which could impact adversely on the futures position. If an overall interest or exchange rate forecast that appears feasible implies large adverse futures movements, a decision to do the arbitrage could be aborted.

The five major types of arbitrage are now discussed, using this conceptual framework. In each case the practical difficulties in carrying out what may appear to be profitable arbitrage strategies are pointed out.

A. Cash and carry arbitrage

One of the most important inputs into the determination of basis—the difference between cash and futures prices—is the cost of carry. The cost of carry imposes an upper bound on the level of basis. Otherwise it would be possible for an investor to borrow funds, purchase a financial instrument in the cash market, hold the instrument for later delivery against a short futures position, and then undertake delivery to earn a riskless profit. This would fulfil our simple definition of arbitrage. If the basis is higher than the cost of carry, an arbitrage trading opportunity should exist.

Cash and carry arbitrage is illustrated first with the gilt-edged contract on LIFFE; it also applies to Treasury bonds and other long-term financial futures in the United States. The way to analyse cash and carry arbitrage is to compare the current price of the cash instrument with the futures settlement price at delivery implied by the prevailing futures price of the instrument. The LIFFE futures contract is based on a standard 12% 20-year gilt-edged stock. Many different gilt-edged stocks are deliverable against the standard contract, and price factors are used to convert the price of the standard gilt into an equivalent price for the actual gilt to be delivered. The settlement amount at delivery is then calculated as,

$$\text{Settlement amount} = [\text{Closing price} \times \text{Price factor} \times 500] + \text{Accrued interest}$$

Price factor: price per pound nominal value of the specific stock at which the stock has a gross redemption yield of 12% minus the undiscounted amount of accrued interest.

Accrued interest: undiscounted amount of accrued interest on a £50,000 nominal value contract as at the day of delivery.

Below is a specimen of the LIFFE tables for deliverable gilts.

Delivery month		Treasury 10.5% 19 May, 1999	Treasury 13% 14 July, 2000	Exchequer 12% 22 Jan., 1999–2002
	D	14.3836	17.8082	16.4384
June 1982	F	0.8922103	1.0737879	1.0006156
	A	172.60	−783.56	−854.79
Sept. 1982	F	0.8924524	1.0725734	0.9996972
	A	1,495.89	854.79	657.53

D = Accrued interest per day on £50,000 face value
F = Price factor as percentage of par
A = Accrued interest on £50,000 face value as of last day of month prior to delivery month.

The information in the table can be used to work out whether a cash and carry arbitrage is feasible. Suppose on 1 July, 1982, it was observed that the Treasury 10½% 1999 was trading at 80-04 in the cash market and the September gilt futures contract was priced at 89-16. The trader wants to know if a cash and carry arbitrage is possible if his financing cost is 13⅜% per year.

First, a time-security grid for the cash and carry operation is drawn up (see Exhibit 7.3). We

Exhibit 7.3: Cash and carry arbitrage

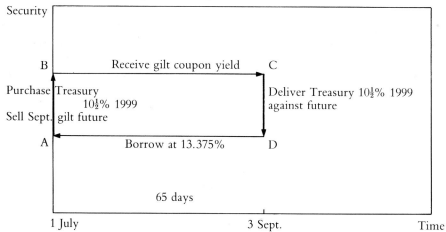

140

assume the transaction is carried out with a single gilt futures contract.

Transaction 1: AB	£40,062.50{500 × 80-04} borrowed at 13.375% Purchase £50,000 nominal Treasury 10½% 1999
Transaction 2: BC	Receive accrued interest of £1,495.89 + £43.15★
Transaction 3: CD	Deliver gilt. Receive principal payment equal to 89-16 × 0.8924524 × 500 = £39,937.25
Transaction 4: DA	Repay loan Cost is £40,062.50{1 + (0.13375 × 65/365)} = £41,016.73

★ 3 extra days accrued interest 1 Sept.–3 Sept.

In this case the arbitrage ratio is

$$\text{Arbitrage ratio} = \frac{£41,476.29 \ (39,937.25 + 1,495.89 + 43.15)}{£41,016.73}$$

$$= 1.0112$$

And the actual cash profit to dealing in one gilt futures contract is

$$\text{Arbitrage profit} = £41,476.29 - £41,016.73$$

$$= £459.56$$

We can also calculate the relevant sensitivities:

Treasury 10½% 1999:	$- [0.0112 \times 80.125] \times 32 = (29/32\text{nds})$
September gilt future:	$[0.0112 \times 89.5] \times 32 = 32/32\text{nds}$
Sterling 65-day rate:	$- \left[0.0112 \times \dfrac{365}{65}\right] \times 10,000 = (629)$ basis points

This particular cash and carry arbitrage appears to be very insensitive to moderate changes in the transactions prices and rates. It is the nice simple example of cash and carry arbitrage found in all the text-books. A similar technique could be applied to determining whether cash and carry opportunities exist for Treasury bonds and GNMAs. However, the trading profit is only certain for this type of transaction as long as the futures price does not move away from its original value—an unlikely assumption in today's volatile interest rate markets. The calculation of gain when the futures closing price is not equal to its starting price looks somewhat different.

Net gain = [Closing price of futures contract × Price factor × 500]

   + Accrued interest

   − Interest cost

   − Purchase cost

   + [Futures contract initial price − Futures contract closing price] × 500

It is obvious that the purportedly riskless arbitrage profit is actually dependent on the movement in the futures price between the date of the sale of the contract and the closing date of the contract. This can be illustrated by comparing the cash and carry gain in the example above with the gain (or loss) to the position if the closing price has moved to 85-00 and 94-00 respectively.

Case 1: Futures price moves from 89-16 to 85-00

$$\text{Net gain} = [85\text{-}00 \times 0.8924524 \times 500]$$

$$+ \ 1,495.89 + [3 \times 14.3836]$$

$$- \ 954.23$$

$$- \ 40,062.50$$

$$+ \ [89\text{-}16 - 85\text{-}00] \times 500$$

$$= £701.54$$

Case 2: Futures price moves from 89-16 to 94-00

$$\text{Net gain} = [94\text{-}00 \times 0.8924524 \times 500]$$
$$+ \ 1{,}495.89 + [3 \times 14.3836]$$
$$- \ 954.23$$
$$- \ 40{,}062.50$$
$$+ \ [89\text{-}16 - 94\text{-}00] \times 500$$
$$= \ £217.57$$

So, when the futures price moved against the open futures position, the profit to the arbitrage was almost halved, and could have disappeared altogether if the adverse futures movement had been more severe. Simple cash and carry arbitrage is certainly not riskless. The problem is the role of the conversion factor: the settlement price is determined by the price factor, whereas the gain or loss to the futures contract is not affected. The degree of risk will be greater, the further away the price factor is from unity. If the price factor is unity, there is no problem.

$$[\text{Futures closing price} \times 1 \times 500] + ([\text{Futures initial price} - \text{Futures closing price}] \times 500)$$
$$= \text{Futures initial price} \times 500$$

Thus the impact of the change in the futures price washes out when the conversion factor is unity, but not otherwise. So, a more sophisticated strategy for a true cash and carry arbitrage is needed.

The price factor risk has to be eliminated from the system, and the simplest way to do this is when starting the cash and carry to sell futures contracts in the amount of £50,000 × price factor rather than the full face amount of £50,000. In the example, we would like to sell futures contracts to the value of £50,000 × 0.8924524 or £44,623 initially, with any extra contracts needed to ensure delivery of exactly the £50,000 nominal of Treasury 10½% stock purchased being bought or sold on the notice of delivery day. The profit or loss from movements in the futures price will be earned on an open futures position of £50,000 × price factor, but the proceeds from delivery will be for a futures position of £50,000, with futures contracts of £50,000 (1 − price factor) being sold on the notice delivery day and called for delivery immediately. The net gain to the transaction becomes:

$$\text{Net gain} = [\text{Futures closing price} \times \text{Price factor} \times 500]$$
$$+ \ \text{Accrued interest} - \text{Interest cost} - \text{Purchase price}$$
$$+ \ [\text{Futures initial price} - \text{Futures closing price}] \times \text{Price factor} \times 500$$

$$= [\text{Futures initial price} \times \text{Price factor} \times 500]$$
$$+ \ \text{Accrued interest} - \text{Interest cost} - \text{Purchase price}$$

This is the original expression for the profit from a cash and carry transaction, if there is no change in the futures price, i.e. weighting the size of the open futures position by the price factor has eliminated the price factor risk.

In practice the trader cannot purchase fractions of the £50,000 gilt futures contract. He would have to do the cash and carry arbitrage in sufficient size that a round number of futures contracts could be sold at the start of the trade and on the notice of delivery day. This could be difficult to achieve in practice.

For example, in the case discussed above, where the relevant conversion factor was 0.8924524, to get even an approximately riskless position would involve the purchase of £2.5 million face value of Treasury 10½%, the sale of 45 September gilt contracts on 1 July and the sale of a further five contracts on 1 September. It could be difficult to sell so many contracts in the financial futures market. Below is the gain for this weighted position in the case when the futures price moves from 89-16 to 94-00, to compare it with the unweighted position when the futures price does not change.

142

$$\text{Net gain} = [94\text{-}00 \times 0.8924524 \times 500] \times 50$$
$$+ [1{,}495.89 + [3 \times 14.3836]] \times 50$$
$$- 954.23 \times 50$$
$$- 40{,}062.50 \times 50$$
$$+ [89\text{-}16 - 94\text{-}00] \times 500 \times 45$$
$$= \pounds 22{,}128.68 \ (= 50 \times \pounds 442.57)$$

The net gain per £50,000 of stock of £442.57 is very close to the gain of £459.56 in the no price change case. The weighting has succeeded in eliminating most of the risk attributable to the price factor.

An alternative strategy is to alter the amount of the cash gilt purchased. For example, given the price factor in the example above of 0.8924524, the investor could sell one gilt futures contract of nominal value £50,000 and purchase cash gilts to the tune of £50,000/0.8924524 or £56,025 nominal of Treasury $10\frac{1}{2}\%$ 1999. This reverse system of weighting will be more practical, since it is possible to buy cash gilts in significantly smaller denominations than futures contracts. It will still be necessary to purchase additional futures contracts immediately prior to delivery. But the total number of contracts to set up an approximately riskless position would be rather smaller: we could manage by buying £450,000 nominal of Treasury $10\frac{1}{2}\%$ 1999 and selling eight gilt futures initially and a final one immediately before delivery. The net gain to this transaction when the futures price moves to 94-00 at delivery is:

$$\text{Net gain} = [94\text{-}00 \times 0.8924524 \times 500] \times 9$$
$$+ [1{,}495.89 + (3 \times 14.3836)] \times 9$$
$$- 954.23 \times 9$$
$$- 40{,}062.50 \times 9$$
$$+ [89\text{-}16 - 94\text{-}00] \times 500 \times 8$$
$$= \pounds 4{,}208.16$$

This is effectively a net gain of £467.57 per £50,000 nominal stock.

These cash and carry strategies have other ramifications when the position is long cash and short futures. First, the short can deliver the gilt to the market at any point during the delivery month. He will choose the day which provides him with the most benefit. If there is an upward sloping yield curve, the tendency will be to deliver as late as possible in the delivery month because the short will wish to earn the difference between the high coupon yield on the gilt and the lower cost of financing for as long as possible. If there is an inverted or downward sloping yield curve, the short will deliver the gilt earlier in the month.

Second, there is an alternative strategy to the one discussed earlier when carrying out the cash and carry with the cheapest deliverable stock (this concept was discussed in Chapter 3). At any point in time there will be one gilt which will give the maximum arbitrage gain to a cash and carry transaction. Currently on LIFFE the cheapest deliverable stock is Treasury $15\frac{1}{2}\%$ 1998, which has a conversion factor for March 1983 of 1.2446. Suppose we carried out the simple cash and carry with this gilt:

$$\text{Buy } \pounds 1{,}000{,}000 \text{ nominal } 15\tfrac{1}{2}\% \ 1998$$

$$\text{Sell } 25 \left(\frac{1{,}000{,}000}{50{,}000} \times 1.2446 \right) \text{ gilt futures contracts march 1983}$$

When it comes to delivery the short has two choices: he can get rid of the excess five gilt contracts immediately before delivery, or he could buy additional gilts in the market to deliver against the excess short contracts in the futures market. This opportunity to earn additional extra returns if cash gilts are priced below futures prices at delivery is termed *the wild card* in the United States.

What happens if there is an observed arbitrage profit to selling a cash gilt, buying gilt futures contracts, and taking delivery against the contracts in due course? The transaction can be illustrated by two cases: first, where the arbitrageur already holds the cheapest deliverable stock in his portfolio; the second, where he does not.

Case 1: Portfolio containing Treasury 15½% 1998
        Sell £1,000,000 nominal Treasury 15½% 1998
        Buy 25 March gilt futures

The transaction is standard. The proceeds of the sale are invested for an appropriate number of days in the money market. At delivery the excess contracts are sold, or additional stock taken if there is a price advantage. If the implied interest rate, or repo rate, from the transaction is less than the rate at which the funds can be invested, an arbitrage profit exists.

There are, however, a few wrinkles that arise because the short is in control of the delivery process. The existence of positive or negative carry should determine the delivery date. But, there is always the possibility that the short will deliver earlier or later in the delivery month than expected. If this happens in the case above—say the short delivered at the beginning rather than the end of the month—the settlement value of the gilt would need to be borrowed for an additional 31 days until the fixed maturity money market investment matured. If short-term rates moved substantially over the life of the arbitrage, this would introduce another element of risk into the transaction.

Another risk is that the short might deliver a stock other than the cheapest deliverable stock: but in that case there is, by definition, a profit to be achieved by selling the stock actually delivered and switching back into the Treasury 15½% 1998. The only conceivable problem that could arise is if a new stock is issued between the transaction date and the delivery date on such terms that it became the cheapest deliverable stock. In that case, reselling the stock delivered if it is the cheapest deliverable and swapping back into the Treasury 15½% 1998 might have a cost which would offset some of the arbitrage profit. These factors become even more evident in the second case.

Case 2: Portfolio does not contain Treasury 15½% 1998

The arbitrage in this case must consist of two separate components; a switch of an actual cash gilt holding into Treasury 15½% 1998, a cash and carry arbitrage, and a reverse switch of the gilt delivered against the future into the original gilt. To see how this might work, suppose the portfolio manager decides to sell his holding of £1,000,000 nominal of Treasury 10½% 1999. He needs to work out the appropriate number of futures contracts to buy. He does not need as many as before because he only wants to obtain enough nominal value of Treasury 15½% 1998 to enable him to repurchase £1,000,000 nominal of the Treasury 10½% 1999; i.e. the first part of the switch is a notional one handled by altering the number of futures contracts, and the second part of the switch would be done in the cash market.

Sell £1,000,000 nominal Treasury 10½% 1999, price = 96-24

Buy 19 gilt futures contract March 1983

$$\text{Number of contracts} = \frac{\pounds1,000,000}{\pounds50,000} \times \frac{96\text{-}24}{128\text{-}12} \times 1.2446 = 18.76$$

Price factor Treasury 15½% 1998 March 1983 = 1.2446

Market price Treasury 15½% 1998 = 128-12

At delivery the excess four contracts are sold, or additional stock purchased, and delivery is taken on 15 contracts giving, on the assumption of Treasury 15½% 1998 being delivered, £750,000 nominal of stock. This in turn could be swapped into £995,155 of the original Treasury 10½% 1999 if the switch ratio had remained constant. The small discrepancy with the original £1,000,000 is due to the fact that it is not possible to put on fractions of futures contracts which are required by the hedge ratio of 18.76.

Although the arbitrage portion of this trade enjoys a locked-in rate of return, save for the small risks discussed earlier, the possibility of a change in the switch ratio between Treasury 10½% 1999 and Treasury 15½% 1998 constitutes a major risk to the profitability of the trade. In choosing the stock to sell, the manager will want to sell those stocks that currently look expensive in terms of the Treasury 15½% 1998. Nonetheless, the prices of bonds of different duration will react differently to changes in interest rates. Hence, the arbitrage profit is not independent of yield curve changes. This type of cash and carry should, therefore, be seen as a sophisticated trading strategy rather than a true arbitrage.

The process for cash and carry transactions on Treasury bond futures trading on the Chicago Board of Trade is exactly the same. The conversion tables however, are slightly different, giving all combinations of maturity and interest rates that are equivalent to a yield of 8.00%. A small sample of such a table is presented below.

Coupon rates

Term	$7\frac{3}{8}\%$	$7\frac{1}{2}\%$	$7\frac{5}{8}\%$	$7\frac{3}{4}\%$
18	0.9409	0.9527	0.9645	0.9764
18-3	0.9404	0.9522	0.9641	0.9760
18-6	0.9402	0.9521	0.9641	0.9761
18-9	0.9396	0.9517	0.9637	0.9757
19	0.9395	0.9516	0.9637	0.9758
19-3	0.9390	0.9511	0.9633	0.9755
19-6	0.9388	0.9510	0.9633	0.9755
19-9	0.9383	0.9506	0.9629	0.9752
20	0.9381	0.9505	09.629	0.9753

Source: Financial Publishing Company, Boston MA Pub. No. 765. 1979

Suppose you saw Treasury bonds $7\frac{5}{8}\%$ (15 February) 2002-07 trading at 81-00 on 1 July, 1982 and the current September futures price trading at 83-10. If your cost of finance was 12% would it pay you to cash and carry?

The cash and carry analysis procedure is exactly the same as for the long-term gilt contract on LIFFE. First, identify the conversion or price factor. When invoicing for delivery on the CBT, the maturity is calculated in complete quarters with no rounding up. On 1 July, 1982, $7\frac{5}{8}\%$ Treasury bonds of February 2002-07 were callable in 19 years, seven months and a few days, which is a maturity for invoicing purposes of 19 years and six months. From the table, the conversion factor for these bonds in 0.9633. The daily accrued interest for such bonds is approximately $20.95. The net gain to the arbitrage is then calculated in the usual way.

$$\text{Net gain } [83\text{-}10 \times 0.9633 \times 1,000]$$
$$+ \$3,812.50^1 + \$398.05^2$$
$$- \$1,837.48^3$$
$$- [81\text{-}00 \times 1,000]$$
$$= \$1,628.00$$

[1] Interest on the bonds is paid half-yearly on 15 August and 15 February. Therefore $3,812.50 is paid to the bond-holder on 15 August.
[2] A further $398.05 accrues between 15 August and 3 September, the first delivery date.
[3] This represents 69 days interest at 12% on the purchase price of $81,000.

Once again this set of cash and futures prices appears to present an arbitrage opportunity. The potential profit would be slightly greater than that indicated, because the $3,812.50 of accrued interest paid on 15 August could have been reinvested for 19 days at a market rate of interest. Again, to make the transaction nearly riskless, when actually doing this cash and carry, the same sort of weighting procedure, discussed in the gilt-edged case above, has to be done.

Similar procedures will apply for GNMA cash and carry arbitrage with one notable exception. The CBT GNMA collateralized depository receipt contract, which is the most widely traded of the GNMA contracts, involves the delivery not of actual GNMA certificates but of a CDR backed by GNMA certificates. Assuming the short buys actual GNMA certificates in the cash market, and originates a CDR for delivery, he will not actually hand out the certificates until the CDR is surrendered. Hence the trader does not know for how long he will need to continue to finance his GNMA cash position. This makes cash and carry arbitrage very risky and difficult for GNMA CDR futures contracts.

The CBT does trade a certificate delivery GNMA futures contract, which involves the delivery of actual GNMA certificates, and is therefore suitable for cash and carry operations. But the liquidity of the contract is extremely poor, making arbitrage trading in sufficiently large volume almost impossible. For all these reasons, GNMA cash and carry arbitrage is probably not an operational strategy.

Cash and carry arbitrage, therefore, is normally confined to Treasury bond operations on the

Chicago Board of Trade, and long gilt transactions on the London International Financial Futures Exchange, and perhaps to a modest degree, 91-day Treasury bill contracts on the IMM.

It is worth the trader recognizing that no matter how carefully he plans his arbitrage strategy, no strategy involving open futures positions can ever be truly riskless, because of the system of initial and variation margins. Unanticipated margin calls, and the cost of financing them, will clearly impact upon the arbitrage profits illustrated earlier. Every serious trader must carefully analyse the potential impact of adverse marking to market developments before implementing a trading strategy. Given that arbitrage profits will be small relative to potential open position and spreading profits, adverse margin developments could affect the profitability of this type of trading more than most.

For taxation purposes the implied repo rates and cash market rates are calculated on a gross basis. In practice a fund manager or other arbitrageur will wish to feed his corporate tax rate into the equations shown to arrive at after-tax equivalent returns. In many cases arbitrage profits which appear significant in gross terms may disappear when individual tax rates are taken into account.

In practice, anyone contemplating this type of arbitrage will need to obtain computer systems that constantly monitor gilt and bond prices and futures prices to assess potential profits. If such profits appear large relative to variation margin risk and commission charges, a transaction may be attractive. However, cash and carry strategies are more complex than the nice simple examples normally presented. Given the complexities, this type of arbitrage will probably not be as popular as some of the others.

B. Futures and forward-forward arbitrage

This type of arbitrage is simpler to implement than cash and carry arbitrage, and is a fairly common type of arbitrage trading in financial futures markets. To obtain forward-forward rates does mean that the trader needs access to the money and interbank markets. Hence, this type of arbitrage is generally confined to banks and other large financial institutions.

There is a close connection between the cash yield curve and the futures market yield curve. The simple expectations theory of interest rates states the following

$$1 + \frac{\Gamma_2 t_2}{Y} = \left(1 + \frac{\Gamma_1 t_1}{Y}\right)\left(1 + \frac{\Gamma^\star (t_2 - t_1)}{Y}\right)$$

where Γ_2 = annual interest rate on an instrument of maturity t_2 days

Γ_1 = annual interest rate on an instrument of maturity t_1 days

$\Gamma^\star$ = annual interest rate on an instrument of maturity $(t_2 - t_1)$ days, in t_1 days time implicit in the yield curve

Y = number of days in the year: 365 days for sterling time deposits on LIFFE, 360 days for Eurodollar time deposits on LIFFE and the IMM

So if Γ_2 is the annual rate of interest on a 180-day sterling time deposit and Γ_1 is the rate on a 90-day sterling deposit, we can find the implicit rate on a 90-day sterling time deposit for a 90-day period starting in 90 days time. More simply, if you have a six-month rate and a three-month rate, you have an implicit value for the three-month rate in three months' time.

This forward-forward rate is exactly what the price of a futures contract represents—an interest rate commencing at some point in the future. If we were to estimate the implied three-month interest rate for September from the cash yield curve, and compare that with the rate implied by a September futures contract, and found them to be significantly different, an arbitrage trading opportunity should exist.

This type of arbitrage can be illustrated by using the time-security grid (Exhibit 7.4). On 15

December it is observed that 90-day Eurodollar interbank rates are 11–11¼% and 181-day Eurodollar interbank rates are 11½–12%. March Eurodollar futures on LIFFE with a delivery date of 15 March are trading at 87.00.

Exhibit 7.4: Forward-forward versus futures arbitrage

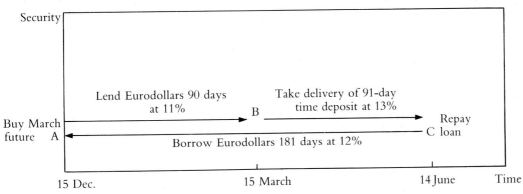

Transaction 1: A   Borrow Eurodollars for 181 days at 12%
Transaction 2: AB $1 invested for 90 days at 11% yields

$$\$1 \times \left\{ 1 + \left[0.11 \times \frac{90}{360} \right] \right\} = \$1.0275 \text{ at } B$$

Transaction 3: BC $1.0275 invested for 91 days at 13% yields

$$\$1.0275 \times \left\{ 1 + \left[0.13 \times \frac{91}{360} \right] \right\} = \$1.06127$$

Transaction 4: C   Repay Eurodollar borrowing

$$\text{Cost} = \$1 \times \left\{ 1 + \left[0.12 \times \frac{181}{360} \right] \right\} = \$1.06033$$

So, the arbitrage ratio is:

$$\text{Arbitrage ratio} = 1.06137/1.06033 = 1.00098$$

A profitable arbitrage appears to be possible. The sensitivities can be worked out in the usual way:

$$\text{90-day Eurodollar lending: } 0.00098 \times \frac{360}{90} \times 10,000 = 39 \text{ basis points}$$

$$\text{181-day Eurodollar borrowing: } -0.00098 \times \frac{360}{181} \times 10,000 = (20) \text{ basis points}$$

$$\text{Eurodollar future implied rate: } 0.00098 \times \frac{360}{91} \times 10,000 = 39 \text{ basis points}$$

How would this work out in terms of a cash transaction?

Step 1: Borrow $1,000,000 for 181 days at 12%. You commit yourself to repay $1,060,333 in 181 days time.
Lend $1,000,000 for 90 days at 11%. You will receive $1,027,500 in 90 days time.
Buy one March futures contract at 87.00.

Step 2: Receive repayment of $1,027.500 from 90-day Eurodollar lending.
Invest $27,500 at March cash market 91-day rate of 12⅞%.
Take delivery of $1,000,000 Eurodollar time deposit at interest rate of 13%.

Step 3: Receive $1,032,861 for Eurodollar time deposit.
Receive back $27,500 plus interest at 12⅞% equals $28,385.
Pay back Eurodollar borrowing at a cost of $1,060,333.

$$\text{Net gain} = \$1,032,861 + \$28,385 - \$1,060,333$$

$$= \$913$$

There is a slight difference between this profit of $913 and the theoretical profit implied by the arbitrage ratio of $980. This arises because the reinvestment rate for the $27,500 of interest on 15 March was slightly lower than the 13% implied in the futures price. This difference implies a degree of risk in the arbitrage strategy. Consider what would have happened if the Eurodollar three-month rate had fallen to 6% by March: while the 13% on the futures contract of $1,000,000 is guaranteed, the return on the $27,500 would have fallen. The net gain would look rather different.

$$\text{Net gain} = \$1,032,861 + \$27,917.08 - \$1,060,333$$
$$= \$445.00$$

Doing the forward-forward/futures arbitrage in this way involves taking a view on the future evolution of interest rates. The way to remove this risk is to buy enough futures contracts so that the 13% is guaranteed on the interim interest payments as well as the overall borrowing position. In the case illustrated, the interest after three months was $27,500, and a guaranteed rate of return of 13% on it for 91 days was needed. But the minimum size of the Eurodollar futures contract is $1,000,000. So, to be able to lock in the interest income return, the minimum number of contracts to match the principal sum would be $1,000,000/$27,500 = 36.4 or approximately 36. To create an almost riskless forward-forward/futures arbitrage, the trader therefore would have to borrow $36,000,000 for 181 days, lend $36,000,000 for 90 days, and purchase 37 Eurodollar futures contracts. While such sums are not large in the context of the Eurodollar market, they do suggest that this type of arbitrage trading will be restricted to large financial institutions and corporate investors.

This kind of arbitrage will probably look even better from the point of view of a bank. In the example above, the trader lent at the bid rate and borrowed at the offer rate. A bank would be doing the reverse: taking in money for 181 days at 11¾% and lending for 90 days at 11¼%. This would increase the arbitrage ratio from 1.00098 to 1.002676. The appeal of this type of arbitrage to banks is evident.

In practice, this type of arbitrage will probably be confined to the banking community, not only because of the bid-ask spread advantage, but because non-banks may find it difficult to borrow for periods different to the standard one-month, three-month and six-month maturities. The cost of financing initial margin, which could be substantial at least on LIFFE, or the adverse impact of marking to market have also not been taken into account. Finally, losses on the futures position need to be paid immediately, while the locked-in gain is not received until the final interest payment on the transaction.

C. Interest and foreign exchange futures combination arbitrage

A third type of financial futures arbitrage involves the use of combination positions of interest rate and foreign exchange rate futures. Domestic interest rate futures can be combined with foreign exchange futures to construct artificial interest rate futures denominated in foreign currencies (see Chapter 5). The arbitrage aspect of these constructs is to compare them with the actual foreign currency rates, and if they are different, arbitrage profits should be possible. The example given in our initial discussion of arbitrage (see p. 138) was one of this type. We will work through this again, looking at the implied transactions to see whether this kind of arbitrage trading is feasible.

	Sterling deposit future	Eurodollar deposit future	$/£ future
September	86.50	85.60	1.7985
December	86.40	85.60	1.8049

There is an arbitrage ratio of 1.0008 to buying sterling time deposit futures, selling Eurodollar time deposit futures, both for September delivery, and buying the sterling/dollar future for September and selling the sterling/dollar future for December. However, getting

148

hold of the arbitrage profit is easier said than done. The problem is the standardization of contract size.

The trader's first thought might be to buy one £250,000 September sterling deposit future and sell 10 foreign exchange futures of £25,000 each. The trader would then be committed to delivering £449,625, but the minimum transaction size in Eurodollar futures is $1,000,000. Even if the trader purchased two sterling contracts and sold 20 foreign exchange contracts, he would require only $899,250 to deliver against the FX contracts, while committing himself through the Eurodollar future to paying 14.40% on $1,000,000 from September to December. Moreover, to avoid further risk he would need to put on further foreign exchange contracts in September to lock in the exchange rate on the dollar interest payments he is committing himself to make in that month.

The standardized nature of the futures contracts makes it almost impossible to make arbitrage of this kind riskless. The small size of the foreign exchange contracts necessitates putting on a very large number to match the size of the interest rate contracts, so that commission costs could be heavy enough to outweigh profits.

A more sensible approach is probably to carry out the interest rate transactions in the futures market, but lock the exchange rates in the forward market where odd transaction sizes are common and commission costs are much lower. The numbers below illustrates the arbitrage if forward exchange rates are equal to futures exchange rates.

Example

Step 1: 30 April
    Purchase 20 June sterling deposit futures at 86.50.
    Sell nine June Eurodollar deposit futures at 85.60.
    Buy £5,000,000 forward for June delivery at 1.7985.
    Buy $9,320,100 forward for September delivery at 1.8049.

Step 2: June delivery date
    Take delivery of 20 sterling time deposit at an interest rate of 13.5%. You pay £5,000,000 and will receive £5,168,287.50 in September.
    Deliver against nine Eurodollar time deposit futures—interest rate 14.4%.
    You receive $9,000,000 and commit to pay $9,327,600 in September.
    Pay $8,992,500 to receive £5,000,000
    Invest spare $7,500 at prevailing market rates.

Step 3: September delivery date
    Receive £5,168,287.50 for sterling time deposits.
    Purchase $9,320,100 for a payment of £5,163,776.30.
    Recover $7,500 plus any accrued interest.
    Make payment of $9,327,600 to Eurodollar time deposit owners.

$$\text{Net gain} = £5,168,287.50 - £5,163,776.30 + (\text{interest on } \$7,500)$$

$$= £4,511.20 + \text{any accrued interest.}$$

Use of the forward market in foreign exchange makes this type of arbitrage very feasible. But it does mean that this trading strategy is really only relevant for banks and other major financial institutions. Such financial futures arbitrage will be an interesting adjunct to current interbank money market and forward exchange market arbitrage for the major money market banks.

Like most arbitrages, this one could be done using smaller quantities of contracts, on the assumption that prices will return to a non-arbitrage position prior to delivery. In that case, the position could be unwound for a profit without any of the complexities outlined above playing a part. However, such a strategy is still risky, since the restoration of equilibrium may not occur before the first delivery date.

D. Short-term and long-term spread arbitrage

The spreads on LIFFE gilt futures contracts correspond to a short-term interest rate between the two contract months; the same rationale also applies to T-bond and GNMA spreads. The implicit short-term rate is calculated as the sum of the yield equivalent of the spread plus the effective running yield on the long-term instrument calculated from the nearby futures price.

This relationship could be useful in spread trade analysis, but it may also provide an arbitrage opportunity. Supposing the implicit three-month yield starting in September is calculated from the September–December T-bond spread. This can be compared with the implicit yield in the September 91-day T-bill futures price. Since they are both three-month rates on government instruments, they should be the same. If they are not, an arbitrage profit ought to be available.

Consider the following information set on 10 November. The IMM December T-bill future is trading at 90-86. The December T-bond future is trading at 93-12 and the March T-bond is trading at 93-14. Is an arbitrage profit available?

This can be worked out through the loop in the time-security grid (Exhibit 7.5).

Exhibit 7.5: T-bond spreads versus short-term rates arbitrage

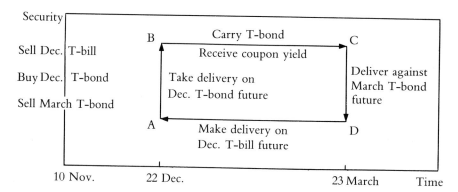

Transaction 1: AB   Borrow $93-12 at 9.48%* and take delivery of $100 nominal T-bonds 8% 20-year.

Transaction 2: BC   Receive accrued interest on T-bond equal to $1.9945 at C.

Transaction 3: CD   Deliver $100 nominal of 8% 20-year T-bonds.
Receive $93-14.

Transaction 4: DA   Repay loan

$$\text{Redemption value} = 93\ 12/32 \left[1 + \left(0.0948 \times \frac{91}{360} \right) \right] = 95\text{-}20$$

* This is the effective yield on the T-bill: Effective yield $= \left[9.14 \times \frac{91}{360} \right] \Big/ \left[100 - \frac{9.14 \times 91}{360} \right] \times \frac{365}{91} = 9.48\%$

The arbitrage ratio is less than one.

Arbitrage ratio = 0.997982 ([93-12 + 1.9945]/95-20)

If we carried out the transactions represented by the arrows shown in the loop, we would lose money. So our natural reaction is to try the arbitrage the other way round. We would be able to make a positive arbitrage profit by buying the December 82 T-bill future and selling the December–March T-bond spread. The arbitrage rate will then be:

Arbitrage ratio = 1.002022

And again we calculate the sensitivities in the usual way.

T-bond Dec. future:	0.002022 × (93-12) × 32 = 6/32nds
T-bond March future:	(0.002022 × 93-14 × 32) = (6/32nds)
T-bill Dec. future:	$0.002022 \times \dfrac{360}{91} \times 10{,}000 = 80$ basis points

This looks a good arbitrage, relatively insensitive to small movements in the various futures prices. It also illustrates an important point: that if going round the loop one way shows a loss, going round the other way may well produce an arbitrage profit.

At first sight it would appear that the correct ratio of contracts in the arbitrage would be one T-bill to 10 T-bond spreads, since the T-bill contract is $1,000,000 face value and the T-bond contract is $10,000 face value. But this is the correct ratio only when an 8% 20-year T-bond is delivered. It will not be the case in practice. Many different bonds are deliverable against the T-bond contract, and the conversion factors used in invoicing equate yield to maturity, not running yield. The running yield on the bond on which delivery is taken in December could be very different to that of an 8% 20-year T-bond, and this could make a big difference to the net arbitrage profit. Secondly, the money that needs to be put up to buy the T-bill will not necessarily be simply 10 times the invoice amount of the bond the trader chooses to deliver. These technical difficulties can be illustrated with some numbers.

Example

The trader decides to sell the T-bond spread and buy the December T-bill. He chooses to make delivery with the $7\frac{5}{8}$% T-bond (15 February) 2002–07. The relevant conversion values for December and March are both 0.9637 (*see* Exhibit 3.8).

Step 1: 10 November
   Buy one December T-bill future at 90-86.
   Sell 11★ December T-bond futures at 93-12.
   Buy 11★ December T-bond futures at 93-14.
   ★ A closer approximation of T-bill cost/T-bond invoice amount.

Step 2: 22 December
   Take delivery of a 91-day T-bill. Face value $1,000,000. Discount yield 9.14%. Payment is $976,896.
   Deliver $1,100,000 of face value of $7\frac{5}{8}$% 2002-07 T-bonds
   Invoice amount received $1,019,678.20 [(93-12 × 0.9637 × 1000) + Accrued interest] × 11
   Interest payment of $41,937.50 on 15 February.
   Invest $844.70 surplus in money market.

Step 3: 23 March
   Receive payment of $1,000,000 for T-bill.
   Take delivery of $1,100,000 face value $7\frac{5}{8}$% T-bonds.
   Invoice amount $998,110.29 [(93-14 × 0.963 × 1000] + Accrued interest] × 11
   Receive $844.70 plus interest.

Ignoring the minor amount of interest on the $1,146.50, the net gain to the arbitrage position can be calculated.

$$\text{Net gain} = \$1,000,000 - \$976,896 + \$1,019,678.20 - \$41,937.5 - \$998,110.29$$
$$= \$2,734.41$$

This arbitrage looks feasible if a little complicated. But there are various reasons which suggest it will be difficult to achieve in practice. The arbitrage gain of $2,734.41 is significantly different to that implied by the arbitrage ratio. This is because the running yield on the $7\frac{5}{8}$% bond is less than the running yield on the standard 8% 20-year bond after adjusting for the price factor. This is controllable when the arbitrage calls for the trader to sell the T-bond spread, since the seller of the nearby contract has the choice of which contract to deliver. Were it the other way around, however, the trader would have no idea which T-bond would be delivered to him, so he would not be able to calculate the effective yield on the T-bond spread in advance. This would make the arbitrage impossible.

Even in this example, the technique presents difficulties. The case involves a trader who delivers the $7\frac{5}{8}$% T-bond against the nearby leg of the spread. But it was assumed that the same bond would be delivered back to him. The trader in practice will not know the actual bond he will receive until it is actually delivered, nor will he know the date in the delivery month on which delivery will be made. Thus the invoice amount is unknown, and there may be a gap between the receipt of the funds from the T-bill and the payment on the second leg of the T-bond spread. Such a gap could involve additional financing.

It was also assumed that the closing prices on the futures contracts are equal to the prices when the arbitrage position is set up. This is unlikely in practice, and changes in price will have effects on the cash gains or losses similar to the cash and carry arbitrage example worked out earlier. More complex weighting of the T-bond spread, both with respect to the T-bill position, and for one spread leg to another, will be necessary.

Thus, delivery complications and the sensitivity of effective spread yields to the contracts delivered generally make this type of trading relatively risky. The fact that T-bond spreads yields and T-bill futures yields are often significantly out of line in the markets suggests that arbitrage trading is restricted in this area. It is probably better simply to put on the arbitrage in the hope prices will adjust before delivery, and close out before delivery even at a loss, rather than enter into the complications outlined above.

In addition, potential arbitrage profits have been determined in terms of the standardized 20-year 8% T-bond. Many traders would believe that this arbitrage calculation should be carried out in terms of the implied spreads on the cheapest deliverable instrument, since this will be the one most likely to be delivered and redelivered. This will alter the notional rate of return considerably, as can be seen from a LIFFE gilt example.

We have the following set of information:

$$March\ gilt\ futures\ price\ =\ 100\text{-}09$$
$$June\ gilt\ futures\ price\ =\ 99\text{-}25$$

$$March\ price\ factor\ for\ Treasury\ 15\tfrac{1}{2}\%\ 1998\ =\ 1.2446$$
$$June\ price\ factor\ for\ Treasury\ 15\tfrac{1}{2}\%\ 1998\ =\ 1.2416$$

$$March\ sterling\ deposit\ future\ price\ =\ 90.25$$

Using this information we can calculate the interest rate implied in the gilt spread.

$$Cash\ outlay\ (2nd\ Wed.\ March) = [100\text{-}09 \times 500 \times 1.2446] - £445.89\ [Accrued\ interest]$$
$$= £61,959.13$$

$$Cash\ inflow\ (2nd\ Wed.\ June) = [99\text{-}25 \times 500 \times 1.2416] + £1,486.30\ [Accrued\ interest]$$
$$= £63,430.50$$

$$Effective\ interest\ rate = \left[\left(\frac{63,430.50}{61,959.13} - 1\right) \times \frac{365}{91}\right] \times 100$$

$$= 9.53\%$$

That compares with the rate in the sterling time deposit futures market of 9.75% for the same period; hence there is a potential arbitrage profit of 22 basis points available. This might be too small to be attractive to the average arbitrageur.

This implied repo rate can also be compared to the rate which would be calculated by the original method.

$$Purchase\ £100\ nominal\ 12\%\ 20\text{-}year\ gilt\ for\quad £100.28125\ (100\text{-}09)$$
$$Sell\ £100\ nominal\ 12\%\ 20\text{-}year\ gilt\ for\quad £\ 99.78125\ (\ 99\text{-}25)$$
$$Receive\ accrued\ interest\ of\ £12 \times 91/365\quad £2.99178$$

$$Implied\ interest\ rate = \left[\left(\frac{99.78125 + 2.99178}{100.28125}\right) - 1\right] \times \frac{365}{91} = 9.97\%$$

Hence, calculating the implied interest rate in the gilt spread using the cheapest deliverable stock gives a rate about 44 basis points lower than calculating it using the standardized gilt on which the futures contract is written. In general, it is probably better to use the rate implied by the cheapest deliverable gilt or T-bond. However, some traders prefer to treat the future as an independent instrument. It is an empirical question as to whether the spread in the market tends to return to that implied by the standard bond or that implied by the cheapest deliverable instrument.

E. Simple inter-market arbitrage

The simplest type of arbitrage arises when an identical financial asset is priced differently in two markets. For instance, a trader could arbitrage the LIFFE or IMM foreign currency contracts and the interbank forward market. Take the following set of rates.

Example

$$Forward\ interbank\ market\ for\ June\quad 1.7650$$
$$IMM\ \$/£\ futures\ contract\ for\ June\quad 1.7615$$

Step 1: Buy 10 IMM June contracts of face value £250,000 equivalent to $440,375.
Sell interbank £250,000 forward equivalent to $441,250 for 9 June delivery.

When the markets come back into line under the pressure of arbitrage trading, the trader can close out his position.

Step 2: Sell 10 IMM June contracts at $1.7500 equivalent to $437.500.
　　　Buy interbank £250,000 forward at $1.7500 equivalent to $437,500 for 9 June delivery.

Gain on IMM position = ($2,875)

Gain on forward position = $3,750

Net gain on arbitrage = $875

If the two markets did not come back together before the delivery date, the trader could take delivery on the IMM contracts and deliver the £250,000 to satisfy his forward commitment, locking in the same profit.

Arbitrages of this kind could also be carried out between the two Eurodollar deposit contracts on LIFFE and IMM.

F. Summing up arbitrage

The basic message of arbitrage trading is that although the concept is simple, the strategies are often very difficult to execute in practice. Virtually all of the strategies discussed here (and there are many other strategies used in financial futures markets) are really only suitable for large, sophisticated traders, particularly banks and other financial institutions. Moreover, in relatively efficient markets, price discrepancies tend to be small and last for only short periods. Hence, to earn significant profits, the arbitrageur generally would have to put on relatively large positions, and be very quick to take advantage of temporary price anomalies.

It is also difficult to set up financial futures positions which generate the true riskless arbitrage profits beloved of the textbooks. Delivery complications, problems of contract size, and possible adverse variation margin calls, all serve to introduce risk into theoretically riskless arbitrage situations. In a sense much of the real-world arbitrage trading could just as easily be described as very complicated spread trading. However, the role of commissions plays a bigger role than in spread trading, and the level of arbitrage profits makes this type of trading generally unprofitable for non-members of the financial futures exchanges.

Chapter 8

Investment applications of financial futures

Many of the techniques and methods of analysis used in hedging and trading are also directly applicable to investment decisions where the futures market is used as a means of acquiring a specific asset rather than purchasing the asset directly, or where an investor planning to purchase a particular asset can achieve a higher rate of return from a combination of some other equivalent risk asset and a position in financial futures. This chapter discusses a few examples of such strategies.

A. Hedging a yield curve ride

One of the most common choices available to an investor with short-term funds is between investing directly in an asset of the required maturity but carrying a lower yield, and putting the money in a longer maturity asset at a higher yield, but carrying the risk that when the asset is sold, interest rates will have moved against the investor.

For example, on 20 April, 61-day Treasury bills were yielding 10.70% and 152-day Treasury bills were yielding 11.25%. Without futures, two investment strategies are possible if funds are required on 21 June: buy 61-day T-bills, or purchase 152-day T-bills and sell them on 21 June. It is also assumed that surplus funds can be invested in the money market at 10.50%.

Alternative 1

20 April:	Buy 61-day T-bill. Hold to maturity	
	Discount (61-day T-bills)	= 10.70%
	Purchase price	= $981,869.44
	Gain	= $18,130.56
	Equivalent annual yield	= 11.05%

Alternative 2

20 April:	Buy 152-day T-bill	
	Discount yield	= 11.25%
	Purchase price	= $952,500
	Invest $29,369.44 (981,869.44 − 952,500) for 61 days at 10.50%	
21 June:	91-day T-bill discount yield	= 12.5%
	Sale price of T-bill	= $968,402.78
	Gain on T-bill	= $15,902.78
	Gain from surplus investment	= $522.53
	Total gain	= $16,425.31
	Equivalent yield	= 10.01%

Thus, although the 152-day T-bill discount yield was 55 basis points higher than that of the 61-day T-bill on 20 April, adverse interest rate movements between 20 April and 21 June resulted in an effective loss of annual yield of over 100 basis points.

The concept of T-bill futures trading on the IMM may change the return to the investments dramatically. The sale of a T-bill contract will allow the investor to lock in the rate at which he can deliver the 91-day T-bill to the market. Assuming the price of a June T-bill future with a delivery date of 21 June is selling on 20 April for 88.70, which is an effective discount yield of 11.30%, the basis is favourable for a short hedger. The decision is then to sell the June T-bill futures contract.

Alternative 3

20 April:	Buy 152-day T-bill	
	Discount yield 11.25%	
	Purchase price	= $952,500
	Invest $27,369.44 for 61 days at 10.5%	
	Pay $2,000 initial margin on	
	purchase of June T-bill future at 88.70	
21 June:	Gain from surplus investment	= $486.94
	Deliver 91-day T-bill to market	
	Settlement price	= $87.50
	Receive payment	= $968,402.78
	Receive profit and initial margin	
	from futures contract profit	= 1 × $25 × 120 ticks = $3,000
	Initial margin	= $2,000
	Total gain	= $19,389.72
	Equivalent yield	= 11.82%

Thus the hedged yield curve ride involving the simultaneous purchase of a 152-day T-bill and sale of a T-bill futures contract has actually raised the effective annual yield to 77 basis points above that achieved by the simple purchase of a 61-day T-bill. In this case it is possible that the investor would have had the use of surplus margin funds during the investment period, and hence could have earned even higher rates of return. There is also the possibility that the futures position might have moved against the investor, in which case variation margin calls would need to be met. Nonetheless a cushion of 77 basis points extra annual yield is quite a comfortable one.

This is a classic case of using the futures market to improve the yield on an investment without a major increase in risk. If the date the money was needed did not actually correspond to the delivery day on the contract, an extra element of basis risk would need to be taken into consideration by the investor.

B. Cash market yields versus futures yields (a strip of futures)

Methods for evaluating future prices from the strip yield curve implied by forward-forward prices have already been discussed. Any investor wishing to invest money for periods of up to a year or so should explore the possibilities offered by a sequence of futures contracts. Consider the following set of rates in the Eurodollar market on 15 March:

	Futures prices	**Cash yields**
June	89.73	3-month 10.08
September	89.38	6-month 10.34
December	89.06	9-month 10.46
March	88.82	12-month 10.46
June	88.60	

Using this data, the comparative returns to investing money can be looked at in two different ways. Consider an investor wishing to put his funds away for nine months: he could invest it directly for nine months at 10.46%, or he could invest it for three months at 10.08% and purchase a June Eurodollar time deposit contract and a September Eurodollar time deposit contract. The implied nine-month yield from the June and September contracts would be:

Nine-month implied yield

$$\text{March–June return} = 10.08\% \times \frac{3}{12} = 2.52\%$$

$$\text{June–September return} = 10.27\%(100 - 89.73) \times \frac{3}{12} = 2.5675\%$$

156

$$\text{September–December return} = 10.62\%(100 - 89.38) \times \frac{3}{12} = 2.655\%$$

$$\text{Nine-month return} = \{(1.0252)(1.025675)(1.02655) - 1\} \times 100$$
$$= 7.9440\%$$

$$\text{Equivalent annual yield (March–December)} = 7.944 \times \frac{12}{9}$$
$$= 10.59\%$$

Calculated in a similar manner, the implied six-month and 12-month return from the futures strip are 10.30% and 10.90% respectively.

Hence it looks as if investing money directly for six months is better than investing for three-months and purchasing a June futures contract. But the cash three-month plus futures strip seems advantageous compared to direct cash investments for nine-month and 12-month periods. However, the implied cash-futures rates shown above assume that not only the principal but also the quarterly interest can be invested at the rate implied in the Eurodollar time deposit futures contracts. This is not the case in practice—quarterly interest needs to be invested at the market rate prevailing for three-month funds at the time the interest is paid.

In these comparisons it is also useful to calculate the minimum reinvestment rate necessary to ensure that the cash futures alternative is better than the straight cash investment. In the nine-month and 12-month cases above, the minimum reinvestment rates are 8% and 0% respectively. Thus although there is a possible risk for the nine-month case, the reinvestment rate could fall to zero without altering the dominance of the 12-month cash-futures alternative over the straight cash investment. In this case, the only remaining risk is the possibility that adverse variation margin payments might be necessary on the futures side of the investment. Alternative investments of this nature can be very attractive in certain markets, and all investors with funds of up to one-year maturity to invest should explore the cash-futures alternatives.

C. Using the long-term contracts

One problem with using the long-term interest contracts such as the Treasury bond, gilt and GNMA contracts for investment purposes is that the entire delivery system is under the control of the short. Hence the investor taking delivery does not know which particular security he will receive. However, the concept that these futures will trade off the cheapest deliverable instrument—which in most cases will be the one delivered—has been discussed. Moreover if the short were to deliver a stock other than the cheapest deliverable security, there will be by definition a profit to be had in selling on the delivered stock in the cash market and switching back into the cheapest deliverable stock.

One of the investment possibilities with long-term securities is a cash and carry (which is the same type of hedged yield curve ride discussed with Treasury bill futures). The alternatives are a cash and carry long-term instrument as opposed to, say, an investment in a medium-term instrument. These investment alternatives are particularly important on the CBT where Treasury bond futures contracts trade with good liquidity as far as 10 to 11 deferred quarters.

Thus an investor might wish to consider the alternatives of purchasing a two-year Treasury note for cash, or buying a cash Treasury bond, at the same time locking in the sale price of the bond by selling a Treasury bond futures contract with a delivery date in two years time.

Alternative 1

15 March, 1983	Buy 14% 2011 T-bond at 115-23
	Sell March 1985 T-bond future 71-05
	Conversion factor for 14% 2011 T-bond = 1.6333
	Equivalent parity price = 70-27

Alternative 2

Buy two-year T-bond. Yield to maturity = 13.00%

Results

Alternative 1

Receive interest payments of $70,000 on 15 May, 1983
$$15 \text{ Nov. } 1983$$
$$15 \text{ May, } 1984$$
$$15 \text{ Nov. } 1984$$

$$\text{Total cost of T-bond} = \$1,157,187.50 + \left[\$70,000 \times \frac{130}{181}\right]$$

$$= \$1,207,463.70$$

Accrued interest on 15 March, 1985

$$[70,000\,(1.07)^3 + 70,000\,(1.07)^2 + 70,000\,(1.07) + 70,000]\left(1 + 0.14 \times \frac{130}{360}\right)$$

$$= \$326,508.49$$

Invoice price at delivery
$$= \{(71\text{-}05)\,(\$100,000)\,(1.6333)\} + \left\{70,000 \times \frac{130}{181}\right\}$$

$$= \$1,212,471.2$$

$$\text{Implied yield} = \left\{\frac{\$1,538,979.70}{\$1,207,463.70} - 1\right\} \times \frac{1}{2} = 13.73\%$$

The hedged yield curve strategy, but this time over a two-year time horizon using Treasury bond futures, displays a significant higher yield than the two-year Treasury note purchase. However, we have assumed that we can reinvest the half-yearly interest payments at the nominal yield on the cheapest deliverable Treasury bond. Since this will not be the case in practice, the investor will need to calculate minimum reinvestment rates required to preserve the advantages of Alternative 2 over Alternative 1.

This type of investment transaction can also be carried out in reverse, creating the long-term futures equivalent of the futures strip. Consider the following alternatives, where a portfolio manager has funds immediately available for investment in gilts. For the sake of simplicity, this example uses current yields only.

Alternative 1

20 September   Buy the Treasury 15.5% 1998 (cheapest deliverable gilt on LIFFE) immediately at 129-08.
Current yield = 12.09%.

Alternative 2

20 September   Invest in the interbank market for six-months at 12.25%.
Buy LIFFE gilt futures for March delivery at 102-16

Conversion factor for Treasury 15.5% 1998 = 1.2446
Implied Treasury 15.5% 1998 price = (102-16)(1.2446)
$$= 127\text{-}18.$$
Implied current yield = 12.15%

In this case, delaying the gilt purchase and temporarily investing the funds in the short-term money market but locking in the gilt purchase price through the futures market has resulted in a higher current yield, and yield to maturity, over the life of the gilt, and a higher yield in the short-term as well. In March the investor can either take delivery of the gilt through the futures market, or unwind the futures transaction and purchase the gilt in the cash market. Deferred purchases of long-term assets such as gilts, Treasury bonds, and GNMAs are a facility readily offered by a liquid futures market, and should be considered by portfolio managers with funds for long-term investment.

In addition to delayed purchases of this kind, long-term futures may be bought directly as an investment on grounds of relative cheapness. Imagine the date is 15 April, and the portfolio manager's forecast is that Treasury bonds are going to rise sharply between that date and June. The portfolio manager should aim to acquire the asset that will appreciate most in such a rally.

The general rule is that when prices rise, the best purchase or the cheapest item rises the most. Occasionally the futures market may look cheap compared to all available cash market instruments. This was frequently the case on LIFFE in its early months of trading, when the implied repo rate on gilt cash and carry transactions was well below rates existing in the money markets. In the case above, if the repo rate on the cheapest deliverable Treasury bond on 15 April is below the equivalent money market rate, a straight investment in June Treasury bond futures will generally produce higher returns than a straight cash T-bond purchase in the case of a rally. Such alternative investments should also be borne in mind by fund managers attempting to adjust portfolios in line with interest rate forecasts.

A similar position arises with stock market indices. When hedging, portfolio managers can use stock market indices to protect their portfolios against systematic risk: by selling stock market indices, the beta of an equity portfolio is reduced. The reverse is true as well.

Consider a well-diversified portfolio with a beta of 1.0, where the fund manager is expecting a sharp rise in the market. One alternative strategy is to rebalance the portfolio towards higher beta stocks. But this will involve transactions costs, may take considerable time, and can conflict with long-term considerations. The alternative investment strategy is to buy stock market index futures. By purchasing S + P 500 index futures in dollar amount equivalent to one-third of the existing portfolio, the effective beta of the portfolio is raised to 1.33. If a stock market rally occurs, considerable benefits will accrue to the portfolio.

Example

30 March	$50,000,000 equity portfolio beta = 1.0
	Fund manager expects a sharp rally
	S + P 500 index = 154.02 June S + P index future = 155.10

Alternative 1: No action

| 1 June | S + P 500 index = 167.30 |
| | Portfolio value = $54,000,000 |

In this case the S + P 500 index rose by 8.8% between 30 March and 1 June, while the value of the equity portfolio rose by $4,000,000 or 8%. The performance of the portfolio was in fact slightly less advantageous than its overall beta of 1.0 would have suggested.

Alternative 2

Buy S + P 500 June index futures equivalent to 40% of portfolio:

$$\text{Number of contracts} = \frac{\$50,000,000 \ (0.4)}{154.02 \times \$500} = 259.7 \text{ contracts}$$

| 1 June | Portfolio value = $54,000,000 |
| | Sell June S + P 500 futures at 167.30 |

$$\text{Futures profit} = 260 \text{ contracts} \times \$25 \text{ per contract} \times 244 \text{ ticks} \left(\frac{167.30 - 155.10}{0.05} \right)$$
$$= \$1,586,000$$
$$\text{Total profit} = \$5,586,000 \ (11.2\% \text{ rise})$$

Purchasing S + P 500 index futures to the tune of 40% of the dollar value increases the weighted beta of the portfolio from 1.0 to 1.4. This would lead to an expected rise in the value of the portfolio of 12.3% for a 8.8% rise in the cash S + P index. The actual rise of 11.2% is somewhat less than this, not only because the underlying rise in portfolio value was less than predicted, but because the negative basis between the S + P index spot and the June future was much reduced over the period.

This means that the June futures price did not rise as sharply as the spot index; in fact, it only rose by 7.9% compared with 8.8% for the spot index. Nonetheless the increase in the beta of the portfolio achieved by buying the S + P index futures greatly increased the response of the portfolio to a rise in the overall market. Beta tailoring of portfolios by the purchase and sale of stock index futures clearly has considerable potential for fund managers who believe they can time the market.

D. Complex proxy investments

So far we have dealt with relatively simple investments through futures. However, many of the more complex artificial instruments described in Chapter 7 can be viewed as alternative investments, or proxies as they are generally known. For instance, consider an investor with dollars to invest for a period from 25 July through to mid-December. Alternative investments of equal, or relatively equal risk would be:

(1) Invest dollars for 143 days in money market.
(2) Convert dollars into sterling at the current spot rate; invest sterling for 143 days in money market; convert back at fixed forward rate in December.
(3) Invest dollars for 52 days in money market; buy September Eurodollar futures.
(4) Convert dollars into sterling at current spot rate; invest sterling for 52 days in money market; buy September sterling deposit futures; convert back at fixed forward rate in December.
(5) Convert dollars into sterling at current spot rate; invest sterling for 52 days in money market; buy September sterling deposit futures; sell December $/£ futures.
(6) Invest dollars for 52 days in money market; buy September $/£ futures; buy September sterling deposit futures; sell December $/£ futures.
(7) Invest dollars for 52 days in money market; lock in fixed $/£ forward rate for September; buy September sterling deposit futures; lock in fixed $/£ forward rate for December.
(8) Invest dollars for 52 days in money market; buy September $/£ futures; buy September sterling deposit futures; lock in fixed $/£ forward rate for December.
(9) Invest dollars for 52 days in money market; lock in fixed $/£ forward rate for September; buy September sterling deposit futures; sell $/£ December futures.
(10)–(11) As in (6)–(9). but convert dollars into sterling at spot rate; invest sterling for 52 days in money market; convert back at futures or forward rate in September; buy Eurodollar September future.
(12)–(17) As in (6)–(11) but use forward-forward dollar and sterling rates rather than futures.

This list is not exhaustive; it gives 17 different possible ways of investing dollar funds, i.e. 16 different proxies for the straight 143-day dollar investment, showing the complex investment strategies which are made possible with futures, forward, and forward-forward interest rates and exchange rates. It is comparatively easy to determine the equivalent annual dollar yield for each of the alternatives above. Even so, any investor of short-term funds needs to have access to programmes to evaluate the comparative risks and returns of each of the strategies shown above.

E. Conclusions

The fact that this chapter on investment applications of financial futures is fairly short should not be taken to mean that they are less important than the hedging and trading applications. Many of the hedging applications discussed earlier (in Chapters 4 and 5) are also essentially investment decisions. A fund manager deciding to hedge an anticipated T-bond or gilt purchase, or hedge portfolio value against general declines in interest rates or exchange rates, is making an investment decision.

This chapter illustrates ways of using the futures market to create proxies: mixtures of cash and futures instruments, or sometimes just futures positions which behave exactly like other cash instruments. Of these methods the hedged yield curve ride and the futures strip, either in short- or long-term instruments, are by far the most important.

Important points for investors
1. When investing short or medium-term funds, always investigate whether a hedged yield curve ride in short- or long-run interest rate futures will lock in a higher yield than the instrument you were going to use.
2. When investing short-term funds, investigate whether a futures strip gives a higher return than a straight investment, but remember the minimum reinvestment rate.
3. When buying long-term assets, investigate whether a deferred purchase via the futures market gives a better return.
4. Always check all the proxies for an investment before deciding which way to do it.
5. Use interest rate and stock index futures to adjust risk of portfolios to better respond to movements in general rates or stock market conditions.
6. Always examine if futures are cheaper than cash.

Chapter 9

Accounting and taxation treatment of financial futures*

A. Accounting issues

Any deal on a financial futures exchange has accounting implications. This chapter highlights and discusses the various accounting matters which have to be resolved before accounts can be drawn up. Practice will differ in every country, but the basic problems which arise are the same.

1. At what stage should unrealized gains and losses be recognized?
2. Should financial futures contracts be treated as commitments?
3. Should the accounting treatment for trading and hedging transactions be the same or should the treatment reflect the purpose of the transactions?
4. What should be disclosed in the financial statements?

The resolution of these problems will depend upon the needs and characteristics of a particular company and the environment in which it operates. Legislation, accounting standards and taxation considerations are not internationally uniform and these all have a bearing on the accounting treatment which should be adopted.

1. Accounting principles

There are no authoritative guidelines on accounting for financial futures in the UK, the United States, or indeed elsewhere.

Clearly the circumstances of each user will be different and the commercial intentions and ramifications of individual transactions will vary. It is thus important, when considering appropriate accounting policies and accounting and reporting systems for financial futures, that users should involve their auditors or financial advisers.

Before discussing any of the specific accounting issues arising from financial futures transactions, it is useful to look at the background to accounting and reporting in the UK and the United States, which are the first two countries to have a financial futures exchange.

United Kingdom

Accounting and reporting in the UK is governed by the Companies Acts which until recently were not prescriptive in terms of profit measurement but were concerned with disclosure and truth and fairness. The development of standards to regulate measurement has largely been left to the accounting profession. The Accounting Standards Committee of the Consultative Committee of Accountancy Bodies has promulgated a number of statements of standard accounting practice (SSAPs) which seek to standardize the treatment of the individual aspects they address. Many of these standards are similar to the international accounting standards (IASs) issued by the International Accounting Standards Committee.

The 1981 Companies Act, implementing the EEC Fourth Directive, adds to the disclosure requirements particularly in terms of the prescribed format of company accounts; it also incorporates certain rules of measurement and embraces the concepts set out in IAS 1,

---

* This chapter was written by Price Waterhouse.

"Disclosure of Accounting Policies". In particular the inclusion of unrealized profits in the distributable reserves of an entity (excluding banks) is prohibited. Realized profits are defined as those profits which fall to be treated as realized in accordance with generally accepted accounting principles, i.e. either in the form of cash or other assets, the ultimate cash realization of which can be assessed with reasonable certainty. This is of particular relevance when considering the accounting and reporting of financial futures transactions.

United States

In the United States there is a considerable amount of literature concerned with generally accepted accounting principles (GAAP) in that country which are normally applicable to all published financial statements. There are no formalized GAAP dealing specifically with accounting for financial futures although the Financial Accounting Standards Board has issued an exposure draft covering disclosure of the effects of such transactions. In addition the American Institute of Certified Public Accountants has issued a discussion paper entitled "Accounting for Forward Placement and Standby Commitments and Interest Rate Futures Contracts". There is, nevertheless, a wide variety of accounting treatments for financial futures transactions in the United States.

2. Principles to be applied

In the absence of any specific guidelines on accounting for financial futures, some guidance may be obtained from the fundamental accounting concepts which are set out in IAS 1. These concepts are:

1. The going concern concept, which assumes that the entity will continue in business for the foreseeable future.
2. The accruals concept, under which revenue and costs are accrued, matched and dealt with in the accounting period to which they relate.
3. The consistency concept, whereby like items in the accounts and from period to period are treated consistently.
4. The prudence concept, which says that revenue and profits are not anticipated but are recognized only when realized and provision is made for all known liabilities.

The application of the going concern and consistency concepts is straightforward in relation to financial futures transactions and warrants little attention. There is, however, an apparent conflict in this instance between the accruals concept and the prudence concept. This particularly concerns the recognition of realized profits and the matching of the results of hedge transactions in the futures market, and is considered in the section on accounting issues.

In addition to the fundamental accounting concepts some further guidance may be obtained from accounting practice in respect of forward foreign exchange transactions as these have a number of similarities with financial futures transactions. Although the accounting treatment for forward foreign exchange transactions is not completely uniform, the common practice is to revalue forward positions on a buy back or liquidation basis (this has been given the name "marking to market" in the United States). This approach recognizes the cost or benefit which would arise on closing out the position and hence recognizes unrealized profits and losses on open positions.

Valuation to market

The timing or recognition of profit and loss on financial futures transactions is fundamental to the accounting for open positions. If an active and liquid market provides the opportunity for positions to be closed at any time, it follows that a decision to keep a position open is no different in principle from a decision to close out. It would be incongruous to recognize one type of decision and not the other.

This view leads to the conclusion that open positions should be revalued to market value, i.e. the closing price on the day in question (mark to market). The difference between the aggregate value thus obtained and the aggregate value of the positions at their contracted prices will be the profit or loss on open contracts at the valuation date. The profit or loss for the accounting period would be this profit or loss on open contracts together with the profit or loss realized on contracts closed during the period less any profit or loss on open contracts at the beginning of the accounting period.

Hedging – principle of symmetry

The aim of a hedger is to reduce risk by protecting himself from the impact of price changes. It seems logical that the accounting treatment should so far as possible reflect this purpose. It is appropriate, therefore, to defer profits and losses arising both from the revaluation of open positions outlined above and those realized from closed hedging positions so that they can be recognized and offset against the effect of price changes on the asset or liability being hedged. In this way the commercial intention of the hedge transaction is properly reflected in accounting terms. This is a fundamental difference from the accounting for trading transactions and raises a number of further issues which are considered separately in the section on hedging. The main issues are the determination of whether a contract is for hedging purposes and the treatment of realized profits and losses in the period of deferral.

Related costs

In practice it is likely that the incidental costs of hedging transactions and any interest earned or incurred as a result of the cash flow from initial and variation margins would not be material and that the interest element would be virtually impossible to identify. These items should strictly be accounted for as part of the result of the hedge; however, it may be appropriate for these items to be recognized in the profit and loss account as and when they arise.

The policy above clearly advocates the recognition of unrealized profits and, relating this to the fundamental accounting concepts, may appear to lean towards the accruals concept and away from that of prudence. The conflict is apparent rather than real as the overriding requirement is for accounts to show a true and fair view. The following arguments help to support a mark to market policy:

1. An effective financial futures market should ensure that profits or losses are instantly realizable.
2. Because there is this opportunity for management to close out a transaction in the market, a profit or loss is effectively realized when the market rate moves and does not depend on a formal decision to close out. Such profits and losses should be recognized in the period when the market movements occur.
3. The mark to market approach is consistent with the predominate practice of banks and others in accounting for forward foreign exchange transactions. Indeed in this context, 'unrealized' profits and losses from forward foreign exchange transactions have been accepted by the UK Accounting Standards Committee as realized, and therefore can be regarded as eligible distributable reserves.
4. The mark to market basis prevents the possibility of manipulation which might otherwise result from management's flexibility either to leave open or to close out contracts on a selective basis.
5. Management can evaluate performance only by reference to current market values of all open contracts.

Balance sheet treatment

Consideration of the balance sheet treatment of the asset or liability underlying the futures contract depends on the legal nature of such contracts whereby title does not pass until delivery. Actual delivery or receipt of underlying assets is not essential as contracts may be, and normally are, closed prior to delivery. It is therefore appropriate that the underlying assets and liabilities should not be shown on the balance sheet. This treatment, reflecting the economic reality of the transaction, is consistent with that adopted for forward foreign exchange transactions.

Funds put up to the clearing house (or, a public order member) to cover initial margins, (a form of collateral) remain on the balance sheet of the depositor as an asset; they are unlikely to be other than current in nature. The method of calculation of initial margins varies from exchange to exchange; on LIFFE they are based on net uncovered positions in each month for each contract with a reduction where remote straddle positions exist.

The balance on account with the clearing house will be increased by:

(a) further remittances of funds;
(b) profits from contracts closed out and reduced by:
— withdrawal of funds,
— losses from contracts closed out, and
— amounts debited by the clearing house in respect of fees, accommodation charges, etc.

The sum of this balance and any variation margin on open contracts represents the member's total equity with the clearing house, which must be maintained, on a daily basis at a level sufficient to meet exchange initial margin requirements. Total equity may exceed this requirement, in cases where the member has either:

(a) allowed profits on settlements to accumulate in his account in preference to immediately withdrawing cash, or
(b) not withdrawn cash in respect of reducing initial margin requirements.

Exactly the same considerations apply to:

(a) non clearing members *vis-à-vis* their clearing members
(b) customers *vis-à-vis* their LIFFE public order members (or futures commission merchants, on US exchanges).

The daily computation of initial/variation margin requirements and maintenance of cover accounts applies to all participants in the financial futures markets. Those participants who take on client business should be able to bring together all client balances on the one hand, and all "omnibus" balances with clearing houses or clearing members on the other, into opposing control accounts which can be reconciled on a daily basis.

Trading

A trader is someone who intends to profit from backing his view of how prices will move while at the same time being prepared to assume the risk this involves.

As in the case of a foreign exchange dealer or a dealer in securities, it is appropriate to revalue the open position to market value and to accrue fully any unrealized profit or loss. It would also seem appropriate to accrue the full amount of the dealer's turn or commission at both dates if this was considered material.

3. Hedging

The aim of hedging is to reduce the risk of loss through adverse price movements in interest rates or currencies by taking positions in financial futures contracts to cover existing or anticipated cash market positions. The hedger is therefore seeking protection from the impact of price changes and it is desirable in accounting for hedging transactions to reflect this objective. In general the results of hedging transactions should be treated so that they match the effects of interest or currency rate changes on the transaction that the hedge is designed to cover. By relating the cash and futures transaction in this way it provides symmetry of accounting for the cash and futures transactions. Before looking at the criteria for determining a hedge as opposed to a trade, it is worth reviewing some of the different reasons for hedging.

Types of hedging transaction

There are clearly a number of different circumstances in which hedging may be appropriate. However there are perhaps three main types of hedge which should be highlighted for the purpose of discussing the accounting treatment.

164

Hedging a currency receipt or payment

This is an obvious use of the futures market and a practice which is well established on the forward foreign exchange market. The aim of the hedge is to lock into an available currency rate to avoid the risk of the currency weakening (receivable) or strengthening (payable) in relation to the local currency. In order to reflect this in the accounts the result of the hedging transaction should be deferred and adjusted against the local value of the receipt or payment when recognized.

Hedging an interest yield

The aim of this hedge is to protect an interest yield or the cost of funds during a stated future period, either in respect of existing or anticipated assets or liabilities, by locking into an available interest rate. In order to reflect this in the accounts, gains or losses on the hedging transaction should, if appropriate, be deferred and written off in the profit and loss account over the period that the hedge is intended to protect. This will obviously be dependent on the structure of the individual hedge. The intent underlying the hedge is the most important criterion.

Hedging an existing asset or liability

The aim of the hedge is to preserve the value of an asset or limit the extent of a liability. In order to reflect this in the accounts, again it may be necessary to defer the hedge profit or loss and recognize this when the hedged asset or liability is revalued or realized. The appropriate accounting for this will also depend on the way the hedged asset or liability is itself treated in the accounts.

4. Criteria for determining a hedge

In order to prevent possible abuses of the difference in treatment between trading and hedging, it is necessary to distinguish one from the other.

The intention of hedge transactions is to manage and limit the risks of an enterprise. As market conditions change, management's view of the risks which they are seeking to limit by means of an existing hedging transaction may also change. The management of a hedging programme should be considered as just one aspect of risk management, which is a dynamic process. These factors suggest that identification of, and accounting for, hedging transactions may in some circumstances be difficult and complex. Neither the accountant nor the auditor should expect to apply rigid and inflexible rules in meeting the challenge of providing useful information to management and of giving a true and fair view in published financial statements.

Nevertheless, it is possible that there will be limits on the extent to which an accounting system can reflect all hedging transactions. Before undertaking hedging activities, the accounting implications should be carefully considered by management. It is important that the auditors of the enterprise should have been involved at an early stage to help agree the basic principles to be applied.

Ground rules should be set to identify hedging transactions which are most suitable to the activities of the business. The following three criteria might be considered in this process:

1. Intent. The transaction should be intended to be a hedge so that the accounting reflects the economic substance. This will also involve evidence of management's intention that the transaction is a hedge and identification of its exact purpose. Thus at the time the futures transaction is entered into, its purpose should be specifically identified and documented, including the asset or liability being hedged and the period over which the hedge is intended to be effective.
2. Correlation. The price of the futures contract and the hedged asset or liability should show a high positive correlation so that they will move in the same direction and with similar magnitude. This will involve matching the futures contract as closely as possible to the hedged asset or liability in terms of the sensitivity to interest rate changes, principal amount and delivery date or maturity.
3. Certainty. In the case of anticipatory hedges (i.e. in respect of a transaction intended to occur at a future date) there should be a reasonable expectation that the cash transaction will be fulfilled. This will obviously be demonstrated by experience.

The three criteria above are similar to those set out in the US Financial Accounting Standard on foreign currency translation (FAS 52) when it considers hedging of foreign currency positions. FAS 52 suggests that, to qualify as a hedge, a transaction should be both "designated" and "effective" as a hedge. These equate to the intent and to the correlation/certainty criteria set out above.

In this context, therefore, the first criterion of intent is fundamental. If the intention is that the transaction is a hedge, it should be possible to record that intention and the reasons for it, at the time the transaction is made. Furthermore in order to properly establish internal control it will be necessary to record the nature and intent of the transaction so that it can be subsequently monitored and reported to management in an appropriate manner.

The second criterion of correlation is more factual. Reasonable correlation, or a reasonable expectation of correlation, is a factor upon which management should have satisfied itself prior to entering a hedge transaction, by reference to information to which others, including the auditors, should similarly be able to refer.

The third criterion of certainty will not always be relevant. When it is relevant, that is with regard to anticipated cash transactions, management will need to be clear about their plans for future cash transactions and it would not be unreasonable for the auditor to expect to see that management has established a good track record in planning effectively and subsequently actioning its plans by entering into the cash transactions anticipated.

Nevertheless, even with the criteria established for treatment as a hedge, some difficult assessment may need to be made. It is likely that the auditor will prefer an assumption that a transaction is a trading transaction, rather than a hedge, unless it can be reasonably shown that the hedge criteria are satisfied, especially where the deferral of losses is in question. This would not seem unreasonable. The prudence concept, it may be argued, suggests that both losses and profits are immediately reflected in the profit and loss account; however, it may be evident that, in order to show a true and fair view, the matching concept should be followed and the loss or profit be deferred as a hedging item. This would seem to be consistent with the spirit of IAS 1.

5. Hedge accounting

Clearly, in the light of the foregoing, the criteria for hedging transactions should be established by management, preferably in consulation with the auditors, in recognition of the risks and circumstances of the business. It is appropriate for a record to be maintained which will demonstrate that transactions comply with these criteria and the more complex the hedging activity, the more detailed these records may need to be.

The following paragraphs outline some of the practical problems that might arise.

General hedges

The consideration of hedging transactions has so far been based on hedges for single assets; however, there will be situations where hedges are part of general asset/liability management and based on aggregates of assets and liabilities rather than individual items. There is no reason why this should necessarily invalidate hedging treatment although the criteria may have to be refined to accommodate the identification of the aggregate assets and liabilities being hedged.

Rolling hedges

In general hedging contracts would normally extend at least until the date of the anticipated cash market transaction, otherwise an exposure would exist between the time the futures contracts are closed out and the time when the cash market transaction is made. Avoidance of this exposure can be achieved, particularly in the case of transactions well into the future, by the use of successive futures contracts. For example, by closing out a position for one delivery month and simultaneously opening an equivalent position for a subsequent delivery month, thereby "rolling" the hedge forward to the later date. The use of this technique may be necessary because the date of the anticipated cash market transaction has been delayed; alternatively it may have been necessary to open the original hedge position in a delivery month earlier than the anticipated date of the cash transaction because no contract for the later delivery month was available.

Providing the rolling forward of the hedge can properly be viewed as an integral part of the hedge operation, and this will be a particularly relevant question where anticipated hedge transactions have been delayed, then it should be appropriate for the relevant futures transactions to be accounted for as part of the hedge. This may entail successive hedge transactions being deferred so that the total hedge profit or loss can be accounted for in the appropriate manner. A similar argument might be applied in cases where rollover occurred because there was insufficient activity (i.e. liquidity) to make the appropriate delivery month attractive and therefore a series of contracts are taken until that distant month becomes sufficiently active, as delivery moves closer.

Discontinued hedges

There will be occasions when hedges are discontinued. This may happen for a variety of reasons. For example, the anticipated cash market transaction may not take place. In this case it would seem appropriate to treat the entire result of the hedge transaction as a trading transaction as soon as it becomes apparent that the anticipated cash market transaction will not take place.

A hedge may also be discontinued because management's expectations of the trend in interest rates or currency rates has changed, i.e. their view of the risks which the hedge was designed to give protection against has altered. This could arise when:

1. contrary to original expectations rates have moved so as to put the hedge into a loss making position; or
2. rates have moved in the direction anticipated so that the hedge shows a profit and management then considers that the remaining risk of further movement in rates does not warrant continuation of the hedge; or
3. rates have not moved significantly but, because of changes in external factors, management now considers that the original risk which was hedged has reduced to the point where continuation of the hedge is not warranted.

Discontinuation of the hedge in these circumstances is likely to present problems to the accountant in monitoring and recording these transactions and to the auditor in assessing management's intentions. However, it would seem appropriate to consider accounting for the result of such futures transactions as a hedge, provided management's intentions in this respect can be clearly established.

In the case of a hedge transaction being left open after the point when the relevant cash transaction has taken place, or after the point when the hedge had been deemed to be discontinued, it would be appropriate for the result of the hedge which arose after that point to be treated as a trading profit or loss if it is material.

Inclusion of deferred amounts in the balance sheet

Most hedging transactions will give rise to deferred profits or losses and these will be included in the balance sheet at the period end. The most appropriate manner for including these in the balance sheet will depend upon the circumstances. In some cases it may be appropriate to relate the result of the hedge to the hedged item in the balance sheet, either as a separate amount, possibly adjacent to the hedged item, or as an adjustment to the amount shown in the balance sheet in respect of the hedged item. In the majority of cases, however, it is likely to be appropriate to include the hedge result as part of current assets or current liabilities, without separate disclosure of the amount concerned.

Valuation of a hedged asset

In cases where the hedge is to protect an asset value, valuation of the asset either at cost, the lower of cost and market value, or market value may affect the recognition of the hedge result.

In cases where the hedge is intended to protect the value of an underlying asset, the resulting net book amount, comprising the cost or carrying value of the asset plus its hedge result, should be reviewed. In particular it may be appropriate to compare this combined amount with the market value, or realizable value, of the underlying asset being hedged.

The original book amount for the hedged asset should not be compared to its market value in isolation since this could indicate the need for an amount to be written off to the profit and loss account in circumstances where a hedging profit has been received which partly or wholly offsets such a write-off.

It is possible that the criteria and records needed to monitor complex hedging transactions will be excessively difficult to establish and maintain; in these cases it may be necessary to treat the futures transactions as trades rather than hedges. It is important that management has an understanding of the differences between this accounting treatment and the commercial intention of the transactions and appreciates that accounts prepared on this basis may not reflect in an ideal manner the outcome of their decisions.

6. Disclosure in financial statements

Having considered the determination of the results of financial futures transactions, this section considers their possible disclosure in financial statements.

United Kingdom

Disclosure in UK statutory accounts is governed by the Companies Acts 1948–81 and Statements of Standard Accounting Practice. The Companies Acts contain no specific guidance on disclosure in this area, and as indicated earlier there is no accounting standard which deals specifically with financial futures. Several published standards, however, do cover relevant areas which need to be taken into account, for example disclosure of accounting policies and disclosure of contingencies, and the Companies Acts do contain certain requirements and exemptions for particular categories of business, such as banking. In addition, current best practice on disclosure, particularly in areas similar to financial futures such as forward foreign exchange, should be considered, although unfortunately, there is a wide variation in standards of disclosure between companies and particularly a lack of disclosure of details of foreign exchange transactions.

United States

In the United States, in contrast, a draft accounting standard was issued in November 1980 which dealt with the disclosure of transactions concerning interest rate futures and related activities. Broadly this proposed the following disclosure:

1. A description of the accounting practice adopted, including methods of accounting for contracts and recognizing gains and losses.
2. The contract amounts and market values of all long and, separately, all short positions on open contracts at the balance sheet date.
3. The amounts of any unrealised gains and unrealized losses on open contracts at the balance sheet date that have not been recognized in income.
4. The net amount of unamortized gains or losses on closed contracts at the balance sheet date that is included in the cost or basis of assets and liabilities.

This provides a useful guide to some of the areas for possible disclosure. These are considered in the following paragraphs, under four main headings:

1. Activity and accounting policy
2. Unamortized gains and losses
3. Open positions
4. Hedging and trading results

Activity and accounting policy

The disclosure of the types of transaction undertaken and the accounting policy adopted must be the most important disclosure requirements. A possible accounting policy which might be appropriate would be as follows:

> "Financial futures transactions are valued at closing market prices and resultant profits and losses are included in trading results except those in respect of specifically designated hedge transactions which are deferred and released to profit and loss account over a period in accordance with the original intent of the hedging transaction".

This accounting policy note could be expanded to cover more detailed points such as hedges of the capital value of assets where the cost base of the asset is adjusted and the detailed method of calculation of amortization.

Unamortized gains and losses

The deferring of gains and losses is not a particularly common accounting practice and there is limited practical experience of its disclosure. Deferred gains and losses will comprise realized and unrealized elements. There will be realized profits or losses on closed contracts. The gains or losses on open contracts could be viewed as unrealized although some or all of these will be reflected by amounts of variation margin received or paid. There may be a case for distinguishing between the results of closed contracts and those of open contracts.

Where amounts are disclosed this could be either the net or gross amount of all deferrals. Consideration would also need to be given as to whether it is necessary to disclose the lengths of various periods over which such deferred amounts are amortized to the profit and loss account.

The distinction between these categories of deferred gains and losses is perhaps a little arbitrary. Furthermore in the majority of cases the amounts involved may not in themselves be material either to the profit and loss account or the balance sheet. The unusual nature of deferred realized losses is not in itself a reason to require disclosure of the amount involved particularly in the circumstances of financial futures. Furthermore the disclosure of deferred gains or losses, or the period over which they are to be amortized, would reveal only a part of the hedging activity involved and by itself might be misleading.

Open positions

The most striking factor about disclosing open positions is that there may be a considerable number of open positions at any one time representing substantial contract values. Bearing in mind the nature of futures contracts and that delivery is unlikely, the value of open positions may not be a particularly useful figure. Of more relevance is the potential impact of, and sensitivity to, price movements on open positions. This will clearly be a very much smaller number and quite possibly not be material in terms of the profit and loss account or balance sheet.

There would seem to be only limited benefits in disclosing open positions. Financial statements do not generally provide a comprehensive summary of the various risks to which an enterprise is exposed. Financial organizations do not normally disclose those assets or liabilities which are at fixed rates of interest and those which are at variable rates. Furthermore they do not normally disclose the basis or frequency of the review of interest rates on assets or liabilities which carry variable rates. Against this background, disclosure of open trading positions or open hedging positions might be considered anomalous.

It may be appropriate, however, to ensure that the possible effect of hedging transactions does not render other accounting disclosure misleading. For example, if a fixed rate liability such as a loan stock has been hedged so as to cause the effective interest cost to reflect changes in market rates, it might be misleading for the accounts to continue to indicate that the interest cost was fixed.

Hedging and trading results

Many of the considerations which apply to the possible disclosures discussed above would apply equally to the disclosure of hedging and trading results, particularly if these were to be analysed in any detail. In the majority of countries it is current practice not to disclose detailed components of the profit and loss account except where specifically required. Profits and losses from trading transactions might most appropriately be reported under other operating income whilst those arising from hedging transactions might most appropriately be netted against the relevant profit and loss item which was being hedged.

Summary

The purpose of disclosure is to enable a reader of a set of accounts to assess the impact on the business (including risk) of the item disclosed. Materiality is obviously a fundamental consideration. There is a wide range of possible disclosures but no specific requirement or overpowering case for any particular one. In the absence of authoritative guidance and until an accepted market practice envolves, this must be a matter of judgement by management and their auditors. Nevertheless a comprehensive accounting policy must be an essential starting point and this should be disclosed whenever involvement in financial futures can be regarded as material.

B. Taxation considerations

The taxation regulations in each country are different, but in each country of operation the same questions have to be addressed. This section identifies the major questions and their resolution in the United States and the UK, the first two countries to operate a financial futures exchange. The major questions are:

1. Is the company a trader or a non-trader?
2. Is a particular transaction a revenue one or a capital one?
3. Are unrealized gains and losses taxed or only realized ones?
4. Do the answers to the above questions have any tax planning implications, particularly if assessment is made on a realized basis?

United States

In general, users of financial futures contracts fall into three broad categories for taxation purposes:

1. Dealer—a seller who profits from a markup or commission on the goods sold.
2. Trader—a seller engaged in a business or trade but who profits from price fluctuation.
3. Investor or speculator—one who profits solely from price fluctuation and income earned on property held.

Dealers' gains and losses are normally taxed as ordinary income transactions, whilst a trader or investor/speculator would normally receive capital tax treatment. A hedger is treated for tax purposes in accordance with the motivation for the hedge, but a hedge directly related to a business will be ordinary income or loss.

There are detailed rules for the identification of long-term as opposed to short-term gains and losses, and the short sale rule is designed to counter the creation of short-term losses matched by long term gains. Although judicially unproven, lack of economic profit potential could result in the denial of loss relief.

A dealer in financial futures is required to maintain and value his stock in accordance with official guidelines. This means that for taxation purposes, he can value his closing stock at market value or at the lower of cost or market value, but the potential profit or loss not yet realized on futures transactions cannot be included in closing stock since they represent unclosed transactions. However, unrealized profits or losses on open futures trades that are hedges can be included in taxable income when this is a common industry practice which results in the clearest method of identifying profit for the period and is consistently applied.

170

Traders, investors and speculators are not taxed on unrealized profits or losses as the taxable event occurs only on completion of the trade.

In the Economic Recovery Tax Act of 1981, legislation was introduced to substantially reduce the potential for abuse of tax straddles. This legislation introduced a number of important developments, The main ones being:

1. It restricted the recognition of losses arising from straddle positions in any year to the extent by which they exceed certain unrealized gains from offsetting positions. There is provision for carry-over of restricted losses.

2. It required all regulated futures contracts (RFCs) to be marked to market at the close of a fiscal year, thus, recognizing only net gains or losses realized or unrealized. Certain RFCs can, by election, be excluded from this but effectively they will then be included in the rule described in the previous paragraph.

3. It required that 60% of the net position recognized in (2) would be long-term gain or loss and 40% short-term gain or loss. Ordinary income or loss would not be taxed at regular tax rates.

4. Except in the case of certain syndicates, hedging transactions are exempt from these rules. A hedge must, for this purpose, be identified as such before the close of the day on which it was entered into.

United Kingdom

Until financial futures trading has been operating for several years in the UK, no normal practice will be established. However, initial guidelines were produced by the London International Financial Futures Exchange and were agreed with the Inland Revenue. The guidelines are reproduced below (the actual text is in italics) but as they were written for tax specialists, some explanation is also provided.

1. *Banks, financial trading companies and insurance companies, with the exception of their life funds, will in general be taxable under Schedule D Case I.*

   This means that they will be treated as trading in financial futures, the main points being that:
   (a) they will be taxed at income rates;
   (b) no investment income surcharge will be made for individuals; and
   (c) the losses are widely offsetable.

2. *As regards transactions carried out by other corporate bodies or individuals, there will be a primary assumption that any profits or losses are of a revenue nature but each case must depend on its own facts. It may be arguable that where a hedging transaction is specifically related to an underlying capital transaction, capital treatment should be afforded to the financial futures transaction.*

   For everyone else (including investment trust, unit trusts and pension funds, etc) the treatment will be either Case I or Case VI.

   Where an isolated transaction is undertaken for the purpose of hedging against a capital movement, e.g. a possible future sale of gilts or the acquisition of a new subsidiary with a purchase price denominated in a foreign currency, then the Revenue conceded that capital treatment might be arguable. In practice this probably means capital treatment for a genuinely isolated transaction, but the Revenue would resist strongly any attempt to obtain capital treatment for regular transactions even where the purpose was a capital hedge.

   The Revenue do not accept that an unidentified asset, which is not intended to be delivered, can be an asset of a capital nature, and are not persuaded in this matter by the existence of an underlying but separate transaction which is of a capital nature.

3. *Individuals would normally be assessed under Schedule D Case VI, but where an individual has an existing financial trade or trades actively through his own or a leased seat on the market, he will probably be assessed under Schedule D Case I.*

   Individuals will be taxed under Case I if they have existing financial trade, or trade actively through their own or a leased seat. Individuals who merely work as dealers but carry out some transactions for their own account will be assessed under Case VI.

4. *Companies which do not have an existing financial trade could also be assessed under Schedule D Case VI. Whether or not the activities by any person amount to trading is a question of fact. That*

171

transactions in financial futures are carried out by a company rather than an individual may be a factor to be taken into account (see Lewis Emanuel & Son Ltd v White 42 TC 369 and also Cooper v C & J Clark Ltd Tax Leaflet 2875) but the Inland Revenue does not consider it conclusive of trading.

The same basic principles apply to companies, although there is no investment income surcharge, but the Lewis Emanuel case is a problem for the Revenue. Most companies should therefore, on current case law, get Case I treatment for regular and reasonably frequent transactions.

Timing of assessment

5. *The normal rule for assessment under Schedule D Case I is that profits or losses may not be anticipated for tax purposes. Consequently, profits or losses in financial futures transactions would normally be taxed or allowed only when realized. A profit or loss could be treated as realized either when matched contracts are acquired, which is perhaps technically more correct, or when the clearing house is notified of set-off. Either approach, if consistently applied, should be acceptable unless the time of set-off were to be manipulated for tax reasons.*

    Case I treatment normally means that the treatment follows the accounting treatment, except that unrealized profits and losses are extracted from the profit and loss account for tax purposes.

    The question still remains as to when a profit or loss is realized. This is an important question, since if the answer is known, the incidence of profits and losses can be controlled. It could be:

    (a) when a matching contract is acquired;

    (b) when the clearing house is notified of settlement; or

    (c) when the automatic daily settlement to market system operates.

    Realization for tax purposes occurs when the profit or loss is ascertained with accuracy and has been earned or incurred.

    As regards LIFFE, alternative (a) is probably technically more correct than (b), since once the matching contract is acquired the profit or loss is established and the settlement date cannot change that fact. At present (c) means that a daily profit or loss is legally realized for clearing members, so for them (c) is correct. For non-clearers (c) will be correct if their clearing-member is using the same system, if not, (a) is correct, but (b) will be accepted by the Revenue if it is not manipulated for tax reasons.

6. *Although the normal rule would not permit the taxation of unrealized profits or the deduction of unrealized losses, the accounting treatment may be acceptable for tax purposes if the treatment of unrealized profits and losses is even-handed and consistent. However, profits or losses which have been realized at the year-end but deferred in the accounts would need to be brought into account for tax purposes.*

    If the accounting policy was to take up unrealized losses only, a widely accepted treatment for futures transactions, this would result in a constant deferral of profit, which the Revenue would not accept, but if both unrealized profits and losses are taken up, the Revenue would not require adjustments for tax purposes.

    There is a rider on this guideline in that accounting treatments for hedges frequently result in the spreading of a financial futures profit or loss in accordance with the life of an underlying transaction. If this results in the deferral of a profit or loss which has been realized, it must be adjusted for tax purposes.

7. *Assessments raised under Schedule D Case VI will be on realized profits.*

    The accounting treatment will not be accepted for Case VI although, in practice, this is unlikely to be significant since most taxpayers assessed under Case VI will not have sophisticated accounting systems.

8. *For capital gains purposes, contracts which do not run to delivery will probably be regarded as unconditional contracts to acquire the underlying asset and would therefore be subject to the normal rules of identification. For this purpose, it is thought that assets would be identified with each other where there are dealings in the same contract for the same delivery month.*

    Capital treatment will be rare but where it is granted, taxation is on a transaction by transaction basis and it will be necessary to identify each sell contract with a buy contract. This will usually be fairly straightforward since capital treatment will probably only be available to isolated transactions but there are special capital gains tax identification rules which apply to dealings in "assets without earmark", which the underlying assets are. Essentially, any sales will be matched with a buy contract for the same contract and delivery month, firstly against any buy contracts acquired in the previous 12 months on a first in, first out basis, and then against earlier contracts on a last in, first out basis. Any instructions for set-off given to the clearing house are disregarded in the above identification rules.

Exchange conversion

9. *All dollar-based transactions will, in theory, be required to be converted into sterling at the date of the relevant contracts. This means that the trader may be exposed to exchange rate movements on the full consideration for the contract. There will, however, be a matching dollar cash transaction which will neutralize this movement and the trader should only be taxed on the sterling equivalent of the real gain.*

Exchange conversion is hopefully a minor point. The problem lies in the underlying principle of UK tax law that all transactions must, in theory, be converted into sterling at the date of the transactions. Since five out of the seven contracts are dollar-based, this point needs to be considered.

If one just looked at the underlying transaction, the trader would be exposed to dollar/sterling movements on the full contract price as well as the price movement on the contract, e.g.

			Dollars	**Rate**	**Sterling**
1.6.83	Buy	DM 2,500	1,000	1.50	667
1.9.83	Sell	DM 2,500	1,100	1.45	759
			$ 100		£ 92

However, in this situation the trader has in effect sold dollars on 1.6.83 (in exchange for DM) which he does not buy/acquire until 1.9.83. He therefore has a dollar transaction which can alternatively be described as follows:

Buy	$1,000	at	1.45	690
Sell	$1,000	at	1.50	667

Exchange loss	(23)
Sterling profit as above	92

Taxable profit	£ 69	(= $100 at 1.45)

The guidelines confirm that this matching dollar transaction is accepted as valid by the Revenue.

Non-residents

10. *Membership of the exchange may not of itself constitute a permanent establishment, but if a booth is rented or other premises are available in the UK, this could well amount to a permanent establishment.*

Non-residents must be divided up into those having the benefit of a double treaty and those who do not.

The guideline refers to a "permanent establishment". This is essentially a tax treaty definition which, for these purposes, can be translated into a "taxable trading operation situated in the UK". A non-resident with treaty protection will only be taxable in the UK if he trades here through a permanent establishment.

The guideline in effect states that mere membership of the exchange will not render a treaty-protected member taxable in the UK. If, however, he rents a booth or acquires office accommodation in the UK which is used for trading on LIFFE, then this would constitute a taxable trading operation in most circumstances.

11. *Where a non-resident uses an independent broker to execute his transactions, then unless he has any other links with the UK, he would probably be protected from UK taxation under the terms of most double taxation treaties. If, however, he does not have the protection of a double taxation treaty, income would be attributable to him.*

An independent broker, which means unconnected by ownership or commercial dependency, would not constitute a permanent establishment under the terms of most double tax treaties. The position is, however, more complex if there is no such treaty which will apply, for example, to most Arab states.

If the non-resident trades actively through a UK broker, he may be taxable, as explained earlier, in that he is trading through an agent in the UK. Clearly, however, recovery of tax is a problem. In order to recover tax, he must be assessed and an assessment can only be served effectively in the UK. The administrative legislation, therefore, provides for assessments to be served on the UK agent, whether or not he handles the profits derived from the trading activities.

This legislation will not apply where:

(a) the broker is not carrying on the regular agency of the non-resident, or
(b) the broker carries on the *bona fide* business of a broker in the UK and receives regular rate commission for the service.

In practice, therefore, although income may technically be attributable to some non-residents trading through a general broker, the Revenue do not have the mechanics available to recover any tax.

Capital gains—delivery

12. *Although the contracts would normally be regarded as unconditional contracts to acquire the underlying asset, this may not be correct in the case of a long gilt contract which runs to delivery. Since it is only on delivery that the asset is properly identified, the Revenue consider that such contracts are conditional upon identification and that, therefore, for capital gains purposes, the purchase or sale does not take place until the asset is identified.*

The guidelines only really cover transactions which never run to delivery. Where a contract runs to delivery, the tax treatment will, in effect, ignore the financial futures transaction and treat it merely as a method of buying or selling what is actually delivered.

For capital gains purposes, the precise timing of a disposal or acquisition is frequently important and in addition, there is specific legislation defining the date of acquisition or disposal where an asset is bought or sold under a contract. Essentially, the date of such a transaction is the date of the contract, unless it is a conditional contract, in which case it is the date the condition is fulfilled.

Except for the gilt contract, all the LIFFE contracts are regarded as unconditional and the effective date of sale is therefore the date of the contract. The gilt contract is, however, regarded as being conditional upon identification of the gilt to be delivered, and therefore the effective date of the transaction is the date of identification of the gilt to be delivered. This is important for gilts, because gilts held by a non-trader in gilts for more than 12 months are tax-free on disposal. Therefore, this 12 months will be calculated by reference to the date of identification. This may seem harsh on a person acquiring gilts via the futures market since his date of acquisition will be delayed, but it is equally advantageous to the disposer who can lock into a disposal price and yet delay the disposal for tax purposes until the 12 months are up.

Conclusion

This overview of the current and anticipated practices in the first two countries to operate a financial futures exchange highlights the main taxation problems which need to be considered. Because of the difficulty and uncertainty of the actual interpretation of the relevant legislation, it is recommended that anybody who wishes to use financial futures anywhere in the world should first consult his taxation advisor.

Chapter 10

Regulatory and macro-economic aspects of financial futures

There has been much discussion over the extent to which financial futures markets need to be regulated. Concern has been voiced over the potential impact of financial futures markets upon the underlying market for cash instruments, particularly the Federal debt markets in the United States. The 1979 study of interest rate futures markets conducted by the US Department of the Treasury and the Federal Reserve system raised concerns over the adequacy of both government and exchange regulation of financial futures markets.

This chapter explores: the current regulatory system for financial futures trading in the United States and the UK, and assesses whether further and more detailed regulation of these markets is necessary relative to other financial markets.

The primary responsibility for all commodity futures trading activity in the United States lies with the Commodity Futures Trading Commission (CFTC), whose re-authorization bill, following its first seven years of life, has now passed through the US Congress. All futures contracts traded on US commodity exchanges have to be approved by the CFTC, and even comparatively minor rule changes or modifications to futures contracts have to be submitted to the CFTC for approval. The Congressional debates on the re-authorization of the CFTC have been intense, and there has been a dispute between the CFTC and the Securities Exchange Commission over the assignment of responsibility for regulating stock index futures contracts and options on financial futures and cash instruments. However, the primary responsibility for regulating financial futures trading will continue to lie with the Commodity Futures Trading Commission.

The regulatory activities of the CFTC have tended to be concentrated on the contract and exchange trading rules approval process. But the CFTC does possess the authority to initiate reviews of and, if necessary, order changes in futures contract rules which may contribute to the potential for market congestion or manipulation. In order to deal with problems which develop while a contract is trading, the CFTC has the authority to collect futures and cash market information for the purpose of conducting adequate futures market surveillance. During emergencies, the CFTC has the authority to take such actions as it believes necessary to maintain or restore orderly trading in a futures contracts. Among additional powers which have been proposed for the CFTC are ones to set position limits for traders in the futures markets, and to grant the federal government authority over futures margin requirements.

In addition to direct controls over the futures markets, the CFTC has also exerted considerable pressure to improve disclosure requirements by major participants in futures market trading. In particular a new rule 21.03 gives the CFTC wide powers to demand information from futures commission merchants, foreign brokers, and US brokers with foreign clients. If market participants refuse to supply the CFTC with the relevant information, the CFTC will have the power to direct the exchange concerned and all futures commission merchants to trade only for liquidation for the offending trader. The type of information which can be demanded from the futures commission merchant or foreign broker is quite specific.

This chapter is an extended version of an article "Financial Futures: Costs and Benefits" published in *The Banker*, October 1982

(1) The name and address of the person in whose name the account is carried; or if the person is not an individual, the name of the individual to contact regarding the account.

(2) The total open futures and options contracts in the account.

(3) The number of futures contracts against which delivery notices have been issued or received, and the number against which exchanges of futures for cash have been transacted during the period of time specified in the call.

(4) Whether the account is carried for and in the name of another futures commission merchant or foreign broker.

(5) For the accounts which are not carried for and in the name of another futures commission merchant or foreign broker, the following: (a) the name and address of any other person who controls the trading of the account, and (b) the name and address of any person who has a 10% or more beneficial interest in the account.

Disclosure rules of this kind conflict with traditional commercial secrecy in many countries, and several non-US commodity exchanges have expressed considerable reservations concerning CFTC attempts to impose US rules on non-US corporations and exchanges. This looks like being a battle that will continue as the CFTC's insistence on full disclosure strengthens.

Apart from the re-authorization of the CFTC, and the extension of disclosure, the main new development in futures regulation in the United States has been the establishment of the futures industry-sponsored National Futures Association. The National Futures Association is the US commodity futures industry's first self-regulatory association. The quoted aims of the NFA are:[1]

(1) To strengthen industry self-regulation by regulating those segments of the futures industry that were previously outside the scope of other self-regulatory organizations.

(2) To control self-regulatory expense by eliminating duplication of effort.

(3) To provide uniform standards to eliminate the overlap and conflicts that are inevitable when there are different groups regulating one industry.

(4) To remove unnecessary regulation constraints in order to aid effective regulation.

Just as the US authorities are willing to see a move towards more self-regulation in the commodity and financial futures industry, so the mood in the UK, which has been characterized almost exclusively by self-regulation, seems to be shifting in favour of some formal regulatory system. This has been partly spurred by the Gower Report.[2] The Gower Report was concerned about the balance between statutory controls and self-regulatory controls, and proposed rules to regulate brokers through a registration procedure which could be given statutory backing. It remains to be seen whether a major degree of formal regulation of futures trading will be introduced over the next few years.

One of the reasons why there is a feeling in the United States that futures markets, and financial futures markets in particular, require a different and perhaps more severe system of regulation than other financial markets, is the high degree of leverage obtainable in such markets. On either the IMM or LIFFE, an individual trader can establish a long position of $1,000,000 in three-month Eurodollar time deposits for an initial payment of only $2,000. Brokers will need to set very stringent rules for individual clients using these markets, particularly given the system of marking to market discussed earlier. Even so, it is important, in such volatile markets, in order to maintain the exchange's reputation, that small investors are fully protected. This has been a subject of considerable concern to the regulatory authorities in the United States, partly in response to a number of commodity frauds perpetrated on US investors, and greater regulation over individual commodity trading is likely.

The advent of financial futures trading in the UK may well bring increased individual investor involvement in futures markets, which in turn will increase pressure on exchanges to bring in better rules for the protection of individual investors. For, whereas commodity speculation is an alien world to the average small investor in Europe, speculating on interest rate

---

[1] These publicly stated aims are drawn from an article by Susan Bard, Manager, Public Affairs for the NFA, entitled "A Look at the NFA", *Futures World*, 26 August, 1982.

[2] *Review of Investor Protection*, published by Her Majesty's Stationery Office, June 1982.

and exchange rate movements may have considerably more appeal. European financial futures exchanges such as LIFFE will need to be conscientious in educating their public about the characteristics of financial futures, and more specifically in making sure that brokers are punctilious in dealing with non-corporate clients. It is also worth remembering that one of the features of the clearing systems associated with financial futures trading is that only clearing members' transactions are fully guaranteed by the clearing house. Small traders still need to rely on the financial resources of their individual brokers, and recent cases in the commodity markets suggest that the UK system of self-regulation has weaknesses in this area.

Apart from individual investor protection, arguments about the costs and benefits of financial futures, and hence the need for additional regulation, have concentrated on four main areas. First, does the existence of financial futures increase the opportunity for speculators to manipulate interest and foreign exchange rates to earn abnormal profits? Second, does speculation or overtrading in the financial futures market cause excessive volatility in the underlying cash markets, with a resultant negative impact on activity in the real economy? Third, could financial futures trading have adverse effects on government funding and monetary policy? And, finally, does financial futures trading divert funds that might be invested in the stock or venture capital markets.

Corners and squeezes

The first area of concern is whether corners and squeezes could be prevalent in financial futures markets. A corner is defined as a situation where an investor or group of investors obtains control over the entire deliverable quantity of a commodity or a financial instrument, and is thus able to force holders of short futures positions to buy from him or settle at whatever price the holder of the corner chooses. Such a situation seems unlikely in most financial futures markets, simply because of the dollar or sterling amount of deliverable supplies. The current LIFFE gilt futures contract specifications allow for over half of all traded gilt-edged stocks to be deliverable. The US T-bond contract also has a wide range of deliverable bonds. In both the United States and UK markets, most short-term interest rate contracts also specify a wide range of instruments available for delivery, with increased use of a cash settlement option.

While corners are unlikely, there is some anecdotal evidence that squeezes may occur in financial futures markets. A squeeze is a situation where, although an investor has not entirely cornered the whole deliverable supply, he or she owns enough to exert some significant pressure on prices. The general pattern is for the speculator to build up simultaneously a large cash position plus a large long position in the corresponding futures contract, and then take delivery forcing up prices of the deliverable commodity. Problems of this kind tend to arise when the deliverable commodity or financial instrument is very tightly specified. The most obvious example is the Treasury bill contract traded on the IMM. Below are some statistics for deliveries of these bills.

Contract deliveries as % of eligible bills

1979			1980		
	March	15.0		March	21.2
	June	33.0		June	21.6
	September	25.0		September	14.6
	December	43.0		December	55.6

* No figures available after end 1980.

It is apparent that deliveries as a proportion of deliverable supplies, and as a proportion of futures outstanding, have been high. While a recent report by the CFTC could find no direct evidence that a squeeze had occurred, there is potential for some degree of market manipulation when the deliverable instrument is so tightly specified. This is presumably a major reason why the Bank of England has been so reluctant to allow the introduction of a Treasury bill futures contract in the UK. However, the absence of such a UK contract does mean that discount house banks have no direct hedge instrument for a sizeable proportion of their reserve assets.

The lesson of these delivery problems seems to be that the exchange can allow a wide variety of deliverable instruments, which generally means that hedging performance is impaired, or can allow the alternative of cash settlement as LIFFE has done for its short-term financial futures, and which is the sole settlement method for Eurodollar contracts on the IMM and all the stock index futures traded in the United States. The problem remains, even with cash settlement, that a speculator could force price changes in a thin cash market, thereby squeezing a bigger futures market. Thus it will be extremely important for the regulators to keep a close watch on cash/futures price relationships around delivery dates.

Destabilizing speculation

What is the potential impact of financial futures trading on underlying interest and foreign exchange rates? Virtually all academic research on futures markets suggests that the existence of such markets reduces the volatility of underlying spot prices. The direction of causation in such arguments is that high volatility in the cash markets induces or improves prospects for futures contracts. At the same time they increase potential profits for speculators buying when they think prices are cheap and selling when they think they are dear, thus dampening the amplitude of any price swings.

While people can speculate without futures markets, the low margin requirements and high leverage factors of futures markets make it easier and less costly. Moreover, whereas short selling is rather difficult for speculators in the cash market, it is easy in the futures market. Thus, the argument runs, the existence of futures markets makes speculation easy, and speculation tends to reduce price volatility. Since the futures and cash markets are tied together through arbitrage operations, the existence of futures markets tends to reduce price swings in the underlying cash markets.

One might equally well argue exactly the opposite case. If futures trading is characterized by destabilizing speculation and therefore excessively volatile prices, and this is transmitted to spot markets through arbitrage, this would increase price volatility in the spot markets. However, this would only happen if the majority of speculators forecast poorly and thus took incorrect decisions about when prices are too low or too high. In the long run, such speculators who consistently get it wrong would be driven from the market.

One possible case for permanent destabilizing speculation has been put forward, generally known as the lemming theory of speculation. This is characterized by the existence of a small body of efficient speculators who consistently make money, and a large constantly replenished body of inefficient, amateur speculators who lose larger sums. The professional speculators might find it more profitable not to attempt to forecast the true equilibrium interest rate or exchange rate, but rather what the naive speculators think is the equilibrium price. In other words, professional speculators might still buy when the price is too high if they believe they will be able to resell the contracts at even higher prices to amateurs.

This classic description of a speculative bubble, if applicable to some periods of futures market trading, would certainly involve untoward fluctuations in underlying cash markets originating in the futures markets. While nobody would suggest that this would be a permanent feature of financial futures trading, recent experience in the commodity markets suggests it could be an occasional problem. This whole question merits, as the CFTC points out, further empirical study. If speculative bubbles are more common in futures markets than in the stock or bond markets, this could suggest that more formal regulation of financial markets might be necessary.

Monetary policy

The impact of financial futures markets on underlying interest rates may not be confined to relative volatility. Despite their monetarist leanings, governments and central banks remain interested in the maturity profile of interest rates.

Suppose the UK government wishes to reduce short-term interest rates. Standard economics would suggest that a temporary relaxation of monetary policy will, through short-term liquidity effects, reduce the level of rates, albeit at the cost of higher interest rates in the future as expectations effects begin to dominate in the medium-term. Governments have historically liked to make use of these short-run liquidity effects. But supposing you have a set of good liquid futures markets: short-term interest rates determined six, nine and 12 months out are likely to reflect the medium-term expectations impact of looser monetary policy, and these rates will feed back through arbitrage to the cash markets. If so, the existence of futures markets could interfere with, and offset, government control over the cash market and short-term interest rates.

In other words, futures markets tend to offset the monopoly benefits of governments and central banks being the sole suppliers of short-run liquidity to the financial markets, and hence could impact on government control over the yield curve.

This could seriously interfere with funding strategies of the traditional type, where rates are raised to artificially high levels to encourage funding through expectations that the next interest rate move must be downwards. This type of operation has been particularly prevalent in the UK. Believers in efficient markets would tend to take the view that this is all to the good, since there seems to be no recognized theory of why the national interest benefits from one type of yield curve or another. But governments have rarely adopted an efficient markets approach to the economy, and the current US and UK governments are no exception.

The question of the shape of the yield curve also has relevance to the design of the long-term T-bond contract on the CBT and the gilt contract on LIFFE. We have already described how a whole range of T-bonds and gilts are deliverable against such futures contracts, with the actual invoice price being adjusted so that the delivered instrument has the same effective yield to maturity as the standardized T-bond or gilt underlying the futures contract. Delivery for such contracts can be initiated on any day of the delivery month. Since the conversion factors are published well in advance, from the point of view of the futures markets all deliverable instruments will be characterized by a fixed price relationship to each other.

Should sets of relationships not correspond to actual relative prices in the cash market, arbitrage opportunities would exist: for example, one might be able to make a riskless profit by simultaneously buying gilt-edged stock in the cash market, selling the future on LIFFE and making delivery against it. Eventually, we may see the actual gilt yield curve shifting towards the fixed relationship one imposed by the conversion values. When this happens you may end up with a yield curve for all deliverable instruments completely fixed and independent of market sentiment and government policy for the delivery months in the year, and probably virtually so for the other months as well.

This may seem to the authorities bizarre, especially as conversion values based on equating yields to maturity abstract from market inflation expectations, risk and liquidity premiums. If the government for some reason wanted to manipulate the longer end of the yield curve, it might look a little askance at the fact that this would automatically yield windfall arbitrage profits to financial futures exchange members.

Arguably considerations of this kind would make central banks reluctant to see financial futures exchanges trading contracts that span the entire yield curve. The reaction of the Federal Reserve to the new CBT T-note contract will be interesting in this respect. Any system of futures trading that interfered with the traditional manipulation of the yield curve by the government to promote government funding would lead to considerable pressure from the authorities in the UK.

Advocates of financial futures markets, however, might stress the offsetting benefits. There is a clear argument that if a mechanism is provided by which institutional investors such as pension funds and insurance companies can offset some of the price risk of government bond purchases through the futures market, the average price at which the bonds can be sold may be increased.

There is almost universal agreement in the United States to the proposition that the ability of underwriting firms to hedge Treasury bond issues in the futures markets has significantly reduced Treasury bond interest rates, at a time when alterations in monetary policy has led to very large swings in Federal funds and other interest rates. This argument would apply to corporate borrowing costs as well, and the presence of financial futures markets could benefit any potential revival in the corporate debenture market in the UK.

The benefits are also not strictly confined to the average level of government and private sector borrowing costs. One of the characteristic results of increased uncertainty in financial markets over the last couple of decades has been an increased reluctance on the part of banks to lend at reasonable fixed rates of interest. What has happened is a shifting of interest rate risk to the borrower, thereby increasing the overall level of interest rates.

If, therefore, the use of financial futures allows interest rate risk to be shifted instead to traders and speculators, the general level of rates reflecting the fundamental demand and supply for loanable funds should be lower. Moreover it could be argued that the use of financial futures and other financial innovations allows banks and other financial institutions to respond more efficiently to changes in the financial environment, and this will also act to lower rates. Finally, it is difficult not to agree with the CFTC view that the ability to hedge interest rate risk should create a lower risk of insolvency for financial and other corporations than would be the case if hedging were not possible. Lower bankruptcy risk will lead to a lower cost of debt finance for both financial and non-financial corporations. This argument does rely on corporations generally using the futures markets for hedging rather than outright speculation, and provides some justification for the approaches of both the CFTC and the US tax authorities which support legitimate hedging activities of commercial banks and industrial corporations but discourage trading and speculation.

A cynic would argue that experience of the US markets simply does not square with such arguments. The US markets are not widely used by institutional hedgers, but are dominated by futures market professionals and commodity pools and individual speculators. There is nothing necessarily wrong with this—the vital role of traders and speculators on providing liquidity has already been discussed. But it is mainly the hedging aspects that fit in with the macro-economic and social benefits of futures markets. The London International Financial Futures Exchange must hope that, with the big institutions tending to dominate its membership, hedging activity will develop earlier and at a more vigorous pace than in the United States. If this does not happen, defending the economic benefits of LIFFE against potential critics will be more difficult.

Diversification of funds

The other macro-economic worry expressed concerning financial futures markets is the problem of the diversification of funds. This has two aspects. First, investors' attention could be diverted to financial futures markets away from the cash markets; second, the cash markets and venture capital markets in general could be starved of actual funds by futures markets' operations. The first problem is more likely to occur than the second, for although futures markets are a zero-sum game, merely shuffling funds among market participants, and therefore unable to affect the aggregate supply of loanable funds, they tend to lead to a concentration of information gathering and processing on the underlying financial instruments on which the futures contracts are written. Hence there will be a net shift of information activity from studying returns on real investments and underwriting activities to studying the features of the few interest rates on which futures contracts exist.

The contrary view argues that since information is available free in futures markets, particularly with the open outcry system, then there will actually be more resources available for information investment in non-futures markets.

Most of these arguments are far-fetched and could essentially be used against any financial innovation. But there could perhaps be an impact on investors' willingness to accept risk. We do not know whether investors' risk preference structures will alter with their increased ability to shift interest rate and exchange rate risks. And it is difficult not to have a sneaking sympathy with criticisms that some of the most skilled minds in the community spend a lot of their time developing new types of contingent claims (a contingent claim is defined as an asset whose value is a function of the value of an other asset) rather than improving the potential for investment in the underlying real economy.

Conclusions

The existence of financial futures markets do raise problems for the regulators and the conductors of macro-economic policy. Traditional problems of regulatory structure such as the possibility of squeezes and corners are no different to those in existing cash markets, but there is a greater necessity to protect small investors in these markets, since there is substantially more retail trade in financial futures markets than in other commodity futures markets. More study is also needed on the influence of these futures markets on the underlying cash markets.

The direct advantages of futures trading are fairly clear. Futures trading tends to increase liquidity and reduce search costs for financial transactions, and hence tends to narrow bid-ask spreads.

Holders of cash positions may well be able to close out such positions in the more diffuse, anonymous futures market more easily and at better prices than in the cash market. The futures market facilitates and reduces the costs of going short, so that prices will no longer be dominated by the more optimistic set of investors, and thereby will provide more accurate information on people's expectations in the market. The risk-transference and hedging facilities of financial futures markets should, on the whole, lower the overall cost of funds both for public and private sector borrowing. And the existence of the clearing house should lower interest costs simply through reduced risk of default on transactions.

Yet there are problems from the government's point of view. In the long-run the existence of financial futures markets is likely, for example, to reduce the Bank of England's ability to alter artificially the structure of short-term interest rates, and restrict official manipulations of the yield curve. This will be emphasized as the number of contracts traded on LIFFE increases. As a free market economist, I would regard this result as no bad thing. Financial futures markets, like most other financial innovations, appear to be generally good for the overall economy as well as for financial markets.

Appendix 1: Glossary

Actuals	The physical or cash financial instrument, as distinguished from a financial futures contract.
Arbitrage	The simultaneous purchase and sale of similar financial instruments in order to profit from distortions from usual price relationships.
Basis	The difference between the cash price of a financial instrument and the price of a financial futures contract.
Basis point	A measurement of the change in yield levels for fixed income securities. One basis point equals 0.01%.
Bear	A person who believes prices will move lower.
Bid	An offer to purchase a specified quantity of a financial futures contract at a specified price.
Break	A rapid and sharp price decline.
Broker	A person paid a fee or commission for acting as an agent in making contracts, sales or purchases. A floor broker is a person who actually executes someone else's trading orders on the trading floor of an exchange.
Bulge	A rapid and sharp price advance.
Bull	A person who believes prices will move higher.
Buy in	A purchase to cover, offset or close a short position.
Buy on close	To buy at the end of the trading session at a price within the closing range.
Buy on opening	To buy at the beginning of a trading session at a price within the opening range.
Call	A designated buying and selling period resembling an auction under the control of a chairman to establish price ranges for futures contracts.
Cash commodity	The actual commodity or instrument as opposed to futures contracts based upon that commodity.
Cash market	The underlying currency or money market in which transactions for the purchase and sale of cash instruments to which futures contracts relate are carried out.
Cash price	A price quotation obtained or a price actually received in a cash market.
CFTC	The Commodity Futures Trading Commission, which is an independent Federal Agency set up in the United States to regulate futures trading.
Chart analysis	The use of graphs and charts to analyse and predict market behaviour.
Clearing house	The organization which registers, monitors, matches and guarantee trades on a futures market, and carries out financial settlement of futures transactions. It could be a division of the futures exchange, or a separate subsidiary corporation of the exchange, or an independent body. In the case of the Chicago Board of Trade, the clearing house is the Board of Trade Clearing Corporation, a separate corporation. LIFFE trades will be cleared through the International Commodities Clearing House, a totally independent firm owned by the major UK banks.
Clearing member	A member firm of the clearing house. Each clearing member must also be a member of an exchange, but not all members of an exchange are also members of the clearing house. All trades of a non-clearing member must be registered with, and eventually settled through, a clearing member.
The close	The period at the end of the trading session, officially designated by the exchange, during which all transactions are considered to be made "at the close".
Closing price	The price at which transactions are made just before the close on a given day. Frequently there is not just one price, but a range of prices at which transactions were made just before the close.
Closing range	The high and low prices at which transactions took place during "the close".
Commission	The one-time fee charged by a broker to a customer when a position is liquidated either by offset (q.v.) or delivery (q.v.).
Commission broker	A member of an exchange who executes orders for members and non-members for the sale or purchase of financial futures contracts.
Contract	A financial futures contract is a binding agreement to make and take delivery at a specified date of a fixed quantity of a specified currency or fixed interest instrument.
Contract grade	The type of cash instruments listed in the rules of the exchange that can be used when delivering cash commodities against futures contracts.
Contract month	The month in which futures contracts may be satisfied by making or accepting delivery.
Cover	To offset a previous futures transaction with an equal and opposite transaction. Short covering is a purchase of futures contracts to offset an

earlier sale of an equal number of the same delivery month. Liquidation is the sale of futures contracts to offset the obligation to take delivery of an equal number of futures contracts of the same delivery month purchased earlier.

Cross hedging	The hedging of an open position in a futures contract of a different, but related, cash instrument.
Current delivery (month)	The futures contract that will become deliverable during the current month.
Day order	An order that is placed for execution, if possible, during only one trading session. If the order cannot be exercised that day, it is automatically cancelled.
Day trading	Refers to establishing and liquidating the same futures position or positions within one day's trading.
Deferred futures	The more distant delivery months in which futures trading is taking place.
Deliverable names	Financial instruments, specified in the rules of the exchange, which may be offered when making delivery of an actual instrument in satisfaction of a futures contract.
Delivery	The tender and receipt of an actual financial instrument or cash in settlement of a futures contract.
Delivery month	A calendar month during which delivery against a futures contract can be made.
Delivery notice	The written notice given by the seller of his intention to make delivery against an open, short (q.v.) futures position on a particular date.
Delivery points	Those locations and facilities designated by futures exchanges at which the financial instruments covered by a futures contract may be delivered in fulfilment of such a contract.
Delivery price	The price fixed by the clearing house at which deliveries on futures contracts are invoiced.
Diffence account	In the UK, an account given to a client by a broker when a position is closed.
Discount	The amount by which the price of one futures contract is less than another, or less than the cash market price of the underlying instrument.
Discretionary account	An account over which any individual or organization, other than the person in whose name the account is carried, exercises trading authority or control.
Eligible margin	The cash or other collateral which the exchange specifies that members may accept from their customers to satisfy initial and variation margin requirements.
Equity	The residual value of a futures trading account, assuming its liquidation at the then current market price.
Evening up	Buying or selling to offset an existing market position.
Exchange	The market in which the purchase or sale of financial futures contracts take place, generally through open outcry.
Exchange of cash for futures	The simultaneous exchange of a specified quantity of the cash instrument for the equivalent quantity in futures.
Financial instrument	The actual currency, fixed interest security or deposit which is specified in a financial futures contract.
Fill or kill order	An order at a specified price which must be offered or bid three times. If not filled, it is cancelled immediately.
First notice day	The first day on which notices of intention to deliver actual financial instruments in fulfilment of a given month's financial futures contracts is authorized.
Floor broker	A member who is paid a fee for executing orders for clearing members and their customers.
Floor trader	An exchange member who executes his own trades by being personally present in the pit or place provided for futures trading.
Forward contract	A cash market transaction in which two parties agree to purchase and sell a commodity at some future time under such conditions as are mutually agreeable. In contrast to futures contracts (q.v.), forward contracts are not standardized.
Forward months	Futures contracts calling for a deferred delivery.
Fundamental analysis	The prediction of market behaviour and price trends by analysis of underlying factors of demand and supply (contrasted with technical analysis and charting).
Futures contract	A term used to designate all standard contracts covering the sale of financial instruments or physical commodities on a futures exchange.
Give-up	At the request of the customer, a brokerage house which has not performed the service is credited with the execution of an order.

GNMA	Government National Mortgage Association; a US government agency that approves the issue of mortgage-backed securities with repayment of principal and interest fully guaranteed by the US Treasury.
GTC	Good till cancelled. Open orders to buy or sell at a fixed price that remain effective until executed or cancelled.
Heavy	A market in which there is a large number of selling orders overhanging the market without a corresponding number of buying orders.
Hedging	The purchase or sale of a futures contract as a temporary substitute for a cash market transaction at a later date. This usually involves taking a futures position equal and opposite to an existing or anticipated cash market position.
Hedger	A person who hedges.
Implied repo rate	The difference between the current cash price and a futures price expressed as an interest rate.
Initial margin	The deposit a customer must make on purchasing or selling a futures contract.
Inverted market	A futures market in which the nearer months are selling at a premium to the more distant months.
Kerb trading	The execution of transactions after the close of the official market.
Last trading day	The final day during which trading may take place in a particular delivery month. Futures contracts outstanding at the end of the last trading day must be settled by delivery of the specified financial instrument, or settlement may be made in cash at the option of the buyer in certain contracts.
Life of contract	Period between the beginning of trading in a particular future and expiration of trading in the delivery month.
Limit move	The maximum fluctuation in price of a futures contract permitted during one trading session, as fixed by the rules of the exchange.
Limit order	An order given to a broker which has restrictions on its execution. The customer specifies a price, and the order is executed only if the market price equals or betters that price.
Liquidation	Any transaction that offsets or closes out a long (q.v.) or short (q.v.) position.
Liquid market	A market where buying and selling can be accomplished with ease, due to the presence of a large number of interested buyers and sellers prepared to trade substantial quantities at small price differences.
A long	A person who has bought one or more futures contracts to establish a market position, and who has not yet closed out that position through an offsetting sale.
Long hedge	The purchase of a futures contract in anticipation of actual purchases in the cash market.
Long of the basis	Refers to a person who has purchased the cash instrument and hedged it with sales of the corresponding futures contract.
Margin	An amount of money deposited by traders of futures contracts as a guarantee of fulfilment of the futures contract.
Maintenance margin	The minimum margin which a customer must keep on deposit with a member at all times.
Margin call	A demand for additional funds because of adverse price movement on an open futures position.
Mark to market	The daily adjustment of an open futures contract to reflect profits and losses on open contracts resulting from price movements occurring during the last trading session.
Market order	An order to buy or sell a futures contract that is to be executed at the best possible price and as soon as possible.
Maturity	Period within which a futures contract can be satisfied by delivery, i.e. the period between the first notice day and last trading day of a futures contract.
Maximum price fluctuation	The maximum amount the contract price can change, up or down, during one trading session, as defined by exchange rules.
Minimum price fluctuation	The smallest increment of price movement possible in trading a given contract.
Nearby	The nearest active trading month of a financial futures market.
Net position	The number of futures contracts bought or sold which have not been offset by opposite transactions.
Nominal price	Price quotation on a futures contract for a period in which no actual trading took place.
Notice day	A day on which notices of intent to deliver, pertaining to a specified delivery month, may be issued.

184

Offer	Indicates a willingness to sell a futures contract at a given price.
Offset	The liquidation of a purchase of futures through the sale of an equal number of contracts of the same delivery month, or the covering of a short sale of futures through the purchase of an equal number of contracts of the same delivery month.
Omnibus account	An account carried by one futures commission merchant or broker with another in which the transactions of two or more persons are combined rather than designated separately.
On opening	The specification of execution of an order during the opening or as soon thereafter as possible.
Open contracts	Contracts which have been bought or sold without the transactions having been completed or offset by subsequent sale or purchase, or actual delivery or receipt of the underlying financial instrument.
Open interest	The cumulative number of futures contracts which have been purchased and not yet offset by opposite futures transactions, nor fulfilled by delivery.
Open order	An order which is good until cancelled or executed.
Open outcry	Method of dealing on futures markets involving verbal bids and offers which are audible to all other market participants on the trading floor or pit.
Opening	The period at the beginning of the trading session officially designated by the exchange during which all transactions are considered to be made "at the opening".
Opening price (or range)	The price or price range of transactions recorded during the period designated by the exchange as the official opening.
Original margin	The initial deposit of margin money required to cover a specific new futures position.
Overbought	A condition under which heavy liquidation of weakly held long futures positions appears imminent.
Oversold	A condition under which heavy covering of weakly held short futures positions appears imminent.
P + S	A purchase and sale statement sent by a broker to a customer when his futures position has changed, showing the number of contracts involved, the contract prices, the gross profit and loss, commission charges, and the net profit and loss on the transactions.
Paper profit	The profit that would be realized if open futures contracts were liquidated as of a certain time or at a certain price.
Perfect hedge	A hedge in which the change in the futures price is identical to the change in the cash market price.
Pit	An octagonal area on the trading floor of an exchange, surrounded by a tier of steps upon which traders and brokers stand while executing futures trades.
Point	The smallest increment of price movement possible in trading a given futures contract, equivalent to the minimum price fluctuation.
Position	An interest in the market, either long or short, in terms of open contracts.
Position limit	The maximum number of speculative futures contracts a person (or possibly group of persons) can hold as determined by the regulatory authorities or by the futures exchange.
Position trading	A type of trading involving the holding of open futures contracts for an extended period of time.
Premium	The excess of one futures contract over another, or over the cash market price.
Price limits	The maximum price advance or decline from the previous day's settlement price permitted for a contract in one trading session by the regulations of the exchange.
Primary market	The principal underlying market for a financial instrument.
Pyramiding	The practice of margining additional futures trades using accrued profits to previous futures transactions.
Rally	An upward movement in prices following a decline.
Range	The high and low prices, or high and low bids and offers, recorded during a specified period.
Reaction	A decline in prices following an advance.
Recovery	A price advance following a decline.
Registered representative	An individual registered with the exchange and the regulatory authorities to solicit customer business for his firm.
Repurchase agreement	The selling of a security by one party to another at the same time that the other party enters into an agreement to resell the securities to the first party at a predetermined price and date.

Round turn	A complete futures transaction in which an individual long or short position is closed out by an opposite futures transaction, or by making or taking delivery.
Scalp	To trade for small gains. Scalping usually involves establishing and liquidating a futures position quickly, always within the same trading day.
Settlement price	The daily price at which the clearing house clears all trades. The settlement price is determined by reference to the closing range, and is used to determine margin calls and invoice prices for deliveries.
A short	A person one who has sold a futures contract to establish a market position and who has not yet closed out this position through an offsetting purchase.
Short hedge	The sale of a futures contract to lock in the current interest rate or exchange rate and thereby eliminate or lessen the possible decline in value of ownership of an approximately equal amount of an actual financial instrument.
Short of the basis	A transaction in which a person has sold the cash financial instrument and hedged the position with a purchase of financial futures contracts.
Short selling	Selling something which is not currently owned, in the hope of buying it back at a lower price.
Short squeeze	A situation in which a lack of supply tends to force prices upwards to the disadvantage of those who are short.
Speculator	A person who buys or sells futures contracts in the hope of profiting from subsequent price movements.
Spot	The characteristic of being available for immediate or nearly immediate delivery.
Spot price	The price at which a spot or cash commodity is selling.
Spread	Refers to the simultaneous purchase and sale of futures contracts for the same instrument for delivery in different months, and to the simultaneous purchase and sale of futures in different but related instruments for delivery in the same or different months. The aim is to benefit from a favourable change in relative prices.
Stop loss order	An order to buy or sell at the market when a definite price is reached, either above or below the price that prevailed when the order was given. Usually used as a method of limiting losses by traders with open positions.
Straddle	Purchase in one market and simultaneous sale in another market of the same futures contract; or the purchase of one futures contract against the sale of a different futures contract.
Switching	Liquidating an existing futures position and simultaneously reinstating that position in a different maturity future on the same financial instrument.
Technical analysis	The analysis of futures markets and future trends of prices by examining the technical factors of market activity such as price trends, volume trends and open interest patterns, often using charting methods.
Tender	Delivery against futures.
Tick	Refers to the minimum possible change in prices, either up or down.
Trading limit	Prices above or below which trading is not allowed in a single trading session. Also limits, defined by the exchange, on any one organization or individual on the maximum number of contracts that may be traded in a given trading day or the maximum net position that may be held.
Trend	The general direction of market prices.
Variable limits	A system on some futures exchanges which allows for larger than normally allowable price movements under certain circumstances.
Variation margin	The gains or losses on open futures positions which are calculated by marking to market ($q.v.$) at the end of each trading day, and credited or debited by the clearing house to each clearing member's account, and by members to their customer's accounts.
Volume	The number of transactions in a futures contract made during a specified period of time.
Wire house	A firm operating a private wire to its own branch offices, or to other firms.

Appendix 2: Contract specifications

This appendix contains the specifications, at the time of writing, for the most important and/or heavily traded financial futures contracts on the world's futures exchange. Although believed to be correct at the time of going to press, neither the author nor Euromoney Publications take responsibility for these descriptions. Exchanges often change contract specifications, particularly in terms of price limits, margin requirements, etc, at short notice. Anyone wishing to trade financial futures should contact his broker or the relevant futures exchange to determine the up-to-date contract specifications.

Part 1: Interest rate futures contracts

1. Chicago Board of Trade

Contract	Face value	Minimum price movement	Maximum price movement	Delivery grade	Delivery months	Price basis
U.S. Treasury bonds	$100,000	$1/32$ of a point or $31.25 per contract	$^{64}/_{32}$ or $2000 per contract	U.S. Treasury bonds maturing at least 15 years from date of delivery if not callable. If callable, with a call date at least 15 years from first day of delivery month. Based on 8% coupon	March, June, September, December	Percentage of par
CDR GNMA	$100,000	$1/32$ of a point or $31.25 per contract	$^{64}/_{32}$ or $2000 per contract	Modified pass-through mortgage backed certificates guaranteed by GNMA based on 8% coupon assuming 30 year maturity prepaid in 12th year	March, June, September, December	Percentage of par
10-year Treasury notes $100,000	$100,000	$1/32$ of a point or $31.25 per contract	$^{64}/_{32}$ or $2000 per contract	U.S. Treasury notes maturing not less than $6\frac{1}{2}$ years and not more than 10 years from first day of delivery month. Based on 8% coupon	March, June, September, December	Percentage of par
Four–six year Treasury notes	$100,000	$1/32$ of a point or $31.25 per contract	$^{64}/_{32}$ or $2000 per contract	U.S. Treasury notes and non-callable bonds maturing not less than 4 years and not more than 6 years from first day of delivery month. Based on 8% coupon	March, June, September, December	Percentage of par
Two-year Treasury notes	$400,000	$1/128$ of a point or $31.25 per contract	$^{96}/_{128}$ or $3000 per contract	U.S. Treasury notes and non-callable bonds maturing not less than 1 year, 9 months and not more than 2 years from first day of delivery month. Based on 8% coupon	March, June, September, December	Percentage of par

1. Chicago Board of Trade–*contd.*

Contract	Face value	Minimum price movement	Maximum price movement	Delivery grade	Delivery months	Price basis
Domestic certificates of deposit	$1,000,000	1 basis point (0.01%) or $25 per contract	60 basis points or per contract	Domestic CDs approved by CBT with original maturity of not more than 6 months and maturing on a business day early in third month following delivery month	March, June, September, December	Index, 100 minus annual yield

2. Chicago Mercantile Exchange (International Monetary Market)

Contract	Face value	Minimum price movement	Maximum price movement	Delivery grade	Delivery months	Price basis
90-day T-bills	$1,000,000 face value at maturity	One basis point (0.01%) or $25	60 basis points or $1,500 per contract	90–92 day U.S. Treasury bills	March, June, September, December	Index, 100 minus annualized discount
One-year T-bills	$250,000 face value at maturity	One basis point (0.01%) or $25	50 basis points or $1,250 per contract	One year U.S. Treasury bills	March, June, September, December	Index, 100 minus annualized discount
Four-year Treasury notes	$100,000 face value	$1/64$ of a point or $15.625	$48/64$ points or $750 per contract	Same issue Treasury notes. Maturity not less than $3\frac{1}{2}$ and not more than $4\frac{1}{2}$ years from first day of delivery month	February, May, August, November	Percentage of par
90-day domestic certificates of deposit	$1,000,000	One basis point (0.01%) or $25	80 basis points or $2,000 per contract	Domestic no-name CDs maturing on a business day not before the 16th of the month after spot month nor after the last day of the month three months after the spot month	March, June, September, December	Index, 100 minus annualized yield
Three-month Eurodollar time deposit	$1,000,000	One basis point (0.01%) or $25	100 basis points or $2,500 per contract	Cash settlement	March, June, September, December spot month	Index, 100 minus annualized yield

3. London International Financial Futures Exchange

Contract	Face value	Minimum price movement	Maximum price movement	Delivery grade	Delivery months	Price basis
Three-month sterling time deposit	£250,000	One basis point (0.01%) or £6.25	100 basis points or £625 per contract	Three-month time deposits at acceptable banks with commencement day the settlement day of the contract. Cash settlement at buyer's option	March, June, September, December	Index, 100 minus annual yield

3. London International Financial Futures Exchange–*contd.*

Contract	Face value	Minimum price movement	Maximum price movement	Delivery grade	Delivery months	Price basis
Three-month Eurodollar time deposit	$1,000,000	One basis point (0.01%) or $25	100 basis points or $2,500 per contract	Three-month time deposits at accceptable banks with commencement day the settlement day of the contract. Cash settlement at buyer's option	March, June, September, December	Index, 100 minus annual yield
Sterling long gilt-edged stock	£50,000 nominal value	$\frac{1}{32}$ of a point or £15.625	$^{64}/_{32}$ points or £1,000 per contract	U.K. gilts with 15-25 years to maturity, based on a standardized 20-year 12% stock	March, June, September, December	Percentage of par

4. Toronto and Montreal

Contract	Face value	Minimum price movement	Maximum price movement	Delivery grade	Delivery months	Price basis
91-day Treasury bill	C$1,000,000	2 basis points or C$50	60 basis points or C$1,500 per contract	84–92 day Canadian Treasury bills	March, June, September, December	Index, 100 minus annualized discount
Canadian long-term government bonds	C$100,000	$\frac{1}{32}$ of a point or C$31.25 per contract	$^{64}/_{32}$ points or C$2,000 per contract	All Canadian government bonds with 18 years or more maturity from delivery month on basis of 9% of coupon	March, June, September, December	Percentage of par
Canadian government mid-term bonds	C$50,000	$\frac{1}{32}$ of a point or C$15.625 per contract	$^{64}/_{32}$ points or C$1000 per contract	Five-year Canadian government bonds on basis of 9% coupon	March, June, September, December	Percentage of par

Note: (1) Winnipeg also trades job lots in 91-day T-bills and long-term bonds, i.e. units of one-fifth the size of the designated board contract. Thus in T-bills the board lot is C$1 million but the basic unit of trade is C$200,000.

5. Mid-America Commodity Exchange

Contract	Face value	Minimum price movement	Maximum price movement	Delivery grade	Delivery months	Price basis
U.S. Treasury bonds	$50,000	$\frac{1}{32}$ of a point or $15.625 per contract	$^{64}/_{32}$ or $1,000 per contract	As for Chicago Board of Trade	March, June, September, December	Percentage of par
90-day U.S. T-bills	$500,000	$\frac{1}{10}$ of a basis point or $1.25 per contract	60 basis points or $750 per contract	Cash settlement	March, June, September, December	Index, 100 minus annualized discount yield

6. Sydney Futures Exchange

Contract	Face value	Minimum price movement	Maximum price movement	Delivery grade	Delivery months	Price basis
90-day bank accepted bills of exchange	$A500,000	1 basis point or A$12.50 per contract	None	Bills maturing 85–95 days from settlement day	Spot month plus next six consecutive months, then financial quarters out to two years	Index, 100 minus annual yield

Part 2: Foreign exchange futures contracts

1. International monetary market (CME)

Currency	Contract	Minimum price movement	Maximum price movement	Contract months
Swiss franc	125,000	$0.0001 or $12.50 per contract	$0.015 or $1,875 per contract	Jan., Mar., Apr., Jun., Jul., Sept., Oct., Dec., and spot month
Mexican peso	1,000,000	$0.00001 or $10 per contract	$0.0015 or $1,500 per contract	As Swiss franc
Deutschemark	125,000	$0.0001 or $12.50 per contract	$0.01 or $1,250 per contract	As Swiss franc
Canadian dollar	100,000	$0.0001 or $10 per contract	$0.0075 or $750 per contract	As Swiss franc
Pound sterling	25,000	$0.0005 or $12.50 per contract	$0.05 or $1,250 per contract	As Swiss franc
Japanese yen	12,500,000	$0.000001 or $12.50 per contract	$0.0001 or $1,250 per contract	As Swiss franc
French franc	250,000	$0.00005 or $12.50 per contract	$0.005 or $1,250 per contract	As Swiss franc
Dutch guilder	125,000	$0.0001 or $12.50 per contract	$0.01 or $1,250 per contract	As Swiss franc

Note: (1) All currency contracts are priced as dollars per unit of foreign currency, e.g. £1 = $1.5200 or 1DM = $0.42.
(2) Delivery involves short delivering face value in foreign currency to the long in exchange for U.S. dollars.

2. London International Financial Futures Exchange

Currency	Contract size	Minimum price movement	Maximum price movement	Contract months
Pound sterling	25,000	0.01¢ per £ or $2.50 per contract	$0.05 or $1,250 per contract	March, June, September, December
Swiss franc	125,000	0.01¢ per Swfr or $12.50 per contract	$0.01 or $1,250 per contract	As pound sterling
Deutschemark	125,000	0.01¢ per DM or $12.50 per contract	$0.01 or $1,250 per contract	As pound sterling
Japanese yen	12,500,000	0.01¢ per 100 yen or $12.50 per contract	$0.01 or $1,250 per contract	As pound sterling

Note: (1) All currency contracts are priced as dollars per unit of foreign currency, e.g. £1 = $1.5200 or 1DM = $0.42.
(2) Delivery involves short delivering face value in foreign currency to long in exchange for U.S. dollars.

3. Sydney Futures Exchange

Currency	Contract	Minimum price movement	Maximum price movement	Contract months
U.S. dollar	100,000	A$0.0001 or $10 per contract	None	Spot months plus next five consecutive months, then financial quarters out to 18 months

Part 3: Stock index futures contracts

Exchange	Contract	Price basis	Minimum price movement	Maximum price movement	Delivery grade	Delivery months
Kansas City Board of Trade	Value Line average index	$500 × index	0.05 index points or $25 per contract	None	Cash settlement	March, June, September, December
Index and Options Market (CME)	S+P 500 composite index	$500 × index	0.05 index points or $25 per contract	None	Cash settlement	March, June, September, December
New York Futures Exchange	New York Stock Exchange composite index	$500 × index	0.05 index points or $25 per contract	None	Cash settlement	March, June, September, December
New York Futures Exchange	New York Stock Exchange financial index	$1,000 × index	0.01 index points or $10 per contract	None	Cash settlement	March, June, September, December
Sydney	Australian Stock Exchange all ordinaries price index	A$1,000 × index	0.01 index points or A$10 per contract	None	Cash settlement	March, June, September, December

Appendix 3: Fundamental and technical analysis of rates

One important factor in futures trading is predicting clearly where cash market interest rates and foreign exchange rates are going to move. Many books have been written on this topic, and no attempt is made here to duplicate them.

The two major approaches to forecasting rates are: fundamental analysis, and technical analysis. Some basic fundamental principles for analysing the evolution of rates are given first.

Fundamental analysis

Interest rates

1. Nominal interest rates are partly determined by real forces and partly by expected inflation.
2. Analyse available economic data to get the best possible indication of expected inflation.
3. Carry out flow of funds analysis to determine prospective changes in equilibrium interest rates.
4. Analyse economic data to try and forecast the business cycle. Use the cycle to predict interest rate turning points, and to predict yield curve shifts.
5. Combine expected inflation numbers and real rate forecasts to get nominal rate forecasts. Compare these with current cash market rates.
6. Maintain a timely economic data-base. Analyse new developments and trends as quickly as possible. Anticipating events ahead of other investors earns the highest returns.

Exchange rates

1. Exchange rate changes are partly caused by real forces and partly by relative inflation.
2. Analyse available economic data to get the best possible handle on relative inflation.
3. Analyse shifts in real demand for a given currency: changes in productivity, portfolio investment attributes, etc.
4. Analyse differences in countries' positions along the business cycle. This can affect real exchange rates for a time.
5. Beware: exchange rates seem to persist at levels not explainable on fundamental grounds for prolonged periods.
6. Try and anticipate changes in market sentiment. Always keep a close watch on political and social developments as well as economic ones.

Technical analysis

The basic feature of fundamental analysis as a tool for understanding movement in interest rates and exchange rates is the analysis of the factors which affect the supply and demand for money and credit. Technical analysis is concerned with studying the market itself—largely by using charts and various statistical techniques to examine whether predictions of the future time-path of interest and exchange rates can be derived from the past history of those rates. This type of analysis argues that the past of a price series has information about the likely future of the series.[1]

The simplest type of technical analysis, and the one most widely relied on in futures market trading, is chart analysis. Basically all chart analysis depends on an assumption that familiar patterns of prices will tend to recur through time and that they can be used to predict the future to some degree. The most common types of chart, which will be supplied by any of the major charting firms, are the bar chart and the point and figure charts. Exhibits A1 and A2 show an example of each. Bar charts map prices against time, showing for each period (which could be a day, week or month) the high price, the low price, and the closing price indicated by the horizontal bar. Such charts are used to see if prices are following familiar patterns, which might include channels, heads and shoulders, double bottoms and other patterns. Any good book on technical analysis will provide a detailed description of possible predictive patterns for bar charts.

---

[1] Two books by Perry J. Kaufman, *Commodity Trading Systems and Methods*, John Wiley and Sons (1978), and *Technical Analysis in Commodities*, John Wiley and Sons (1980), are classics in this field. Another good book is Martin Pring, *Technical Analysis Explained*, McGraw-Hill (1980).

Exhibit A.1: Data display—bar chart

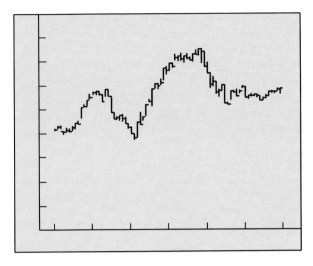

Source: Investor Intelligence Systems Ltd

Exhibit A.2: Data display—point and figure (or reversal) chart

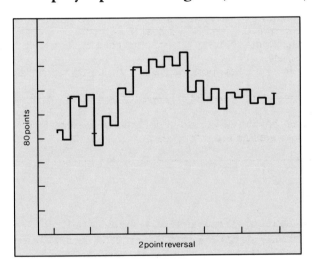

Source: Investor Intelligence Systems Ltd

Exhibit A.2 shows a point and figure chart. Such charts are more complex to produce than simple bar charts, since they do not have a fixed time scale along the horizontal axis. Such charts display only price changes, moving to a new column only when a price reversal has taken place. To avoid too many columns, not all price reversals are recorded: the point and figure chart shown is of the two reversal type; reversals of two units or less are not recorded. The chart shown has a two point scale. That means that a four point move in price is required to establish a new column. The purported advantage of such charts is that they only show trading activity which actually involves reversals in prices. The idea is to look for familiar patterns that can be expected to repeat themselves. In particular, chart analysts use such charts to try and establish price support and resistance levels; a break of the price through such levels is often regarded as an important buying or selling signal.

Many technical analysts also make use of advanced statistical techniques for analysing futures price series, e.g. moving averages, momentum models and Box-Jenkins models. Followers of such techniques as Eliot wave analysis and Gann diagrams use even more complex methods of analysis. Technical analysts also use volume and open interest statistics in conjunction with the price series to improve prediction performance.

Although these techniques are mentioned only briefly, an understanding of the more elementary techniques of technical analysis is important for the financial futures trader if for no other reason than that so many futures market participants do trade on the basis of charts. Trading on the basis of charts also introduces an element of objectivity into trading decisions, which may help the investor to avoid running unnecessary trading losses. In essence, the aim is to develop an appropriate trading rule derived from the technical anlysis. In its simplest form, a trader could try and identify trend patterns, and adopt a trading rule of buying or selling whenever a trend is broken. Limit orders for stop-loss and profit-taking could also be used in conjunction with such a trading rule.

There are as many technical analysis approaches and charting approaches as there are individual traders. This summary gives but a brief flavour of what is available. All traders should be aware of charts, and examine whether their fundamental analysis is in line with the existing chart patterns. Whether an individual trader wishes to go further than that in using technical analysis, will depend on his own experience with these methods.

Bibliography

This bibliography is designed to cover the more important books, articles and pamphlets published in the financial futures area over the last few years. It is strictly confined to financial futures, and is not designed to be exhaustive. It therefore excludes innumerable books and articles on the cash markets, interest rate and foreign exchange rate forecasting, technical analysis and charting, etc. For those interested in pursuing such topics, the reader is referred to the following excellent bibliographies.

Bibliography and Information Source List, Financial Futures. International Monetary Market, Chicago Mercantile Exchange.
Bibliography: Financial Futures, Information Sources. London International Financial Futures Exchange.
Commodity Futures Trading: A Bibliography. Chicago Board of Trade.
An excellent bibliography in Kolb, R. W. *Interest Rate Futures: A Comprehensive Introduction*, R. F. Dame Inc, Virginia, 1982.

A. Financial futures markets

1. Books

Gay, G. and Kolb, R.W. (eds), *Interest Rate Futures: Concepts and Issues*, Robert F. Dame Inc., Richmond, Virginia, 1982.
Hoel, Arline, *A Primer on the Futures Markets for Treasury Bills*, Federal Reserve Bank of New York, New York, 1977.
Kolb, R.W., *Interest Rate Futures: A Comprehensive Introduction*, Robert F. Dame Inc., Richmond, Virginia, 1982.
Loosigian, A.M., *Interest Rate Futures*, Dow Jones-Irwin, Homewood, Illinois, 1980.
Loosigian, A.M., *Foreign Exchange Futures*, Dow Jones-Irwin, Homewood, Illinois, 1982.
Powers, M.J. and Vogel, D., *Inside the Financial Futures Market*, Wiley, New York, 1981.
Rothstein, N. (ed), *The Handbook of Financial Futures*, McGraw-Hill, New York, forthcoming.
Schwartz, E., *How to Use Interest Rate Futures Contracts*, Dow Jones-Irwin, Homewood, Illinois, 1978.
Weberman, B., *Interest Rate Futures: Profits and Pitfalls*, B. Weberman, New York, 1979.
Willett, E.R., *Interest Rate Futures: The Basics*, Willett Institute of Finance, New York, 1979.

2. Exchange publications

Chicago Board of Trade:	*Financial Instrument Markets: Cash-Futures Relationships.*
	An Introduction to the Interest Rate Futures Market.
	Hedging Interest Rate Risk.
	Understanding the Delivery Process in Financial Futures.
Chicago Mercantile Exchange:	*Understanding Futures in Foreign Exchange.*
	Opportunities in Interest Rates—Treasury Bill Futures.
	Opportunities in CD Futures.
	Inside Eurodollar Futures.
	Inside S + P 500 Stock Index Futures.
	Currency Futures Trading for Financial Institutions.
	Opportunities in Stock Futures.
London International Futures Exchange:	*Introduction.*
	Hedging Techniques.
	Trading Techniques.
	Financial Futures: Accounting Principles and Records.
	Internal Control for Financial Futures.

3. Articles

Arak, M. and McCurdy, C. (1979), *Interest Rate Futures*, Federal Reserve Bank of New York Quarterly Review 4, 33–46.

Batchelor, R.A. (1983), *Financial Futures: Price and Open Interest Determination*, Working Paper No. 30, City University, Centre for Banking and International Finance.

Cagan, P. (1981), *Financial Futures Markets: Is More Regulation Needed*, Journal of Futures Markets, 1, 169–189.

Capozza, D. and Cornell, B. (1979), *Treasury Bill Pricing in the Spot and Futures Markets*, Review of Economics and Statistics, 61, 513–520.

Chow, B.G. and Brophy, D.T. (1982), *Treasury Bill Futures Markets: A Formulation and Interpretation*, Journal of Futures Markets, 2, 25–47.

Cicchetti, P., Dale, C., and Vignola, A.J. (1981), *Usefulness of Treasury Bill Futures as Hedging Instruments*, Journal of Futures Markets, 1, 379–387.

Cornell, B. (1981), *Taxes and the Pricing of Treasury Bill Futures Contracts*, Journal of Finance, 36, 1169–1177.

Culbertson, W.P. (1978), *GNMA Futures Trading: Its Impact on the Residential Mortgage Market*, Chicago Board of Trade International Futures Trading Seminar, V, 106–125.

Dale, C. (1981), *The Hedging Effectiveness of Currency Futures Markets*, Journal of Futures Markets, 1, 77–88.

Dew, J.K. and Martell, T. (1981), *Treasury Bill Futures, Commercial Lending and the Synthetic Fixed Rate Loan*, Journal of Commercial Bank Lending, 63, 27–38.

Ederington, L.H. (1979), *The Hedging Effectiveness of the New Financial Futures Markets*, Journal of Finance, 34, 157–170.

Ederington, L.H. (1980), *Living with Inflation: A Proposal for New Futures and Options Markets*, Financial Analysts Journal, Jan–Feb, 1980.

Figlewski, S. and Kon, S. (1982), *Portfolio Management with Stock Index Futures*, Financial Analysts Journal, Jan–Feb, 52–60.

Fitzgerald, M.D. (1982), *Using the Financial Futures Market*, The Banker, April, 105–129.

Fitzgerald, M.D. (1982), *Financial Futures Costs and Benefits*, The Banker, October, 41–52.

Hill, J. and Schneeweiss, T. (1981), *Forecasting Effectiveness of Foreign Currency Futures*, Business Economics, May, 42–46.

Jones, F. (1981), *The Integration of the Cash and Futures Markets for Treasury Securities*, Journal of Futures Markets, 1, 33–57.

Keen, H. (1980), *Interest Rate Futures*, Federal Reserve Bank of Philadelphia Business Review Nov/Dec, 13–22.

Kolb, R.W. and Chiang, R. (1981), *Improving Hedging Performance Using Interest Rate Futures*, Financial Management, Autumn, 72–79.

Leibowitz, M.L. (1981), *A Yield Basis for Financial Futures*, Financial Analysts Journal, Jan–Feb, 42–51.

Leibowitz, M.L. (1981), *The Analysis of Value and Volatility in Financial Futures*, Salomon Center Monograph in Finance and Economics 1981–3, New York University.

Long, R.W. and Rasche, R.H. (1978), *A Comparison of Yields on Futures Contracts and Implied Forward Rates*, Federal Reserve Bank of St. Louis Review, 60, 12–30.

Lovell, M.C. and Vogel, R.C. (1973), *A CPI-Futures Market*, Journal of Political Economy, July/Aug, 1009–1012.

Maness, T.S. (1981), *Optimal versus Naive Buy-Hedging with T-Bill Futures*, Journal of Futures Markets, 1, 393–403.

McLeod, R.W., and McCabe, G.M. (1980), *Hedging for Better Spread Management*, The Bankers Magazine, 163, 255–263.

McEnally, R.W., and Rice, M.L. (1979), *Hedging Possibilities in the Flotation of Debt Securities*, Financial Management, 8, 265–277.

Niederhoffer, V. and Zechhauser, R. (1980), *Market Index Futures Contracts*, Financial Analysts Journal, January–February, 49–55.

Puglisi, D.J. (1978), *Is the Futures Market for Treasury Bills Efficient?*, Journal of Portfolio Management, Winter, 64–67.

Rendleman, R.J., and Carabini, C.E. (1979), *The Efficiency of the Treasury Bill Futures Market*, Journal of Finance, 34, 895–914.

4. Official publications

Hobson, R.B. (1978), *Futures Trading in Financial Instruments*, Commodity Futures Trading Commission, October.

Treasury-Federal Reserve Study of Financial Futures Markets, 1979.

Commodity Futures Trading Commission Study of Financial Futures Markets, 1981.

5. Periodicals

Regularly

Journal of Futures Markets, J. Wiley Interscience Journals, 605, Third Avenue, New York, NY 10158, U.S.A.

Futures World, Metal Bulletin PLC, Park House, 3 Park Terrace, Worcester Park, Surrey KT4 7HY, U.K.

Commodity Magazine, 219, Parkade, Cedar Falls, Iowa 50613, U.S.A.

Occasionally

Journal of Portfolio Management.

Financial Analysts Journal.

Journal of Finance.

Journal of Financial Economics.

Index

Accounting treatment of financial futures 161–70
  Balance sheet treatment 163
  Criteria for determining a hedge 165
  Hedge accounting 166–8
  Hedging
    a currency receipt or payment 165
    an existing asset or liability 165
    an interest yield 165
  Hedging and trading results 170
  in UK 161–2
  in US 162
  Open position 169
  Related costs 163
  Unamortized gains and losses 169
  Valuation to market 162
Arbitrage 7, 62, 137–53
  Arbitrage ratio 139
  Arbitrage trading 119
  Cash and carry arbitrage 62, 139–46
  Closed arbitrage 138
  Futures and forward-forward arbitrage 146–8
  Interest and foreign exchange futures
    combination arbitrage 148–9
  Short-term rate and long-term spread arbitrage 149–52
  Simple inter-market arbitrage 152–3

Basis 62, 63, 82
  Basis relationships 80–4
Beta 104–6

Canadian Treasury bill contract 50
Canadian bond contract 50
Carryable commodity 62
Cash yield curve 83
Cheapest deliverable instrument/stock 60, 143
Chicago Board of Trade (CBT) 4, 32, 38, 40, 42, 49
  CBT 6½–10 year Treasury note contract 49
  CBT two-year Treasury note contract 49
Chicago Mercantile Exchange (CME) 4, 48
Chicago Mercantile Index and Options Market
  (IOM) 4, 48
Clearing house 11–12, 16, 17
Clearing system 16
Commercial banks, hedging for 89–97
  Balance sheet maturity mismatch 89–92
  Hedging an asset purchase 92–5
  Fixed rate funds in dollar currencies 95–7
Commissions 23–4

Commodity Futures Trading Commission
  (CFTC) 2, 67, 175
Convergence 81, 82
Conversion factors (see also Price factors) 33–4, 57–71, 75–6
  of gilt futures 37
  and duration 57
Corners 177
Corporations, hedging for 107–14
  Hedging a corporate bond issue 112–14
Correlation analysis 51–3
  Correlation coefficient 51
Cost of carry 81, 82, 124
Coupon slippage 116

Dealer 170
Delivery
  of contracts 11–12
  of domestic certificate of deposit futures 46–7
  of Eurodollar time deposits 29
  of foreign currency contracts 45
  of GNMA Collateralized Depository Receipt
    (CDR) 41–44
  IMM delivery system of Eurodollar time
    deposits 29
  LIFFE delivery system of Eurodollar time
    deposits 30
  of long-term gilt contracts 36–8
  of T-bill futures contracts 27
  of US T-bond futures 33
Disclosure rules 176
Domestic certificate of deposit futures 46–7
  delivery of 47
Duration 57, 60–1, 76–7, 102, 131

Effective yield
  of T-bill 28
Eurodollar time deposits 29–32
  Delivery of 29
  IMM delivery system 29
  LIFFE delivery system 30
Expectations theory of interest rates 146

Face value of contracts 74
Federal National Mortgage Association 116
Financial futures contracts 1
  Pricing of 9–11
Foreign currency contracts 45–6
  Delivery of 46
Forward-forward futures arbitrage 146–8

Forward-forward market   72
Forward-forward rate   62, 146
Forward markets   2
Fundamental analysis   122
Funds, diversification of   180
Futures/cash relationship   61
Futures, strip of   156

GNMA contract   38–44
   Bond equivalent yield   38
   Cash and carry arbitrage   145
   Certificate delivery contracts   42
     Delivery of   42
     Invoice value of   42–3
   Collateralized depository receipt (CDR)   40–2
     Delivery procedure of   40–41
     Receipt contract   145
   Forward market   39
   Futures   128
   Market   115–18
   Par cap provision   39
   Pass-through yield   38
   Standby market   39
Government National Mortgage Association (*see* GNMA)
Gower Report   176

Hedge
   accounting   166–8
   adjustment   87
   evaluation   87–8
   monitoring   86–7
Hedge design   56
   Hedge effectiveness   56
   Optimal hedge   56
   Optimal hedge ratio   56
Hedge ratio   74
   Face value of contract   74
   Money equivalency   74
Hedgers   67
Hedging   67–118
   Aggressive hedging strategies   80–6
   an asset purchase   92–5
   for a commercial bank   89
   a corporate bond issue   112–14
   for corporations   107–14
   Criteria for determining a hedge   165–6
   Cross hedging   73
   a currency receipt or payment   165
   Discontinued hedging   167
   an existing asset on liability   165
   Foreign exchange hedger   110–12
   General hedges   166
   an interest yield   165
   Long hedge   68
   Mortgage hedging   115–18
   One-off hedge   78
   Portfolio hedging   99
   for portfolio managers   97–107
   Principle of symmetry   163
   Rolling hedge   79, 166
   Rolling strip hedge   78
   Short hedge   68
   Spread hedge   79
   with stock index futures   103–6
   Strip hedge   78
   and trading results   170
   a yield curve ride   155–6

IMM   4, 25, 29, 43, 45, 46
Implicit rate   123
Implied repo rate   64, 146
Interest parity   65
   Interest parity theorem   124
Interest rate probability distribution   71
Invoice price
   of T-bill futures   28
   of US Treasury bond futures   35
Invoice value
   of GNMA certificate delivery contracts   42

Kansas City Board of Trade   47

Linear regression   54–6
   and hedge design   56
London International Financial Futures Exchange
   (LIFFE)   6, 29, 30, 32, 36, 45, 57
Long-term gilt contracts   36–8
   Delivery of   36–8
   Conversion factors   37

Marking to market   80, 137
Margins   12–15
   Variation margin   12
   Maintenance margin   13
Matched book   72
Measurement of return   135
Mismatched book   72
Monetary policy   178
Money equivalency   74

National Futures Association   176
Negative cost of carry   122
Net exposed balances table   70
New York Futures Exchange (NYFE)   48
Non-carryable commodity   62
Non-systematic risk   103–4
NYSE Composite index   48

Orders   18–23
   Alternative order   22
   At the close order   21
   At the opening order   21
   FOK order   20
   Limit order   18, 84
   Market order   18
   MIT order   19
   Scale order   21
   Stop-limit order   9
   Stop and limit order   20
   Stop order   19, 84
   Straddle order   22
   Switch order   23

Parity prices   99
Portfolio managers, hedging by   97–107
Position trading   7
Price factors (*see also* Conversion factors)   75–6
   LIFFE price factors   57–8
   CBT price factors   59
Price limits   24–5
Pricing
   of Treasury bill futures contracts   25
   of US Treasury bond futures   32
Proxy investments   159

Regression coefficients   74–5
Regulation of financial futures markets   175

Risk capital 135
Risk exposure, determination of 69
Rule 21.03 175

Scalpers 133
Securities Exchange Commission (SEC) 175
Sensitivity 139
Settlement price 15
Speculating 119–36
    Lemming theory of speculation 178
    Speculator 170
    Speculative bubbles 178
Spreads (*see* also Trading) 84, 121
    Butterfly spread 131
    Buying the spread 121
    CD/Eurodollar spread 127
    CD spreads 125
    Condor spreads 131
    Inter-contract spreading 125–31
    Intra-contract spreading 122–5
    Pseudo-butterfly spread 131
    Pseudo-condor spread 131
    Selling the spread 122
    Spread broker 133
    Spread of spreads 131
    Spread trading 121–33
    T-bill/CD spread 127
    T-bill spreads 125
    Unweighted spread 129
    Weighted spread 129
Squeezes 177
Standard and Poor's 500 index 48
Statistical analysis 51–6
Sterling time deposit 32
Stock market index futures 48–9
    Hedging with stock index futures 103–6
Strip yield curve 63, 83
Swap price 96
Systematic risk 103–4

Tailing 124

Taxation treatment of financial futures 170–4
    Capital gain on delivery 174
    Exchange conversion 173
    in UK 171–4
    in US 170–1
    Non-residents 173–4
    Timing of assets 172–3
Technical analysis 122
Tick value 26
Time security grid 137
Traders 170
    Day traders 134
    Long-duration traders 134
    Scalpers 133
Trading (*see* also Spreads) 119–36
    Arbitrage trading 119
    Open position trading 119, 120–1
    Spread trading 119, 121–33
    Straddle trading 122
    Timing of 133–4
    Volume 4
Transaction costs 23–4
Treasury bill futures contracts 25–8
    Delivery of 27
    Invoice price of 28
    Effective T-bill yield 28
    Tick value 26

Underwriting application of financial futures 114–18

US Treasury bond futures 32, 128
    Conversion factor 33–4
    Delivery of 33
    Invoice price 35
    Pricing 32–3

Valuation of hedged asset 16
Value Line index 47
Volatility 178

Wild card 143

Author's biography

Dr. M. Desmond Fitzgerald, B.A. (York), Ph.D. (Manchester) is currently Finance for Industry Senior Research Fellow, Centre for Banking and International Finance, and Head of Finance Division, The City University Business School. He is also a Visiting Professor of Finance at New York University.

Previously he has taught at New York University Graduate School of Business Administration, and run the Economic Research Department of Chemical Bank in London. He acts as a consultant on financial futures to Hoare Govett Financial Futures Ltd., and is closely involved in the design and implementation of training courses for the London International Financial Futures Exchange. He is also a senior consultant on energy and minerals developments to the Chemical Bank of New York.

He has published widely in academic and general journals, and has edited (with R. A. Batchelor) a book *Financial Regulation* to be published by Macmillan in 1984. Current research interests include optimal hedging with financial futures, the valuation of options on futures, medieval financial markets, and the relative speed of thoroughbred racehorses.